# From School Delusion to Design

## Also by the Author

*The Systems Thinking School: Redesigning Schools from the Inside-Out*

# From School Delusion to Design

## *Mixed-Age Groups and Values-Led Transformation*

Peter A. Barnard

ROWMAN & LITTLEFIELD
Lanham • Boulder • New York • London

Published by Rowman & Littlefield
A wholly owned subsidiary of The Rowman & Littlefield Publishing Group, Inc.
4501 Forbes Boulevard, Suite 200, Lanham, Maryland 20706
www.rowman.com

16 Carlisle Street, London W1D 3BT, United Kingdom



British Library Cataloguing in Publication Information Available

**Library of Congress Cataloging-in-Publication Data**

Barnard, Peter A.
From school delusion to design : subtitle mixed-age groups and values-led transformation / Peter A. Barnard.
pages cm.
Includes bibliographical references.
ISBN 978-1-4758-1534-4 (cloth : alk. paper) — ISBN 978-1-4758-1535-1 (pbk. : alk. paper) — ISBN 978-1-4758-1536-8 (electronic) 1. Tutors and tutoring. 2. Group work in education. 3. Ability grouping in education. 4. Student-centered learning. 5. School improvement programs. I. Title.
LC41.B365 2015
371.39'4—dc23

2015000452

# Contents

# Foreword

In 2004, I assisted a school district in a redesign process utilizing Jamshid Gharajedaghi and Russell Ackoff's systems work. We challenged many prevailing assumptions and the members of the school community created a beautiful design for the future of their district. Of all the exciting ideas, one stood out from the rest. The team designed a K–12 vertical "homeroom." The idea simultaneously met their desire to build a stronger community through new modes of connection and to solve the problem of performance "dips" every time a child made a transition from one level to the next (elementary to middle school, etc.).

It called for at least one teacher/school employee from each level of the system to be a part of a K–12 vertical "homeroom." The vision was that these groups would meet regularly to learn about one another, assist one another, and build stronger relationships. The belief was that through such purposeful interactions they would see reduced bullying, stronger connections, mutual respect, and mentoring/tutoring. Every student would know at least one teacher from the next "level"—a set of adults who would advocate for them and be there as the child moved from one level to the next, along with a handful of other students. Transitions would be seamless, community would be built, and outcomes would improve. They had visions of parents being included so that parents could build bonds beyond the ones they had based on their child's sports teams and interests.

It was a great design and it never happened.

Almost immediately the reasons why it wouldn't work surfaced to temper the excitement. We couldn't help them see past the schedules, logistics, and time that they viewed as immovable barriers. The truth was that the only barrier was the belief in the legitimacy of the existing structures and almost blind acceptance of those structures as contextually permanent.

What I didn't know in 2004 was that Peter Barnard had already not only envisioned the power of such a simple idea, but had led such work to fruition, which produced the very results we imagined in our design work. I understood systems theory and methodology quite well and I could see how, through system redesign, an idea Barnard calls "vertical tutoring" could become reality. What I hadn't yet learned was how to initiate a "doable" iteration toward this ultimate design, one the community wouldn't reject outright. I also hadn't come to understand and appreciate the true power of community.

To paraphrase Peter Block, "nothing happens but through community." Going further, Block says, "Community exists for the sake of belonging and takes its identity from the gifts, generosity, and accountability of its citizens. It is not defined by its fears, its isolation, or its penchant for retribution" (Block 2008). Education reformers and their ilk have taken us down the path of fear, isolation, and retribution with their industrial-age, command-and-control, humanity-reducing policies and beliefs for far too long and with disastrous results. But I, we, are not guiltless in this. We have for far too long simply rolled over, tried to get along, or tried to engage in debate or complaint. This is no way to create a new future—one filled with possibility, hope, and abundance. Reformers ignore and we, as citizens, have seemingly forgotten the most important word in most school district names. The word is *community.*

In places across America we are beginning to see educators reconnect with their communities, engaging them in conversation and dialogue about what they want for their children. These conversations create fissures within which to begin bringing to life new structures and processes actually designed to create that which our communities are telling us they want. Despite some of this great work, we still are encumbered with a system designed largely to produce the exact opposite outcomes we truly desire.

While it is important to engage the community that is a part of the school's containing system, it is as important to engage the community within the school in ways that unlock the future and that can give us new fissures to leverage important change. In fact, it is in the community within the walls of the school that we educators have the most influence over and can adjust most quickly—and is exactly where we should be starting. Peter Barnard has provided us with a critical resource in this regard—a readable, "doable" map for how to move forward. Blending his understanding of systems thinking with practical experience, Barnard gives us "vertical tutoring." At first glance, it seems somewhat ridiculous and a "been there, done that" idea. Yes, we've done "homeroom" ad nauseam in education, but we did it within the old paradigms and assumptions of industrial-age schooling—not as a design iteration to create something very new and different. Barnard's practices are far more strategic and aligned to the future of education than our past attempts. It is a means to a larger and more important end.

By starting with something somewhat known and accepted by the existing system, Barnard provides us with a strategy to begin challenging the implicit assumptions through new practices. Vertical tutoring introduces the power of community building and subtlety, but powerfully helps us begin to move away from the age- and grade-based structures and beliefs that are largely responsible for holding us in the existing system.

Barnard's counterintuitive but powerful approach helps us reculture schools through a clear understanding of social systems theory, application, and actions that can help move us forward. It gives us a way to break the age- and grade-based structures actually promoting fear, scarcity, and retribution, and begin to replace them with purposeful organizing structures and processes that unlock the gifts, possibilities, and abundance sitting latent in our communities. This is an important contribution to our efforts to move beyond feckless reform to true transformation.

Dr. Trace Pickering
Associate Superintendent, Co-Creator of the Iowa BIG program
Cedar Rapids, Iowa

# Preface

My previous book, *The Systems Thinking School*, was intended to be a last foray into the world of systems thinking and schools. It seems, however, that the book raised questions about the perceived folly of organizing a school with tutor groups formed from students across all grades or year groups. While such a method may seem intuitively wrong to many, for others the idea came as a blessing. A passionate advocate of U.S. public schools informed me that he sent copies to all of his city's school board members advising that they should read the book carefully before appointing their new superintendent!

In many ways this book is precisely about that singular, thoughtful gesture. There is now a growing passion for major systemic change rather than what seems to be more "tinkering at the edge." The fact is that those in charge of schools at whatever level have an awesome responsibility but seem to make predictable mistakes in their judgments and interventions. They appear stuck in a holding pattern of repeat behaviors.

We are not good at improving schools. Why this is so and what to do about it is addressed here as best I can and each chapter summons key witnesses to the cause. Together, they build a picture and inform a better way of thinking about schools. Besides, it struck me that in the unlikely event that the school board members should heed such advice and engage in more counterintuitive learning, there is much more that the unfortunate superintendent of schools might need to know.

Parents, students, and teachers who have contacted me often request more information on mixed-age organization in school. Some have requested a systems thinking primer on school management and leadership; others wanted more on the research basis for vertical (mixed-age) tutoring, including more about the underpinning psychology and the practicalities. Some astute school leaders requested more precise markers regarding the process of change from a school grade system organizationally based on same-age groups to one that depends upon mixed-age groups as their structural platform for improving learning and teaching.

That being the case, this book is a response. It uses the same systems scaffolding as its predecessor and the same starting point: that we are at a hiatus, a point at which one paradigm should be giving way to another, but instead we find ourselves reinventing the past with an unhealthy combination of uncertainty and trepidation. We are at a time when big decisions need to be made and when better judgment is needed.

Meanwhile, the super-resilient, universal, industrial, factory school continues on its merry but damaging way, apparently undisturbed by any crisis of confidence. It seems that there is a global system blindness to the waste that the dominant factory school system creates, based as it is on the central premise of same-age organization.

It seems that every jurisdiction adopts the universal factory model, oblivious to its shortcomings and the harm it generates. All wrongly believe that this year's reforms, the relentless focus on teachers, the weight of research, increased investment, new targets, and curriculum change will somehow get this broken mincing machine operational. History is not on their side.

While many jurisdictions are in denial, the United States at least realizes that it has a *wicked* problem on its hands, a system that all too easily breaks down when faced with social and economic complexity. The unfortunate perception is that such a problem or combination of problems can be resolved with the right fixes and by resorting to the old and familiar industrial reform toolbox.

Yet it is within the power of each and every school to start a process of transformation, one that remodels the school's learning culture by rebuilding the interconnectivity that the industrial same-age model must unavoidably limit. Many schools are doing so, especially in the United Kingdom, Australia, and New Zealand; however, to make such a change requires as much unlearning as relearning, and in turn this requires a more informed understanding of systems. This is because real change requires the past to be left behind, not carried forward. But to unlearn a system requires a clear understanding of how that system works not how we assume it works and what we accept.

As far as schools are concerned, any process of unlearning requires a systems thinking understanding of the *same-age* system in use, and the inevitable distortions and limitations such a system inadvertently creates. In effect, implementing a better system requires managers to unlearn the one in place. Unlearning the one in place requires that the one in use is understood at a far deeper level than is the case. Further, any transformation from one system (same-age) to another (mixed-age) cannot be achieved using the management ideas of the system being abandoned. A change of management mindset or mental model is critical to such a process.

We think we know the school system in use given its familiarity to all of us. Unfortunately, we could not be more wrong. What we know, as we shall learn, is what we *see*. It is one thing to recognize that that there are many problems associated with the dominant same-age factory model of school, and quite another to understand how those problems manifest themselves. Organizational problems hide in the most obscure places and are rarely what they seem: they are complex, elusive, and obscure, and our [biased] judgment calls and explanations are rarely as rational and straightforward as we like to assume. Just as big systemic change in education is firmly stuck in the moribund grip of old bureaucracies and ideas, so our schools as smaller systems are held back by the management assumptions and organizational methodologies of the past.

We depend on what we know even when what we know doesn't work and is rarely all there is. While this says much for our persistence, it says little for our understanding of complex organizations. It is an irony that many call for schools to produce problem solvers and team players, while at the same time being unable to problem-solve schools, let alone say what the problem is! Even some of our best team players and problem solvers watch helplessly as a public service system flirts with meltdown!

As a result, this book takes as its main theme the journey from *delusion* to *design*. Such a journey focuses on psychology with a systems thinking edge, and let me say at the outset that I have no real qualification whatsoever in psychology. I just read, interpret, and apply like most practitioners do, and hope to have understood what I can and get some applications vaguely right. Systems thinking helps, and so does having a second opinion from the expert witnesses included here and from the many hundreds of school teams with whom it has been my privilege to work.

Readers of *The Systems Thinking School* will find themselves retracing some old ground and skipping over known areas: I have tried to explain any technical systems terms used throughout so none of us gets too lost. Also included is more of the interesting research concerning *learning intelligence* now gaining momentum, and its implication for school design.

The systems solution remains the same. There is a certain sequence to systemic change that for me must be entirely school driven. First, schools need to be persuaded to look again at how they operate as teaching and learning organizations (how they *self-organize*), but with a new systems awareness of any inherent biases and assumptions. Then we need schools to consider a systems thinking alternative to their managerial modus operandi.

The formal introduction of mixed-age groups that I call *vertical tutoring* (VT) remains the single most important staging post between where schools are now and where we need them to be. VT is by far the fastest, most effective, and joyous means of securing better schools and is the closest we shall get to transforming schools into the learning organizations they aspire to be. Getting this first step and critical leverage point right is the key; this is the first domino that sets in motion the cumulative redesign of the school as a system and as a learning organization.

If used carefully, this book will help elucidate the past and explain how we got to where we are. It is a journey from delusion to counterintuitive surprises and redesign, and remains the best way to secure the unlearning needed to leave the past behind. It is much of what I have learned as a practitioner, from very many decades of transforming same-age systems into embryonic mixed-age learning organizations (vertical tutoring).

Of course, dissolving one set of problems does not prevent a whole new set of challenges. The key is to get schools to a point at which they are more able to make good decisions and do the right learning things needed for a more secure future. This requires the courage to be different and the ability to spot and barge through any paradoxes and misleading tautologies that tend to blight their landscape.

Whatever the context or culture, each school will need to change the way it goes about managing learning, given the harm it is doing to the many that so bravely walk our school corridors. We must always remember that schools are there to serve the commons, to make the world a better place, not a more dangerous one.

The school has to steer a careful course—one that better protects them from the nonsenses thrown at them. Not only must a school be values driven and have moral and spiritual purpose, but it must also be ecologically connected to all other systems and to itself.

As ever, I have tried to make each chapter stand alone, and this means more repetition than I might wish. It is, so students tell me, how they read!

Hopefully, all of these ramblings will be made clear!

# Acknowledgments

Most of the information and all of the ideas contained in this book have not only been learned from my experience as a teacher and secondary school principal, but also through my work with hundreds of school leadership teams, parents, students, teachers, and support staff who give so selflessly of their time. The thirst for seeking safer and better ways of running a school and for more joined-up management and real innovation remains undiminished and international. I shall always be indebted to my teachers and colleagues in the field.

Otherwise, my thanks remain largely as before. I hope that Professor Frank Duffy will once again welcome this book as part of his growing and prestigious series, "Leading Systematic School Improvement." His selfless efforts in the field of systems thinking have gathered a treasure trove of ideas available to all.

On this occasion I must also extend my thanks to John Seddon. His Vanguard website, books, and essays have been an enormous help whenever I have found myself stuck. His work on service systems in the United Kingdom would certainly have cheered W. Edwards Deming to no end. They have certainly help me understand schools far better, and John's teaching is apparent throughout; even after thirty-eight years of teaching I remain a learner.

Thanks as ever go to Tom Koerner, vice president and editorial director of Rowman & Littlefield Education, for his support, advice, and enthusiasm. This time I shall also mention and thank Carlie Wall, associate editor, who sends me endless incomprehensible forms and generally gets things done. Another special word of thanks goes to Su Wales, a leading educationist and teaching practitioner in the United Kingdom, who, for a bottle of bubbly, kindly read the original draft of this book so many drafts ago.

In Virginia, Patricia George once again foolishly offered to knock all of my scribbling into some sort of readable shape. I tried hard to reduce her workload by attempting to write more in the American vernacular. Having conquered the use of "z" in preference to "s" in most words, the use of "program" for "programme," and the omission of the "u" in words ending in "-our," I discovered two more anomalies that seem to defy logic when crossing the pond. One is to put a capital letter after a colon, something that I simply cannot bring myself to do; the other is to put full stops (for some reason, called "periods" in the United States) inside quotation marks, "instead of outside where they should be." Nevertheless we seem to have arrived at some kind of compromise. I tried to sneak some past Patricia's scrutiny and it is for readers to judge who won this battle.

Otherwise, Patricia is completely unphased and simply makes sense of things: she remains the essence of what it is to be "cool". (Spot where the *period* is and the non-capital letter after the colon!) She has even allowed me to write unedited this single section using U.K. grammar and punctuation.

A good friend, Moira Furber, did a final read-through with me and I am grateful for the care she took and the changes she advised. As part of a post-graduate course in the history of education, Moira reminded me that she studied the Victorian "Payment by Results" method abandoned in the 1890s. It saddened me to say that this century-old model of management is returning with a vengeance today.

Meanwhile, members of my own family cannot understand why I write books on school management and for some time have been urging me to write a raunchy novel of some kind, something likely to sell more copies and perhaps be made into a film! I try to explain that basing such a novel on systems thinking would not be easy, although I am not altogether giving up on the idea!

Since writing *The Systems Thinking School*, the other Patricia in my life (and partner of more years than she allows me to publish) achieved a prestigious Gold Medal at the one-hundredth Chelsea Flower Show in London, for her WaterAid Garden (2013). Once again, the wonderful Ringo Starr was there to support the WaterAid charity and open her garden. As I write, my son, Laurent, is reviewing various music tracks. He now plays with three bands, "Moones" (indie rock), "Gallows" (adorable and frenetic hard-core punk rock), and "Krokodil" (progressive metal), and that means three new albums to be released this side of Christmas.

It remains my good fortune to live with people who are truly more innovative and creative than I am and who are almost certainly better systems thinkers.

As ever, I apologize for any errors, all of which are mine. I have no army of helpers to read and correct my jumbled thoughts. I just hope to have made at least some sense, some of the time. It's an age thing!

# Introduction

> Change will not come if we wait for some other person or some other time. We are the ones we've been waiting for. We are the change that we seek.
>
> —Barack Obama, February 5, 2008

In the fourteenth century, a Franciscan friar called William of Ockham lived in the English village of Ockham in the county of Surrey. He suggested that when there are competing theories that make similar predictions, the simpler one is better. It is a law of parsimony that seeks to cut through any long-held assumptions in its search for truth, and has become known as "Occam's Razor." The *razor* removes the unnecessary dross that builds up over time: systems thinking is like Occam's Razor.

For our purposes, systems thinking is a means of understanding how and why a complex organization like a school works in the way that it does. It wants to know what a school actually does, not just what managers say it does. To do this, it must cut through the dross.

Systems thinking looks at the school as a complete system and tries to figure out how the various human elements, in this case the school's staff, students, and parents, interact to make sense of learning and teaching. In other words, systems thinking tries to make sense of perceived complexity by looking at an organization, in this case a school, as a system with purposes and methods; it seeks to understand what the school does, how it works, and why it works in the way it does. It looks anew at long-held assumptions in order to see more.

This book first seeks to understand and explain the organizational behavior of the school and takes a systems thinking approach. It avoids isolating individual elements like teachers as entities separate from the whole; it is this that makes a systems thinking approach so very different from any reform approach to school improvement.

In return, we are offered fresh operational insights into the school as an organization. This includes the opportunity for those people most involved to make the substantive changes needed to enhance the learning process. If the organization in question turns out to be riddled with problems, the inevitable answer lies in cultural redesign, not fixes and add-ons. Any attempt to fix component elements (such as teachers) or add on an extra bit (such as a new pro-social program) by way of reform is likely to prove ineffective and inappropriate. It is also likely to result in inevitable problems being created elsewhere.

There are latent factors deep within a system's mechanism, the way an organization goes about its work, that cause it to behave in the way it does. The late Donella Meadows (2009) described the fundamentals of systems thinking in this way:

> Once we see the relationship between structure and behavior, we can begin to understand how systems work, what makes them produce poor results, and how to shift them into better behavior patterns. (p. 1)

The universal factory school comes under the heading of what Rittel and Webber (1973) termed a "wicked problem" and Russell Ackoff (1979) called a "mess," one so complex that they cannot be easily defined let alone resolved. Schools are a universal mess despite some jurisdictions being purported to be "better" than others at "education." The fact is, no one really knows what schools are *for,* let alone what they *do* given the variety of explanations offered. The linkage between purpose and method is both insecure and obscure.

The statement that follows may sound ludicrous but it remains a conclusion herein. Schools, when looked at from a systems perspective, are highly dangerous places run by saints. They change nothing and self-perpetuate the disconnected ecology and uncertainty in the world we have. What is claimed for schools is not what *is.*

In his book, *The Black Swan,* Taleb (2011) put the problem more succinctly.

> Living on our planet, today, requires a lot more imagination than we are made to have. We lack imagination and repress it to others. (p. xxxii)

A Black Swan event is one that deviates from what is predicted. Schooling falls into this category. Schools were meant to develop potential, be coherent, adaptive, connected, and enabling, and not to reproduce sameness and practice limitation. Taleb explains how we spend our time "engaged in small talk, focusing on the known, and the repeated."

Otherwise, a Black Swan event is one that

a. Comes as a surprise. No one expected school systems to fail in spectacular ways.
b. Has a major impact socially, economically, individually, and globally. Be your own judge on this.
c. After the event, the causes are rationalized (the imperfect science of hindsight) and event causes nominated. We attach blame to individuals rather than the system in play.

These "causes" include teacher quality, training quality, pay, accountability, social factors, financing, leadership, targets, and curriculum; in fact a whole confusion of elemental parts. We work on the apparent causes despite the circles into which they lead. School systems as they stand are slow-motion train wrecks that appear to have defied explanation, and this means only one thing: we are seeing the problem wrongly.

It is a theme taken up by Alpaslan and Mitroff (2011) in their book *Swans, Swine, and Swindlers: Coping with the Growing Threat of Mega-Crises and Mega-Messes*. The "swans" are illustrated by false assumptions and mistaken beliefs. Left unattended and misunderstood these, like linear school systems, can all too easily turn into major crises. Often what seems to be innocent, benign, and normal turns out to be the very opposite.

Such situations are exacerbated by the "swine" with their "greed, hubris, and arrogance." Then we get the swindlers with their corrupt behaviors exploiting the mess created and adding to it until a crisis forms. The challenge is to design systems that encourage better behaviors and design out the old ones, but that means unlearning the system in play.

## ASSUMPTION

Here is a misguided assumption: Schools operate best when students are organized into same-age groups (grades or years).

While this may seem plausible (after all, hasn't it always been thus and what we *see*?), the outcome of such a decision leads inevitably to two organizational problems: *separation* and *limitation*. The same-age approach to school organization seems so logical. It is used to solve perceived complexity issues and to efficiently manage learning, student numbers, time, and teacher allocation.

What school managers don't understand is that this decision actually creates infinitely more complexity than it seeks to resolve. Understanding how and why this is remains critical to unlearning and to change management. Indeed, when this same-age system is implemented, a chain reaction begins from which there is no obvious management remedy. Problems actually increase in complexity. Things start to spiral out of control and schools end up managing all the wrong things, thinking they are the right things.

We then assume that the system structure is okay, so it must be the people element that is somehow failing and persuade ourselves we are right! There is a case for arguing that the many Black Swans we now have started their formative life in our schools deep within the social and learning relationships that form in same-age structures, the universal factory model, and grand assumption. The factory management processes erroneously assumed to enable such learning and teaching are still with us, still turning messes into crises. We'll pursue this as we go.

Meadows (2009) set out some systems laws to help:

- A system is more than the sum of its parts.
- Many of the interconnections in systems operate through the flow of information.

- The least obvious part of a system, its function or purpose, is often the most crucial determinant of the system behavior.
- System structure is the source of system behavior. System behavior reveals itself as a series of events over time.

The potential for these laws to be usurped and assumed is legion. When I work closely with schools, the gap between the methods in use and the high-value purposes schools claim make almost no sense. In fact, the methods in use result in entirely different outcomes to those assumed. Examine the practices, and the purpose reveals itself and this purpose is rarely what schools claim. Somewhere, somehow, values are lost and assumed in the system operations in play.

Luckily, we can also work backward, and Jeffrey Conklin (2006) offers us a way out. When a (wicked) problem becomes so complex and loaded with assumption, obfuscation, incoherence, and more besides, it is "not understood until after the formulation of a solution." In other words, if the reculturing and redesign solution needed to "dissolve" (using Ackoff's word) the problem of a failing public school system is known, it is much easier to see what exactly is going wrong.

Only then is it possible to redesign the system's underpinning structure to promote the kind of ecological coherence that leads to safer schools, better learning, improved outcomes, and a more identifiable and values-driven purpose. The seemingly simple but surprising start to resolving the mess that schools are in is to ensure that the basic organization of, say, a secondary school is based on mixed-age groups not same-age groups! While this is not full systemic change, it is the start of a systemic change process and without it any viable and worthwhile learning transformation cannot be realized.

Some thirty years ago, I was the new head teacher of a large secondary school. We took the high-risk decision to scrap the same-age tutor groups and make them mixed-age. The simple intention then was to enable better use of assessment data and to improve parent partnership. None of us were aware (absence of systems thinking) that this small change would throw all of our past practice into sharp focus.

It suddenly became clear that what we had been trying to do in our linear way was foolish and delusional. We had persuaded ourselves that the old linear logistics of school organization and our deeper values were the same things and that one somehow assumed the other. We were driven by logistics, not values. By changing from a horizontal (same-age) structure to a vertical (mixed-age) structure, we had inadvertently stumbled on an innovative solution that also enabled managers to see clearly what we had been doing erroneously in the past. This meant we could unlearn the past and grasp a better future.

Same-age school organization, the current universal factory model, is assumed to be benign. The domino effect it creates, however, begins with an industrial mindset and a production process of sifting, sorting, and batching. Once started, it is a difficult process to undo and is mightily resistant to change; it is self-serving and its proponents seek to ensure such a process is maintained in perpetuity.

So there are two contrasting models: one that begins with the idea of separation by age (now global) and one that begins with interconnectivity and mixed-age structures. The latter, at least, is gaining a firm foothold.

Organization by same-age is the unquestioned assumption and the dark secret of the industrial model, the factory school. While this may have made some kind of sense in an industrial age, it makes no sense now. By maintaining such an industrial view of the school as an organization, schools commit to an unpredictable journey, one requiring constant repair and one largely devoid of real purpose and value. This makes schools party to many Black Swan events. In fact, schools are the birthing pools of Black Swan events.

Any separation process decreases interconnectivity. There is a loss of communications and learning partnerships that in turn leads inevitably to limitations in learning. The false assumption is that separation is a means of controlling complexity, and we shall explore this myth later. It does the opposite.

If this is all so, then the remedy is obvious; it is for each school to explore a mixed-age means of organization or *vertical tutoring,* a concept that has been around (seemingly forever for me) but largely unexploited as a viable means of organizing a school. Strangely, this seemingly off-the-wall, counterintuitive, and almost unacceptable notion changes everything for the better and makes learning and teaching easier all around. The problem is that few, if any, in the United States and elsewhere, will believe such a counterintuitive hypothesis and that means there is much explaining to do!

How could the introduction of mixed-age groups for, say, twenty minutes a day and without any accompanying program make a profound difference in the learning capability of a school and make such a significant improvement to the lives of teachers, students, and families? It all sounds frankly ridiculous, until, that is, you think it through from a systems thinking perspective and see it in operation in the many schools that now employ VT as their organizational structure and means of building an interconnected learning support culture.

Of course, this simple change is not all there is. Like any domino effect, organizing schools into mixed-age units sets in progress another and very different chain reaction. It changes a linear model (horizontal or same-age) into a non-linear model. This book centers on that first domino, vertical tutoring, the mixed-age homeroom group, but first, a word of warning.

To implement such a change with limited knowledge of systems thinking is folly and there are many schools that have made the mistake of assuming such a change is easy. Schools have a penchant for copying other schools and when they do so, they ignore training and knowledge and so import as many bad ideas as good. Schools that fail to unlearn linearity can make matters worse by mixing the age groups in their schools but keeping the way they manage the same! They omit the unlearning needed for new learning.

To explain such a crazy notion as VT requires that schools have a reasonable understanding of systems thinking and a willingness to suspend judgment for a while. It also means accepting that the current management systems in use are broken and were never intended for the world we now live in. In fact they are making the world a worse and more dangerous place, and schools should never do this.

But this is jumping the gun. Trying to describe what systems thinking is and how it works is difficult enough. In part, it is an intuitive mix of primitive and ancient thinking, our birthright schema for understanding our environment and recognizing connections and patterns regarding how things work and interconnect. Unfortunately, such intuition can only take us so far and can go very wrong indeed if left uninformed. When things become distorted, broken, and dysfunctional (a wicked problem), it is counterintuition that is more likely to rescue us and return us from delusion to common sense.

We think the system we have is right. We even think it can be fixed rather than systemically changed. And that is the problem: our thinking.

# ONE

# The Way We Think We Think Isn't the Way We Think

> The companies that survive the longest are the ones that work out what they uniquely can give to the world not just growth or money but their excellence, their respect for others, or their ability to make people happy. Some call these things a soul.
>
> —Charles Handy, 1997

How on earth can you write about a universal, organizational model that is so much a prisoner of the past and so ambivalent of human psychology; one that courts so much controversy and one swayed by paradoxes and untested assumptions; a model that at any moment in time is dynamic and static, simple and complex, successful and failing; a system of abandoned values and uncertain purposes run by altruists?

Schools are often the focus of intense frustration and criticism, and attempts to improve them often prove futile, especially in the United States. At least the United States realizes it has a problem. Yet we somehow "choose" to persist with the same reform ideas that have failed again and again. The United States has reached a point at which bold decisions are needed to replace misguided and ill-judged reformational change; yet it is hesitant and stuck and, as ever, it tries to buy its way out.

Schools as organizations are indispensable to us, and yet they seem incapable of utilizing the human resources (teachers, parents, and students) and accumulated knowledge available to them. It makes no sense that our creative, talented, and amazing teachers should be held captive by the past in the way that they appear to be. We need clarity and we need to look at what schools might do to change their circumstances, especially what passes as the normal thinking of school managers.

W. Edwards Deming, the great organizational guru, believed that managers have to change with particular reference to the way they think and work, and this book is a fourth attempt at offering a key to the cell door and highlighting the best escape route (the only one in my view) to systemic change and a brighter learning future.

This means that there are two strange areas to explore. First, we need to understand the nature of the illusions that appear to be at work and lead to delusional management behaviors, judgments, and assumptions. Then we need to see if the systems thinking remedy suggested, mixed-age tutoring (and later, mixed-age teaching) and the values, psychology, and management principles that underpin such a seemingly odd proposal, provide the counterintuitive answers and leverage point needed for school transformation, and then on to systemic change.

Ideally, I should take readers to such schools so you might see this firsthand. Any book is a poor substitute. As it is, on completion of a book or an essay, I realize that not only is there still far more to explain, but that I hadn't quite said what I meant to say in the first place. Systems thinking is like that, and I find myself scribbling again, hoping that this fourth time I'll get closer to seeing the school at work and persuading my teacher heroes and school managers to look again. The problem is that books are never sufficient; they can never replace conversations between people who continue to be so enthusiastic about the wonders that schools somehow perform despite those who have mastery over them.

The problem is that schools are far more complicated, more precious, and more fragile as organizations than we think, and it is difficult to see, let alone describe, the array of multiple system pieces, the elemental parts all working at the same time to form a school's culture. It becomes even more difficult when these are overlaid with emotions like dedication, passion, despair, and love, and when schools are populated by some of the most selfless, brilliant, altruistic, creative, hard-working, and dedicated people we are ever likely to meet.

The most important things that systems thinking can do is explain the vital importance of the school, how wrongly it works as a system, and suggest an alternative. In so doing, it must show how to avoid the trap of tautology, oxymoron, and paradox. Only then can it be redesigned and its prisoners given a key to the cell door.

This must be done in a way that blames nobody. U.S. teachers are as good as teachers anywhere; better, perhaps. They can make a broken system appear to work in a culture made complex by absent policies on well-being and equity, and this makes them special and deserving of a better explanation of the challenges they face.

As things stand, the teacher dropout rate is as worrying as that of their students. In the United States the national statistic surveys do not make for pleasant reading. While 200,000 new recruits begin school each year, around 20,000-plus will quit by the summer. Thirty percent are gone by year three and 45 percent leave schools after five years. Thirty-seven percent of teachers are over fifty and nearing retirement.

The reasons cited are seldom related to salary (less than 20 percent), but instead to organizational factors, a system that doesn't work, whereby the promised support subsystems fail. These include parental support, administrative support, and collegial support, a disconnected system of uncertain values. An excellent overview is offered by Claudia Graziano (2014). You may ask what all of this has to do with mixed-age structure; surely these will only make matters worse!

Same-age systems have to abide by laws of separation and limitation. They start with separation, lead to limitation, and this leads to a whole litany of bad places. Mixed-age systems start by building connectivity and maintaining communication flow. They heal.

The chapters of this book feature significant work by true academics and organizational leaders. Otherwise, to simply present a mixed-age solution to the wicked problem of public schools in the United States and the factory school management system used worldwide, is asking for trouble; the justifications had better be good!

## THE OTHER SYSTEMS, 1 AND 2

To think rationally about schools as organizations requires a firm footing in systems thinking theory combined with an ability to accept that all is not as it seems when we look at schools. Our judgments and the decisions we make seem to depend on two other systems working in some kind of harmony. These are our intuitive selves and our more analytical selves. How we use both to make sense of the circumstances in which we find ourselves is the challenge here. It seems we have a problem seeing the actualité of school.

Daniel Kahneman (2011) wrote a book, *Thinking, Fast and Slow,* that many regard as his seminal work. His topic (in my simple terms) elucidates the way we think and how we go about making sense of our world and why we sometimes get our decisions and judgments so wrong. When this happens, it is all too easy to hurtle off in the wrong direction or, just as likely, to repeat past mistakes. We are ruled more by our intuitive biases and tribal psychology than we think! The world is still reeling from catastrophic financial decisions and assumptions caused by errant economic judgments and biases. We do not have to look far for our Black Swans, swine, and swindlers!

All of this is germane to systems thinking, which seeks to clarify systems flaws using a mix of analysis, data, graphs, stories, and metaphors—any means, objective and subjective, that might help us *see* better and understand more. This enables more effective judgments to be made and better strategies for improvement to be designed.

The fact is that as we navigate the minefield of public education, we are prone to repeat mistakes. We muddle through life guided uncertainly by what Kahneman calls "biases of intuition." While the approach and judgments of those who run school systems may seem rational and perfectly normal, others question what is going on and observe what appear to be obvious errors being made. It seems that people (school administrators included) come across as very certain even when they are wrong. As Kahneman says:

> we normally allow ourselves to be guided by impressions and feelings, and the confidence we have in our intuitive beliefs and preferences is usually justified. But not always. We are often confident when we are wrong, and an objective observer is more likely to detect errors than we are. (2011, p. 4)

We need to take great care when we assume that failing schools are caused by poor teachers and are curable by use of carrots and sticks. All is rarely as it seems.

Systems thinking seeks to be an objective observer. Kahneman introduces us to two "characters" to explain how we go about thinking and making decisions: System 1 and System 2. This is as good a place as any to start us thinking about matters concerning "illusion" and "delusion," so throughout this section, keep school management in mind.

System 1 thinking is effortless, intuitive, and impulsive. It is fast, automatic, and independent, and even finishes other people's sentences. It recognizes patterns instantly and is quick to spot new ones forming and make best-bet assumptions and associations.

In familiar situations, it makes accurate predictions and is rarely short on suggesting strategies for action based on what is known, regardless of whether such suggestions are right or wrong. While we walk along a road, it is System 1 that is absorbing and analyzing a huge array of complex information, forever monitoring the environment for threats and anything unusual. The ways in which schools engage with the complexity they face will be an important feature that follows this chapter.

System 2, however, is slow, lazy, and ponderous, but is who we think of as our *self*. This is the system of our conscious reasoning that governs our beliefs, the choices we make, and decides what action to take, if any. It is our rational thinking. System 2 thinks it is in full control, the sensible one, but the real "action hero," Kahneman advises, is System 1.

While intuitive System 1 comes up with all kinds of instant responses and suggestions, it sometimes requires the slow and lazy System 2 to check for accuracy and put the responses into some kind of order. While we walk along the road, it is System 2 that is mulling over what to have for lunch or an appointment that needs to be kept, while System 1 continues monitoring a whole mess of information. It seeks anything unusual such as pattern changes and anything odd that might grab its attention and requires making sense of and an immediate response.

Between the two system characters, they get a lot right, but they can also make mistakes, especially when System 1 tries its hand at interpreting unfamiliar circumstances like Black Swans that require explanation beyond the knowledge it has. Without sufficient information, System 1 resorts to guesswork based on what it knows, and this can result in biases and inaccuracies being brought into play and simplistic responses and best-bet guesses.

Meanwhile, the work that System 2 does is particularly arduous; it seems that any cognitive, decision-making process requires huge effort and our System 2 tires quickly when thinking. This can be particularly so when working on math problems and even maintaining self-control, something that can be easily lost under pressure.

This is an obvious thinking weakness. Unless System 2 is alert and on the ball, System 1 can jump to all kinds of inaccurate conclusions when information is missing, and so cause System 2 to make mistakes (especially, remember, when System 2 is tired, distracted, or doing hard sums). Biases can all too easily be assumed, pass unnoticed, and go undetected. After all, System 2 is the responsible one!

There are many biases. System 1 will invariably try and believe and make some kind of sense of what it sees, even if it makes no real sense, and this makes our fast and intuitive System 1 "gullible." Trusting intuition has its risks. If at the same time, lazy System 2 becomes "depleted" when called on to think and make a decision, it is possible for System 2 to be unduly influenced and even persuaded as to what is or isn't the case by intuition and assumption, especially given System 1's innate penchant for constructing what appears to be a plausible explanation.

So what has all of this to do with systems thinking and schools? The answer is this: thinking is not as straightforward as we think! It involves dealing with the illusions and/or biases that inform our working assumptions; in turn these can have an impact on research and its interpretation. Much educational research, valuable as it might be, assumes that same-age grouping is operationally benign. This leads administrators to make errant assumptions and judgments. According to Robin Hogarth (2001), even learning can be a "wicked" environment, one in which professionals are just as likely to learn the wrong lessons from experience as the right.

What we see is never all there is, and what we know in the absence of systems thinking is rarely enough. If we continue along a road fed with bias and illusion or fail to realize that these exist, mistakes self-perpetuate. It is wise to seek a second opinion, a systems thinking view. Otherwise, it is possible that our decisions and judgments will not only be fragile and uncertain, but possibly completely wrong and delusional.

The longer we experience this lack of awareness, the longer problems accumulate and wicked messes form; the dross accrues, and as our biases become accepted, this makes them more difficult to counter. In school, our working reality can become distorted. It helps explain how organizations exert such an influence on behavior and on the nature of the mental models used to navigate everyday work and systems.

How can it possibly be that so many jurisdictions put their faith in a factory school system that is so narrowly focused, produces so much waste, does so much harm, and ignores so much potential? Why is it that so much goes wrong in public services that we seem unable to fix? It appears that the way we think gets hung up with familiar patterns, what we think we know, even when the solutions it offers no longer appear to work.

In schools, we have an overreliance on known and familiar reform and managerial strategies as solutions, even though these have previously failed to find the answers we seek. We even have a notion of the school as a "learning organization," discussed later. However, despite all we do and all the elegant descriptors we have, the learning organization is as far off as ever, contrary to those deluded into believing they work in one!

System 1 is forever seeking coherence and it will make up a story to suit what it sees based on the information it has. Problems occur when lazy System 2 simply endorses such beliefs. We jump to conclusions that are not always justified. You can just hear that wonderful Laurel and Hardy phrase as System 2 talks to System 1: "Well, here's another fine mess you've gotten me into."

Kahneman describes the difficulty as WYSIATI (what you see is all there is), and because what we see is never enough, biases creep in to plug the gaps.

The beauty of systems thinking is that it enables us to look again at what we see in a less accepting way. It is a science that appreciates that not all is as it seems. Meanwhile, System 2 is too lazy and depleted to consider any risky redesign alternatives because the math is just too hard, the thinking too demanding, and the personal risk too great. The consensus will always play it safe, despite this being the more risky option. As Charles Handy so often said, such paradoxes are everywhere.

## FIRST DAY

On the very first day of secondary school, students are plunged into a maelstrom of information. They have to learn how to cope in a system, one that will change and shape them and have a lasting impact. Having quoted a scene from one film, here is a quote from another, "Mean Girls."

Cady Heron has been taught at home but now finds herself having to make sense of school life. The screenwriter, Tina Fey, allows us to see the school system from a customer point of view:

> The first day of school was a blur. A stressful, surreal blur. I got in trouble for the most random things—"Where are you going?" "Oh, I have to go to the bathroom." "You need the lavatory pass." "Okay, can

> I have the lavatory pass?" "Nice try. Have a seat." If not that, "Don't read ahead!" "No green pen!" "No food in class!" I had never lived in a world where adults didn't trust me, where they were always yelling at me.

Welcome to school, Cady! Schools manage numbers. In fact, the first thing a school sees is numbers to be managed. The system has rules, lots of them. Cady will also learn about procedures, protocols, practices, principles, and more besides. The rules are there to achieve compliance and prevent chaos. They are backed up by rewards and punishments. The school thinks it is managing complexity because WYSIATI. It is actually creating complexity!

Unfortunately, uncertain attitudes form from learning relationships limited by time and numbers. Cady does not feel trusted or treated like an individual. The individual is hidden in the numbers, grades, and targets, and can stay hidden throughout their time at school.

What is proposed in this book is something entirely different: that the very first meeting between school and student has to be individualized. It has to be fast, clear, and accurate, and the learning relationship that forms between the homeroom or tutor and tutee has to be lasting and based on trust. It is the single most important act of the school.

This means that on entry to school every player's Systems 1 and 2 have to be awake and on the same page, and preferably the same planet. Such a first interface requires preparation, focus, and must be as bespoke as possible. In a vertical system, this is facilitated with ease. In a horizontal system, it is a numbers problem, largely ignored and always delayed.

How this first learning relationship is achieved is critical to learning and psychological well-being, and is set out in detail in *The Systems Thinking School* and re-emphasized here as part of the school redesign process. It is why mixed-age approaches are so important, but to say this at this stage is meaningless to those unfamiliar with the concept and practice of vertical tutoring.

Mixing students by age requires systems thinking. The idea that mixing grades or age groups is the best catalyst we have for full systemic change is counterintuitive. It will be disbelieved and probably dismissed as untenable: biases kick in; there is insufficient information! What you see is all there is and we don't see students organized into mixed-age settings, so we assume it cannot work. It increases complexity—so we think!

In every chapter that follows in this book, Kahneman seems to be there, checking any biases I inadvertently introduce as a systems thinking amateur. All I can claim is that I have made the journey, seen the evidence, and have more than earned my T-shirt. Further, this book appeals entirely to counterintuition! The many secondary teachers and students who work in mixed-age systems as their dominant management and learning culture tell me it has made them so much better and happier—they are my second opinion!

However, schools that attempt such a change in the absence of systems understanding will achieve little in the way of benefit. I can only hope Kahneman never reads this book, something former "friends" tell me I need never worry about!

We need to make inroads, and the next chapter looks at Peter Senge's work, especially the way learning organizations might work. How does he "see" it?

This is where we go next.

# TWO

# The Five Disciplines

> "I couldn't afford to learn it," said the Mock Turtle with a sigh. "I only took the regular course."
> "What was that?" inquired Alice.
> "Reeling and Writhing, of course, to begin with," the Mock Turtle replied; "and then the different branches of Arithmetic—Ambition, Distraction, Uglification, and Derision."
> —Lewis Carroll, *Alice's Adventures in Wonderland* (1865)

To recap, given WYSIATI, we need help not only in seeing more, but in interpreting what we see. Systems thinker Linda Booth Sweeney provides a more than helpful six-step sequence that describes the systems thinking approach. The comments in parentheses and interpretations are my own.

1. First, tell the story (from the nineteenth century to the present and how we got to where we are).
2. Then name the elements. (The main players: teachers, tutors, students, and parents.)
3. Sketch out behaviors over time. (There seems to be almost no change to industrial organizational management behaviors and methods; still command and control in essence.)
4. Make the system visible. (Now examine the organization from a user or customer perspective given that teachers, students, and families are all customers of the system and each other. All provide and receive services.)
5. Look for leverage (or a simple means capable of reculturing organizational learning behaviors to make any changes needed; implement VT and systems thinking training).

6. Share and test (the new system ideas and make them operational; evaluate the change by comparing before and after and then keep innovating, working on the system).

The development of school systems worldwide seems to have stabilized, with the exception of the United States (part of the story of schools). However, this does not make the dominant global factory system in widespread use okay. All jurisdictions should ensure that all students have the opportunity to work in vertical teams at least for part of each school day for reasons that will become very clear as we proceed.

Simply making something appear to work better doesn't alter the deep underpinning meanings, structures, and learning relationships of a school. Neither does it make the world we live in a better or safer place. So we return to Peter Senge and *The Fifth Discipline* (2006) to look again, and to make the school system more visible (as per item 4 above). Given the massive influence of this work, it requires a bit of navigation.

Senge set out much of what we need to better understand systems thinking and its underpinning psychology and philosophy. He connects the past to the present, and the organizations in which we work to the lives we lead and the behaviors we have; he evidentially shows not only how things can go wrong on both counts, but how we might create better ways of organizing work and by implication improving both the life we lead and our ecological well-being. It is for me helpful and unhelpful, a book sometimes hoisted by its own petard. Maybe schools have misinterpreted it?

*The Fifth Discipline* tells the story of "learning organizations." Senge notes that the dominant management behavior over time is one of *command and control* (defined below) and that the unintended consequences of this approach are damaging both spiritually and ecologically. In effect, our organizational behaviors lead to messes, harm, and crises; innovation is stifled and values assumed.

He reminds us how hungry students are to be more involved, to be leaders, to work in teams, and to take more responsibility. He further suggests that much of the answer involves "student voice": the way we listen to students, involve them in the life of school, and allow time for reflective dialogue. Further, Senge points out that the schools we have need to change. The school as an organization has to be able to itself learn, to lead learning rather than be forever behind the learning curve. However, we are not told how to go about such change. There is no obvious leverage point, just disciplinary practice.

I have worked in hundreds of schools that tell me how "student voice" works. I have even been the school principal in such schools. Yet I have not seen a single school that remotely understands what such a concept means, nor have I come across any single school truly able to develop student leadership and responsibility for all. In fact, most do the opposite. Schools that claim otherwise are deluded by the linearity in which they operate. In fact, all of these desirables are more than doable, but not in schools governed by same-age groups that must always practice limitation and separation.

Senge suggests that what we need are communities that learn, ones driven by values and hence the central idea of the learning organization. These organizations will look very different from the ones we have and will be characterized by their ability to practice and master five disciplines. Senge tells us that learning organizations are:

> organizations where people continually expand their capacity to create the results they truly desire, where new and expansive patterns of thinking are nurtured, where collective aspiration is set free, and where people are continually learning how to learn together. (Senge 2006, p. 3)

This provides us with a good picture of what schools should or might be. Senge goes further. He talks of *metanoia*, a Greek word denoting a shift of mind. The learning organization is one that *self-organizes* and so has the capacity to be adaptive and create its own future. It would seem that our schools aren't even close and that any idea of a learning organization is simply a distant aspiration.

Seddon and O'Donovan (2010) were moved to ask the question: "Why aren't we all working for learning organizations?" This is something I'll explore later and in the following chapter. Their take on the reason is the dominant mindset of "command and control" management. In a command and control setup, there is "an obsession with managing the activity of workers." Seddon (2008) suggested that three questions preoccupy management decisions in service sector organizations. These are:

- How much work is coming in?
- How many people have I got?
- How long does it take to do things?

Sound familiar to school? It should. It is the industrial mindset, the mental model of school management and the unmoving obstacle to change, to learning, and to better schools.

Senge offers us "the three-legged stool" as our somewhat odd starter picture for a learning organization. The stool is a metaphor for an organization like a school. It proposes that the "core learning capabilities of teams" (the stool's seat) depends on the three legs of the stool being firmly attached. The three legs are a) understanding complexity, b) reflective conversation, and c) aspiration. In other words, an organization like a school is offered a picture, perhaps a set of descriptors, of the way it might go about its work in a purposeful way, and how it might begin to learn and self-organize through disciplinary practice.

The five underpinning disciplines that need to be mastered are systems thinking (the fifth discipline), personal mastery, mental models, building shared vision, and team learning (dialogue). Taking these on board in any substantive way has to avoid the delusion that they already reflect school practice and are somehow organizationally a priori.

Schools have a problem with change and reform. Look back and the road traveled is littered with failed initiatives, ideas that never worked, and reforms that went nowhere; not to mention the copious amounts of time, investment, and energy wasted. This has spawned a reinvention of the same old tired causes, and today we seem to have as many types of leadership as there are adjectives to describe them: licorice all-sorts regurgitated, laundry lists of desirable traits.

Schools tend to assimilate ideas, but in ways that produce no fundamental changes to organizational behaviors and learning relationships (the command and control mindset). If the fundamental form of the industrial factory secondary school hasn't really changed in a hundred years or so, why should the five disciplines fare any better? Just how long is this all going to take, given what time we have?

This is the crux of the challenge. Schools can grab all the ideas they want from their environment and claim them to be functional and operative ("make them their own" is the common phrase of delusion), but the working fundamentals remain the same. The fundamental form of the linear school based on same-age structure will always be to separate and limit, and it is only when schools see and understand why they can move on as organizations aspiring to deeper learning and even more effective teaching. Senge's idea is to practice the disciplines and to understand the interlinked structures based on "practices, principles, and essences."

To master the disciplines requires distinct stages of learning. It cannot all be done at once. It is a gradual process that involves an understanding of learning and interpersonal learning relationships to develop new capacities. Diana Smith (quoted in Senge, p. 386) advises an approach that includes the following (my interpretations):

- Cognitive capacities: Seeing things more clearly and speaking a new language. This leads to seeing the assumptions in play with greater clarity.
- New action rules: As old assumptions loosen, people experiment with new rules based on new assumptions. They start to innovate and think differently.
- New values and assumptions: People become values-led and these hold under stress. They combat ambiguity and this develops the capacity to learn.

For me, this "three-stage continuum" for developing new capacities or capabilities is precisely the domain of system thinking and subsumes

Senge's other four disciplines. Diana Smith's book (2011) is well worth reading, given its emphasis on relationships and learning.

As things stand, schools are stuck in an organizational paradox between being pro-learning and anti-complexity; they need a systems understanding of the relationships in play and the assumptions that determine methods in use. From inside the school, this paradox cannot be seen, let alone resolved, but it is there all the same and governs each school day.

Student voice is a good idea until schools get hold of it. What students quickly learn from student voice is that no one is listening, and even when they are, no real changes occur. They learn that democracy doesn't actually work all that well in practice. It is the same with the disciplines. The disciplines have not really impacted school change but we like to assume they have. The formulaic way they are presented is unlikely to bring about the systemic change needed. They are important but need care.

If Senge is right, it should be possible to compare the linear (same-age) school system (the dominant factory model) with one based on a mixed-age, non-linear form, one that undoes the industrial command and control ethic. When the two systems are compared (same-age versus mixed-age), what becomes abundantly clear is that the latter can make the journey and aspire to be a learning organization, and the other will eventually perish; a beautiful case of educational Darwinism.

But I need to explain why this is. Senge's basic constructs are grouped under the three embracing headings of aspiration, reflective conversation, and understanding complexity. When these are in place and functional, it is proposed that they provide the means of developing the "core learning capabilities for a team." They enable an organization to learn and self-organize (learn, diversify, adapt, innovate).

As I am unable to draw even the simplest three-legged stool, please imagine you are looking down on one in figure 2.1. If we apply this model to schools, we should expect to see the complete whole, not a two- or one-legged stool unfit for purpose or one that is wobbly. Every leg has to be present and operational.

The actual disciplines are a mix of methods, ideas, and practices that combine in ways that enable an organization to learn. Each is critical to the other; each depicts areas of essential learning. These are:

**Systems thinking:** A problem-solving approach that enables us to see whole patterns, the elements and their interactions from different perspectives. The discipline enables an understanding of complexity and how to resolve it. Without systems thinking, the other disciplines cannot work.

**Mental models:** These are deeply ingrained assumptions, part reality/part distortion, used to rationalize and make sense of what we do. The

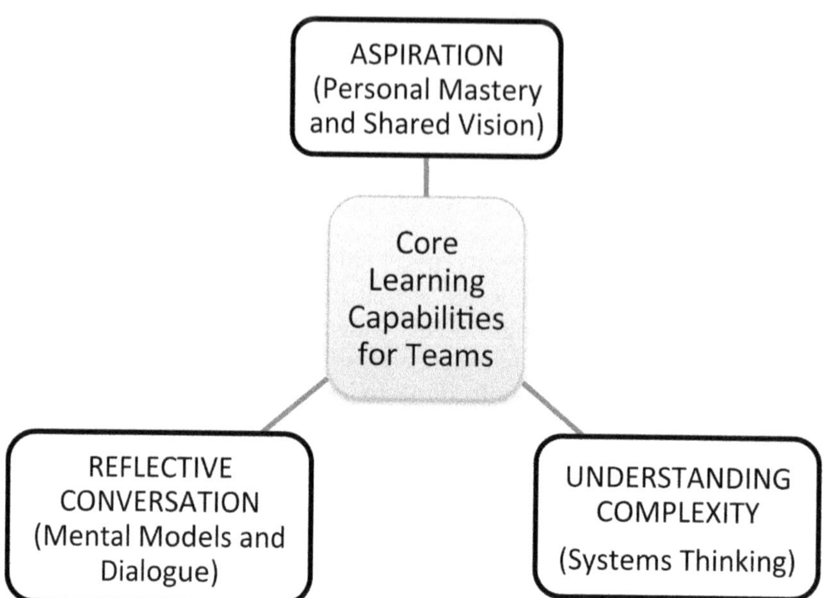


**Figure 2.1.**

discipline is to uncover any errant convictions and expose them to scrutiny. Hence the need for systems thinking.

**Personal mastery:** This is the learning organization's spiritual tiller. This discipline is described by Senge as "continually clarifying and deepening our personal vision, of developing patience, and of seeing reality objectively." Hence (again) the need for systems thinking.

**Building shared vision:** This discipline involves the translation of individual vision into a shared vision. This is not a leadership laundry list but "a set of principles and guiding practices." These should garner commitment rather than compliance. Hence the need for systems thinking.

**Team learning/Dialogue:** Team learning requires the management team to unlearn the existing mental model of their organization in terms of customers and markets. Dialogue, which includes thinking in teams, is the essential attributive discipline. Assumptions have to be suspended or exposed for true dialogue to occur. Hence the need for systems thinking.

The point in question is the inclusion of systems thinking within this list. It is not so much a discipline as the rationale that guides systemic change.

These disciplines appear to cover all the bases for a learning organization to form given the accumulated knowledge gathered from organizations internationally. They seem to be spot-on and familiar until confronted with the very paradox they are intended to counter, the industrial mental model we have of the school and in particular the way school managers view complexity and the thinking they use to control it. It starts with a basic premise: complexity is a bad thing—right? The premise is an errant assumption and built on another assumption: that school managers understand complexity when they see it.

The mental model used by school managers has been honed by a century of largely ineffectual reform. Hence it has become set in its industrial ways and become expert at deflection. The school looks at any new learning "tools," say, the disciplines on offer, and says, "Ah! Yes, we already use these. Here, I'll show you where we keep them! We are a learning organization after all. We all learn here so we must be. We aspire, we reflect, we understand complexity . . . see, we do it all!"

Indeed, a cursory glance at the school might even suggest that schools already conform to the model of the three-legged stool. Surely, it can be argued, schools manage complexity on a daily basis; surely schools and our players engage regularly in reflective conversations (aren't school managers forever in meetings?); surely schools have aspiration covered too. Job done! But look again, get a second opinion, and all is not as it seems. It is all so much illusion and delusion.

These are organizational assumptions: claims on reality. It is all a veil of pretense, words that are superficially assimilated into the language used by schools, and so lead to more delusion over time. More separation and limitation. So how does it work? What grounds can there be for the suggestion that such capable people have got it wrong? The answer is of course the influence of the system itself on how the learning and teaching work is being done and why it is being done in the way it is.

School managers operating grade schools or same-age year systems have no difficulty in explaining precisely how their school works. They will readily say how each of the disciplines nominated by Senge, with the exception of systems thinking (the one they need), is used to achieve learning and teaching ends. But a second glance shows that all is not as it appears.

The incorporation of the five disciplines in any substantive form is assumed. Their existence is at best partial so they can only be used at the most superficial level, one that promotes sameness rather than innovation. They have been customized and adapted for use in schools that operate same-age methodologies, resulting in a mismatch of organizational linguistics. Schools have a habit of grabbing words and redefining them to suit a multitude of behaviors. It is not a fault, but it is a product of the industrial mindset, the mental model in use to explain and rationalize away all things.

The reason is simple. Systems thinking, the discipline needed to understand and engage with complexity, has not so much gone AWOL from schools but was never there in the first place (and still isn't). Senge's grouping of the five disciplines and how they work are only tenuously combined in a loose framework of philosophy and metaphysics. They tend to be descriptors of a learning organization already formed. They do not help schools make the move from where they are to where they need to be.

For me descriptors, even translated into practical activities, are confused with disciplines. This limits their usefulness in removing delusion. But there is an even greater difficulty. Many brought up in systems thinking see systems thinking as a small part of *system dynamics*, as a kind of contributory element or subsystem. It is a view that undermines systems thinking and is a mistaken view. It is the other way around. In the same way, systems thinking is not the fifth discipline at all. If it is a discipline, it is the only one needed.

Without the truer and more precise language of systems thinking, the other so-called disciplines can never work optimally; indeed they can hardly work at all. The result is that the other four disciplines needed for organizational learning can never work as viable learning constructs of change. People cannot themselves easily remove the mental models imposed by the constraints and language distortions and methods of the systems in which they work.

I realize that this takes us into an irresolvable chicken-and-egg situation. Structure truly does influence behavior, just as Senge and Deming say. To change this requires systems thinking, not disciplinary practices alone. Yes, there are obvious linkages, but it is systems thinking that has the answers, the language, and the clarity of purpose. It can be learned quickly by everyone, especially as it is fundamentally common sense.

In fact, the situation is getting worse. Four of the five disciplines have been superficially assimilated by schools and actually work to keep the linear, factory school system the same in perpetuity. Reflective conversations are useless if the system defines what they are, their context, and practice. Ironically, part of the explanation for this is to be found in the disciplines themselves.

In the strangest and most paradoxical of ways, the disciplines reveal an absent truth. The relationship between complexity (the numbers) and the systems thinking needed to handle complexity inadvertently reveal the truer purpose of school.

The key to understanding the universal factory school model, including its same-age structure, is all to do with the way schools perceive and understand complexity. This is the domain of systems thinking. The division of schools into same-age groups based on industrial factory management ideas is a physical process of managing numbers. The model persists even though the justifications have long gone. Because it persists, the justifications we have, set against the damage done, must be assumed.

It seems that the original school blueprint created a mental model and a management psychology so pervasive as to defy change, one able to assimilate, contort language, and defy the learning relationships so essential in today's world. Schools are adamant that they must manage complexity to prevent chaos. What schools do not realize is that they are making matters worse not better, more complex not less.

Cady Heron, going through the school hall on her first day, has to be managed. People have to be managed and follow rules and procedures to prevent chaos. Later, when Cady leaves school, she will manage people in the same way she learned in school, from the system in use.

It is happening now. The nasty management loop for schools is completing itself. Gold stars for great teachers, punishment and reskilling for the rest, disciplines or not. The idea is that people have to be obsessively managed because otherwise they mess up—but they keep messing up. Managers think they can herd cats, managing the wrong things, people rather than systems. Here is their rule and guiding principle: people cannot be trusted; they need control orders and a script to follow!

For schools, complexity involves the management of the large numbers engaged in the teaching and learning process. There are high numbers of students and parents and a small number of school staff. It is an operation that appears to require an industrial solution, one that needs strict controls and engenders compliance. This complexity increases exponentially when parents want to get involved and start to demand a say, so any homeschool partnership too must be carefully limited and reduced to what is manageable. Human interaction is seen as complexity; I needn't point out the obvious learning paradoxes here.

How is this complexity of human learning relationships *managed*? By reduction, separation, and limitation. How else? Schools see no alternative. The five disciplines have to be adapted, reconfigured, and customized as industrial tools used to manage a linear system. The linear school must always distort semantics, meanings, and linguistics, and stretch them to cover all eventualities. Parent partnership, when examined closely, is not partnership at all. Communication too can never be what it is claimed; *communication* is actually not communications (two-way) at all. For schools, it is an information-out system, one way only, and limited at that! The school has it all under command and control!

This indicates the school door we need to enter. As Senge suggests, we need to understand the nature of complexity more precisely than we do. We need to know exactly why the school feels compelled to manage the complexity it perceives by limitation and separation in the way it does.

What was it that Cady Heron said in school that day? "I had never lived in a world where adults didn't trust me." Cady Heron is a systems thinker. She has a handle on systems thinking but soon the school will teach her not to trust; not in the classroom, not by teachers, but through the stymied social and learning relationships of same-age organization. The one that doesn't trust teachers either!

We need to get a handle on complexity and save Cady from assimilation by the Borg.

# THREE

# Complexity and Demand in Systems Thinking

So in a public service-like school, what exactly is complexity in systems thinking terms? The answer is relatively simple. It is the huge variety of customer *value demand* on the school's learning system. The value demand is all that customers need to be able to draw down from the school to live worthwhile and useful lives. Value demand is defined by the customers and the greater ecological system to which we belong, not just by what the school and the bigger school system decides to offer. In essence, the value demand is all that allows a child to grow and develop into who he or she was meant to be.

Parents tell us that what they want and value comprises a long list, *the variety of value demand*. Each is concerned with their unique child. Trawl the research and you'll find value demand expressed by parents in these broad terms:

- They want their child to be taught well and to do as well as possible at school.
- They would like their child to learn stuff, be encouraged and helped, and not be bullied.
- They would like the school to find and recognize their child's talents and realize his or her potential.
- They would like more information on their child's learning and any strategies for improvement.
- They would like to be kept informed and for intervention to be fast when matters go awry.
- They would like to be involved, to be part of the learning process.
- They want their child to aspire, often to do better than they did.

- They would like their child's needs to be recognized and individual attention given.
- They want good learning relationships in the school between students and staff alike.
- They would like someone at school to really know their child well, someone they can talk to at critical learning times.

Note how these values depend on developing learning relationships, the areas that schools eye as complexity to be managed. The school must convince (delude) itself into believing it can somehow deliver on value demand in the industrial form it has. It assumes.

Any failure to absorb and meet value immediately creates *failure demand.* Failure demand takes the form of complaints, reworking, drop-outs, anti-social behavior, and (of course) a loss of trust and increases in both cost and bureaucracy. Enter this trap and things get a lot worse. The list of failure demands is long and expensive; it drains resources, uses up energy, and weakens the school, causing it to require even more back office staff, more money, and external help. It also makes it more difficult to support new teachers and develop their expertise; the list goes on and on. It creates a mess that can quickly become a crisis.

In other words, if the school is unable to absorb the variety of value demand made on its system or simply assumes such demand is being met by the system it has, failure demand is an inevitable consequence. The school, being unable to absorb the complexity of the variety of value demand on its system, tries to control it through limitation and separation, but all that this does is increases complexity (management of failure demand) and make things far worse.

Because same-age systems always perpetuate reductionism and limitation as their single command management strategy, they can never get to terms with the challenge of value demand. Unable to absorb such complexity, the school makes complexity far worse. The practice of separation and limitation in schools is to offer a temporary Band-Aid to a desperate patient. Once the placebo effect wears off, things can take a sudden turn for the worse. Put another way, the school unknowingly recreates the very complexity it seeks to manage through a failure to individualize the service it offers.

There is a wealth of difference between being able to *absorb* complexity and thus being able to predict and respond to it, and *managing* complexity to simply try and reduce it. Without this systems thinking understanding and its accompanying language, the school persuades itself that all is well, customers are happy, and service levels are up to scratch.

The former implies an understanding of the variety of demand on the system, while the latter tends to see only the numbers and assumes that the inherent value demand is being met. The organization ceases to be driven by values in preference for assumption. When you see only numbers, the key management tools are limitation and separation. When you see value demand and meet it, you enter the domain of quality, the defining characteristic of true learning relationships and of interconnectivity.

Schools see such a list (above), the value demand on their system, and, just like the five disciplines, assume that they meet all demands, that these matters are somehow incorporated by what they do. Unfortunately this is a delusion, a redefinition of the facts. Schools may even point, just as they do with the disciplines, to places where each of the above demands is being met. But look closer at any *method in use* and all is not as claimed and provably so. The exponential growth of failure demand proves the self-deception. The organization's assumptions are invalid.

The options for a linear school based on same-age groups are miserably few when faced with large numbers of students and parents (customers) who require a more gold-plated and bespoke service. Its ability to cope with such demand is beyond its means in the form it has. One size has to fit many; complexity has to be reduced, limited, and batched; more money is always needed for increased back office staff to manage failure demand; compliance is all, reforms rain down, and confusion and complications increase.

Complexity for schools is neither viewed as a source of cross-border energy, nor as an opportunity, one better able to guide the school's work and define purpose. Such options are closed off, reduced, and limited. The irony is this: the value demand that customers want from the school is the same as the service that most schools want to give. Because same-age structures are inflexible, high in bureaucracy, and unbending in time, the customer care and individualized learning support needed cannot be effectively delivered; it becomes assumed and subsumed and values get lost along the way. Self-deceit, after all, is a mechanism that enables us to live with ourselves!

It is assumed de facto that same-age grouping is the default state for schools. For teaching organizations like schools, it probably is. For learning organizations, the nurturing of emotional and spiritual intelligence, and the support young learners need, it cannot be so assumed.

The research to support the contention that mixed-age organizations work better is almost entirely absent, despite the growing number of secondary schools that have adopted a mixed-age organizational culture. Why should researchers research the seemingly benign? What is prevalent in research, however, are the positive gains from mentoring, positive psychology, and teamwork, and in a VT school, every child is both a mentor and a mentee, just as every teacher and parent is. VT is learning relationship dependent. It needs the complexity of learning relationships to enable intrinsic learning,

The reason is that we are blind to structure. We see the way a school organizes itself as familiar and benign, so we concentrate on teachers not realizing that they are also system customers similarly constrained by the way the school organizes itself. Teachers have become sorters and batchers with mental models designed to suit, accepting of assumptions and able to rationalize to get through. We deny teachers the opportunity to be the absorbers of value demand that we need them to be and that they want to be.

The linear assumption is deeply embedded and has spread well beyond the boundaries of the school, embedding industrial mental models and preventing change. Its absence from research reflects a global if mistaken view that the same-age way a school structures itself is benign. Nothing could be further from the truth. If same-age grouping is the basic blueprint of industrial school design, then any leverage point for change should focus on mixed-age groups. When this happens, and systems thinking is applied, the model corrects itself. It is a case of Occam's Razor: the simplest (and most counterintuitive) explanation is the best.

As things are, each leg of Senge's three-legged stool damages the other. Each is trying unsuccessfully to support the learning teams, but each is too busy tripping over the inherent assumptions of the other. The failure of the school to understand and absorb the complexity of value demand distorts any reflective conversation; this acts to undermine aspiration, and for any quasi-learning organization like a school, this spells disaster and leads inevitably to an overdependence on extrinsic learning and factory school ethics. It also leads to more failure demand. Loops keep completing themselves in ways that ignore key feedback stocks.

While the three-legged *school* may somehow remain standing thanks to our teachers, it has distinctly wobbly legs and is not one that can be relied on to provide the "core learning" needed by school teams. It cannot become a learning organization, one in ecological balance with itself and other systems. Even when this broken feedback loop somehow completes itself, the school has to fall back on what it knows to solve the nature of the aspiration problem it has inadvertently created. No matter what the linear same-age school does, it is its karma to arrive at the wrong answer and to forever travel a land of unintended consequences.

Same-age grouping is a domino that sets in motion a sequence of command and control, management thinking that cannot meet the increasingly sophisticated variety of value demand the school faces. It makes us stare at the teacher as the culprit rather than the school as an organization. It causes us to think that a new pro-social program or reform will fix things. We think leaders need emotional support when all they need is systems understanding (training against value demand). We keep looking in the wrong place for the solutions we need and the judgments we call: WYSIATI.

The school is a simple linear factory that sifts, batches, and gift wraps students for delivery, ready or not. Along the way the school performs miracles but also causes harm. The many young people who leave school will perceive the world just as they were taught by the school as an organization. It is a largely dog-eat-dog world, uncertain of purpose and composed of a number of separate and wasteful factories damaging to the commons. Grab what you can, destroy the commons, and don't give a hang for Gaia.

It is to Deming I now turn, and the quotation by Senge (2006) in the introduction to *The Fifth Discipline:*

> People failed, he (Deming) realized, because they had been socialized into ways of thinking and acting that were embedded in their most formative institutional experiences. (p. xi)

Could the situation in school be even worse than feared, rippling out far beyond the school boundaries like a global contagion, reducing the common good and damaging interconnectivity among people? This is writ large in *The Fifth Discipline* in a damning paragraph by W. Edwards Deming and quoted by Senge:

> Our prevailing system of management has destroyed our people. People are born with intrinsic motivation, self-respect, dignity, curiosity to learn, joy in learning. The forces of destruction begin with toddlers—a prize for the best Halloween costume, grades in school, gold stars—and on up through university . . . loss unknown and unknowable. (p. x)

To that list of behaviors and underpinning it, I have no hesitation in citing the organization of schools based on same-age practice. This common denominator is the destructive determinant of how the industrial factory school operates. In schools children learn much about human relationships not through programs but through the rules, principles, protocols, policies, procedures, and practices of the school system in use, and when examined, these turn out to be almost the complete opposite of the learning values claimed.

In short, the design of the work determines performance and outcomes, what is achievable. Ergo, changing the design is far more effective than constantly trying to change people. What young people learn in school is repeated in the world of work: the loop completes and self-perpetuates industrial sameness. We then apply the management used in the world of work to the world of school and wonder why it doesn't work. Education is beset by these strange feedback loops frozen in time, self-perpetuating, misleading, and going nowhere fast.

Many others have alluded as much, including Shukla (1994), Belbin (1996), Handy (1998), Kanter (1998), Duffy (2010), Ackoff (2004), Wheatley (2004), Ackoff and Greenburg (2008), Meadows (2009), Drucker (2010), and more besides. It is to the prevailing system of management that we now turn, a system characterized by a number of flaws.

## A WORD ON LEARNING RELATIONSHIPS

In a same-age school there is high dependence on the teacher alone. Unfortunately the teacher has many students to teach and relationships can take an age to form. This endangers learning, adds risk, and poses problems for absorption of value demand, let alone meeting such demand. In a mixed-age school, one in which the home group or tutor group is mixed by age, learning relationships are many. This means that both the capability and capacity for absorbing and meeting the variety of value demands are not only fit for purpose, but of higher quality in all cases.

The home–school partnership is much stronger. All older students mentor younger students. Everyone in school is a leader, a mentor, and a mentee. Time can be flexed far more to suit. This makes the teacher-student relationship both more mature and more secure. There can now be reflective conversations, leadership everywhere, aspiration, value demands being better met, and interconnectivity increased.

When students left my large, vertically tutored, secondary schools, I was always able to write to parents and say that their sons and daughters had taught us so much. I was able to say with confidence that the world would be a better and different place because of their children. I do not think I could do this had I kept to the same-age system that limited and dulled so much human potential, experience, and learning relationships.

For an increasing number of schools, the mixed-age concept remains the best means of escape from the dominant industrial management paradigm in which schools are trapped. But then the mixed-age system is not a solution; it is simply a key for unlocking mental models and allowing imagination and innovation to make a good run for it before the system's prison guards give chase.

Value demand has to be managed by people who are capable, innovative, and trusted to do the value work. Fortunately our schools are full of such people, and parents are anxious to meet them and work with them. All we need is a method, one that puts us back in touch with who we are. A method that sees Cady Heron as an amazing person to be known, listened to, and trusted. We need people in the school who can flex time to get to know her well.

# FOUR

# A Letter, Some Thoughts, and Some Math

> Most people do not listen with the intent to understand; they listen with the intent to reply.
>
> —Stephen R. Covey, *The Seven Habits of Highly Effective People*

Before we get to our letter to parents, we need to pause again. In a world that is not all that it seems, pauses to reflect are advisable. The various McKinsey reports pay little attention to structure, preferring to highlight teachers (instructors) as the key to school improvement and inviting us into a world of tautology. Frank Coffield (2012) identified ten deficiencies in this influential report and the one that followed. Neither report has helped schools or public policy to develop in any substantive way, although the second effort was better than the first.

Neither has changed the basic factory form of schools—quite the opposite. Such reports are systems thinking deficient and, therefore, biased. Whenever people are criticized, it is best to look very closely at the organizations in which they work and then at those so quick to pass judgment. This bunch of misleading tautologies sent governments scurrying in different directions like headless chickens, and today the Program for International Student Assessment (PISA) ensures they continue to scurry. It takes a little time to spot the conjurer's trick if we ever do, but it is there hidden in our biases.

For systems thinkers, truths are usually counterintuitive but really just truths, a best means of describing what is actually happening in an organization as opposed to what good people may think or assume is happening, or wish us to think is happening. Truth sometimes has to be revealed; it is often illusory and counterintuitive, realized only when the illusion is understood and the delusion exposed as false. This is why counterintuitive truths are so worthy of attention.

We need an escape strategy.

*Fowler's Modern English Usage* describes "illusion" as follows:

> an impression that, though false, is entertained provisionally on the recommendation of the senses . . . , but awaits full acceptance and may be expected not to influence action.

A "delusion" is slightly different:

> A delusion is a belief that, though false, has been surrendered to and accepted by the whole mind as the truth, and so may be expected to influence action.

As Fowler says, what a conjuror does, his real action, is a delusion. The conjuror succeeds in deluding us into believing what is happening. What the conjuror performs is an illusion. The belief that the conjuror actually does what he says and appears to do is a delusion. These concepts can be applied to a school system.

If such a system is broken beyond repair and doesn't work, and we keep trying the same repairs believing we can make it work, we are deluding ourselves. Too often facts don't support beliefs when exposed by systems thinking. People are very ready to pass on delusional beliefs to the extent that they sell the illusion to the rest of us. The factory school flatters to deceive.

Once the curtain of illusion is drawn back, it exposes what was hidden, a true picture of what was there all along and shining in its counterintuitive obviousness. If systems thinking does anything, it revels in seeking out counterintuitive truths from the places where they hide and the illusory form they assume. Although as Fowler says, illusion and delusion are sometimes interchangeable, delusion really has a different meaning and requires a different approach to the challenge it poses for schools.

Let me set out some delusional beliefs and assumptions, and feel free to add your own. But before I present such a list, we need some systems thinking information. Herein may be the most important section so far.

## THE LINK AMONG PURPOSE, MEASURES, AND METHOD

We know that schools perform feats of real magic despite being managed by illusionists, so here is the picture stripped down.

A system must have a purpose, and what a system does is its purpose. It is no good being deluded into a world of false claims, publicized aims, and invalid intentions, one in which values are assumed, partnership downgraded, and learning relations swapped for teaching relationships. Today, that purpose is to ensure that children pass tests across an increasingly narrow range of performance criteria using a bar incrementally raised to ensure ongoing grading, standards, and separation.

What is happening is what is important, not the claimed aims, assumptions, and intentions. We know this because it is pass rates that we measure and use to judge performance. We do not measure goodness, resilience, courage, team attributes, helpfulness, thoughtfulness, enthusiasm, and so on. Schools and teachers are judged on numerical objectives.

Here is the rub: what we measure determines the method schools use. If we measure graded pass rates, the method in use tends to reflect this, and that is precisely why we have the schools we have rather than the schools we need. We ignore our customers and instead invite them into an unwinnable and frenetic standards war while the world's stock of goodness declines.

We think in the current linear same-age system:

- That people (our teachers, parents, and students) are the problem that needs fixing when things go inevitably wrong in an organization like a school.
- That "poor" schools have "poor" teachers by spurious definition. They are the guilty ones, not the pre-created social and organizational milieu in which they find themselves.
- That schools can tackle bullying and gang membership using prosocial "programs" (not realizing that schools' operational system itself is often the unwitting cause of such behaviors).
- That teacher reward systems, intensive evaluation by output, and annual appraisals motivate staff and lead to improvement.
- That organizing learning by age is a good idea and that separating peer groups is helpful. The opposite is the counterintuitive truth.
- That poverty, mental health, and welfare can all be discounted as factors affecting learning and teaching. It is all down to the quality of the teacher.
- That great teaching can be coerced through incentives, targets, and evaluation rather than being the product of a great and more purposeful system.
- That test results are all that count as assessment for learning and system outputs.
- That what we measure is what is important, remembering that measures determine method. If we measure exam results, we create an exam system (method).
- That racing to the top is educative.
- That values can be assumed. Schools publish these claims, ergo they must exist.
- That command and control structures work (that we even know what they are).

- That school "policies" rather than better organizational practices can somehow ensure "that every child matters" and "none are left behind."
- That school systems are savvy regarding child psychology, care, and in-group loyalty. There is incongruity here.
- That parent partnership (there can be none in linear schools) can be prescribed, set out, integrated, and made to work.
- That schools can become learning organizations.
- That schools prepare young people for the world of work.
- That pro-social programs are sufficient, essential, and effective for well-being and changing errant behavior.
- That school counselors can replace tutors rather than support them.
- That leaders need visions and that everyone needs targets. Everyone actually needs strategies for improvement (the *how* rather than the *what*).
- That it is possible for school leaders to transform schools humanely without systems thinking knowledge.
- That it is possible to train teachers and managers by ignoring value demand.
- That reforms and other expensive and repeat failures work.
- That throwing money and financial incentives at schools works.
- That there can be formative and summative assessment in a linear model.
- That cherry-picking ideas from schools and other jurisdictions will fix things.
- That the staff and teachers trying to make the school work are what is at fault rather than the way that the school organizes itself as a learning system.
- That a three-tier system whereby children change schools (junior high school to high school) is somehow educationally useful. (This simply damages and sets back essential learning relationships.)
- That super-sized schools are efficient, effective, and save money.

So the list accumulates. The fact is that we are prey to illusion while we seem to thrive on delusion. Such delusional behaviors are, according to Robert Trivers (2011), an unconscious and self-protecting means of dealing with some of life's harsh realities and of securing advantage. But while delusion may be an innate state, it has consequences. Problems arise when we are so immersed in our delusional ways that we can no longer see the wood for the trees.

It is Trivers who describes the contradictions that then arise. The information we seek out causes us to act in a way that invariably destroys the same information. We deny the truth to ourselves and even "project on to others traits that are in fact true of ourselves—and attack them."

To lead us into this maze is my all-time favorite quotation from the systems thinking philosopher and problem-dissolving guru, Russell Ackoff (2004):

> The righter we do the wrong thing, the wronger we become. When we make a mistake doing the wrong thing and correct it, we become wronger. When we make a mistake doing the right thing and correct it, we become righter. Therefore, it is better to do the right thing wrong than the wrong thing right. (p. 2)

It boils down to knowing the right things from the wrong things, and the presence of delusion offers only a 50/50 chance of success: first things first.

Let's write a letter from the school to parents saying how we might change all of the above.

## A LETTER HOME

Set out below is just such a letter from school, and some general thoughts. They include elements relating to a journey from delusion to system thinking design and all hint at the need for a counterintuitive approach to the way schools organize themselves, a change of system at the level of learning relationships. The contents may or may not make sense at this point, given that much of the necessary background information is missing. By the end of the book, however, all should be obvious if it is not already so.

I encourage you to circle back and reread the letter when you have finished the book, and if you are a head teacher, to send it! This letter is one that high schools in New Zealand, Australia, pockets of Europe, and most of the United Kingdom are likely to recognize immediately. I can add to that list schools that I have trained in China, Qatar, Japan, and more. It is one that many schools have already sent.

To most schools in the United States, such a letter will probably come across as fatuous, bombastic, and idealistic—completely unnecessary. Stuff, schools will wrongly claim that they already (delusionally) do. Others might find the reference to terms like VT (vertical or mixed-age tutoring) and systems thinking somewhat odd, curious, and possibly irksome. But having gotten this far, you may be at least intrigued.

Whatever the effect, the reasons for placing this draft letter somewhere near the front of this book will become clear. The first challenge is to persuade schools to at least read it; the second is to understand it; and the third is to send it. This book is here to enable completion of all three stages, but I am happy if schools complete the first and seek a second opinion.

The Universal Linear High School
New York

Dear Parents,

For some time now, ULHS has been investigating an organizational culture called vertical tutoring (VT), a systems thinking approach to the way schools support and promote learning. The key focus of VT is to develop high-quality learning relationships that bring out the best in all who are engaged in the learning process. This includes all students, all parents, and all staff.

As a school, we have been researching this approach, have received professional advice, and have spoken to schools that have adopted VT. We are now in a position to involve all staff, students, and you in these discussions. Moving to a VT system is a significant change and is not without its challenges. We are anxious, therefore, that parents and students feel informed and have an opportunity to comment.

To this end, an information evening for parents will be held on [Insert Date]. Special assemblies will be held for all students and training will be provided for all staff and for older students. Our intention is to enable our students to learn from students in schools that have already moved to a VT system. Set out here is what a change to VT will mean and the reasons for this change.

*So what is Vertical Tutoring?*

The change to VT will see a significant reduction in the size of homeroom or tutor groups, which means that all staff employed by the school in a professional capacity, teachers and non-teachers, will be involved in tutoring for a short time each day. In turn, the new tutor groups will have both a lead tutor and a co-tutor, a significant investment in higher-quality learning relationships. Tutor time will be moved to a new twenty-minute slot before morning break.

The key change, however, involves the composition of the tutor groups. Each new tutor group will be populated by students from all year groups, creating a balance of age, gender, ability, ethnicity, and behavior, so that all groups share a similar profile. It is critical that "friendship" is not a first consideration. Each tutor group would then be allocated to one of eight houses or colleges, creating schools within schools. This is sometimes called a *nested system,* and will ensure that every child is known and valued as an individual.

*Why change?*

This change is caused by our frustration with the linear, peer-based education system. No matter how tutor time is arranged and organized, and no matter how skilled the tutor, the current home-room arrangements fall short of what is needed to support the key areas on which successful learning and teaching depend. Our research shows that a VT culture meets a number of critical learning needs that are not only of benefit to all, but are ones that same-age systems can only aspire to.

In particular, the introduction of VT will enable our school to:

1. Significantly improve parent partnership and parent involvement in the learning process.
2. Provide opportunities for all students, not the few, to develop as leaders and mentors.
3. Establish stronger, lasting, and more substantive learning relationships between students, parents, and the school.
4. Intervene rapidly and effectively when things go wrong or when there are concerns.
5. Develop better learning dispositions and attitudes that research advises and we all know are critical to increasing learning intelligence.
6. Ensure a significant reduction in bullying and gang influence through the new mentoring and in-group loyalty structures.
7. Keep aspirations high by working more closely with students and parents to improve individual and group support.
8. Change the way assessment for learning works so that it better supports learning and teaching.
9. Improve information flow between home and school—so vital to learning and to successful outcomes.

Our research shows that VT is the best and most cost-effective means of ensuring that we deliver on our promises as a school; it will enable us to do our best for all students and to walk the talk of the values we hold dear. VT will also provide a better means of ensuring that every student is recognized, known, and supported. Personal tutors will not only see every child every day, but care passionately about them as young people and as learners. We will build a new and better communications, assessment, and support system around this key learning relationship.

But this is not the only learning relationship that VT enhances. It is also important to us that parents benefit by having a personal but enhanced contact with tutors who not only know each child well, but who can listen to your concerns and ideas. VT will ensure that our partnership with you works effectively.

Students will be in tutor time for about twenty minutes each day; there will not be a formally taught pro-social program during this time. The rest of the school day, evenings, weekends, and social networking time is more than sufficient for students to maintain their current friendships. The intention is that having students of different ages trained in leadership and mentoring, and who are able to assist, guide, and support others through the example they set and the empathy they show, will provide benefits for all students.

We expect the change to VT to make a significant impact on every child's self-esteem, confidence, to the quality of teaching and learning, and to the individual support that the school offers. We want all children to be the kind of leaders that the school needs them to be, that we know they can be, and that they know they have to be in the world beyond school.

Tutors will play a vital role in this process. They will be there to support mixed-age tutoring and mentoring in ways that benefit all students. They will also act as your child's personal mentor, guide, and advocate throughout each student's career at school.

*How will parent partnership be improved?*

Despite the increased complexity of education today, parents are currently given a meager few minutes with a subject teacher each year. This is simply inadequate and is not "partnership" by any stretch of the imagination. Neither are *opportunities* for parents to contact the school sufficient. Parent partnership, the school's working relationship with you, must be built in, not added on as an afterthought.

We are aware that research shows that families and peer groups exert a powerful influence on student outcomes. This is why as a school we need to work more closely with you than has ever been the case, and why we must ensure that students are in groups designed to bring out the best in them.

Our aim is to create a fully interconnected communications and support system, one that is best able to grow the school into a complete learning organization, something that cannot be done given the limitations of our linear and same-age system. A vertical system, with its mixed-age tutor groups, will allow us to develop and enhance the many learning relationships on which achievement depends and with which character best develops.

The key to this change rests in a number of areas, but especially with the role of the tutors and their impact in working with their new mixed-age tutor groups. As principal, I too would hope to make the standard needed and take on one of these vital roles for as long as I can.

Information home will also change. The data sheets will be enhanced to include written strategies for improvement that all parties can understand, use, and discuss. These will include advice on the individual learning dispositions that drive your child's achievement. Reports will also recognize the many other talents each child has and which are deserving of attention.

It is our further intention that full reports on students and other data will be issued at critical times in the student's learning cycle, not at a time convenient to the school. At these critical learning times, parents and students will be invited by their child's personal tutors to take part in an in-depth *deep learning conversation* or *academic tutorial*. These occasions will enable a more complete overview and assessment to be made with regard to progress in learning, besides providing a means of identifying any further support needed. It is envisaged that such an important meeting will last for a minimum of forty minutes and, because of its importance, will take place within the span of a specific week, at a time convenient for both parents and staff. Subject evenings will remain.

It is our intention to be advised by research, to seek out best practice, and to build the supportive learning community that the students deserve and need. This is one that all of us can be proud of and one to which all of us, including our students and yourselves, can make a real contribution.

Please feel free to conduct your own research by typing "vertical tutoring" into any search engine and see for yourselves what schools have to say.

All change is difficult and the best change is sometimes counterintuitive. Hearts and minds have to be won; courage is needed to be different. However, without substantive change to the way we manage our school, it can never become the place of intrinsic learning that our students need it to be, and we can never be the people that you and our students expect and want us to be. Most of us came into teaching to teach the subject we love and to make a difference to the lives of the students you allow us to guide. We believe that VT will enable us to do these things better.

I hope you will be willing to learn more about VT and support the school in this important matter. Feel free to contact me. Your views and support are always important to us.

Yours sincerely,

Principal (ULHS)

P.S. As some have said before, had I more time, I would have written a far shorter letter.

Schools may well look at the ten-point list in the above letter and tick all ten areas as being already in place. They might claim that this is exactly how their school operates already, that there really is no need to change. However, it is important that our System 2s are now more engaged and alert to any misleading and intuitive beliefs. Later, if we are not already aware, we will learn exactly why this initial reaction is so prevalent and delusional.

## AND NOW FOR A FEW THOUGHTS

There are key messages that we need to take with us. These too will become clearer as we go along.

1. Conventional school management thinking is geared toward fixing component parts when things go wrong (such as teachers) and adding bits on (such as new pro-social programs and courses). This approach has a place but is loaded with assumptions as to how schools make work, work, and fails to change the fundamentals of the original industrial blueprint. Such an approach is high on maintenance, requiring a veritable deluge of protocols, policies, and evaluative procedures. Reforms follow the same approach with the same negative outcomes. The industrial school blueprint still in use was designed for a very different purpose.
2. Only organizations that adapt can have use and relevance; they survive. We need our schools to thrive and be adaptive, and this means change. Schools must learn to change themselves and not follow what "appears" to be change. They do not and cannot ever respond well to external micromanagement and reform.
3. Organizations govern our behavior. Schools are divided into functional areas, each with its own modus operandi and targets. This makes retrieval and use of information from all key players difficult and feedback loops close to inoperable, limiting assessment for learning, restricting knowledge, delaying interventions, and reducing learning capability. The five disciplines cannot work.
4. In turn, this silo effect changes behaviors and restricts interconnectivity. What is intended to simplify complexity actually limits information and openness to learning. Paradoxically this actually serves to increase complexity: by acting on a system part to reduce

and control complexity, other parts of the system are affected negatively and so must operate with limited information. The knock-on effect is to reduce learning. This creates failure demand loops (complaints, reworking, etc.) and the need to build in further limitations, such as data sheets as replacements for reports and holistic assessments; an unwanted and ultimately expensive negative feedback loop builds that keeps everything as it is.

5. Changing management thinking and behaviors means abandoning much of what schools consider normal and intuitive, and this unlearning is extremely difficult. Coming to terms with the idea that school managers are inadvertently making things worse, not better (and blaming others), is not easy.
6. The way we think governs the way we work and the performance outputs we achieve. The way we think rests more with the organization we work in than we think. What we think is not necessarily what we know, just as what we see isn't all there is.
7. A school must find a way to develop a deep commitment to holistic and intrinsic learning as an antidote to its industrial ways. This is what school managers wrongly assume and claim to do (see the list in the letter above).
8. Most people are at their best when they are working in productive teams in which they feel valued and able to be creative and party to something greater than themselves. Deming called it "joy" and Haidt called it "happiness."
9. Being able to understand complexity and examine systems through systems thinking is critical to finding a thinking and design way of making a system better (reculturing). It also wards off delusion.
10. When a system becomes stuck, unstable, and weighed down with criticism and advice (a wicked problem) that it cannot resolve, it needs to be enabled to understand more of itself and to unlearn. Only then can it truly learn to help itself and become self-organizing, and be a more reflective (learning) organization.

Finally, we should be prepared for surprises. The last thing any systems thinker wishes to do is produce a ten-point plan when a philosophy driven by sound values is needed. The above are simply some initial thoughts that combine to make a whole, and a few guidelines and principles to map out the geography of the area that schools are being invited to explore. They are definitely not tools and toolboxes! Systems thinking doesn't really do tools and it would be an immeasurable benefit to U.S. management linguistics to ban this metaphor.

Most are reminders to System 2 to be wary of System 1's too easily accepted conclusions, assumptions, and incomplete PowerPoint presentations!

## AND LASTLY, A MATH PROBLEM

At the heart of the school's industrial blueprint is a challenge that persists today. It involves the mathematical specialty of Albert Einstein concerning space, time, and numbers and the relationship between them. The parameters of school design are as follows and will be mentioned throughout as *the math problem*. For any school:

- There are many more students than teachers;
- There are many more parents than teachers;
- There is more knowledge than there are school subjects; and
- There is more learning (positive + negative) outside the classroom than in.

The challenge is to design a school whereby all players, students, parents, and school staff (teachers, support staff, and tutors) are fully interconnected and communicating; one that allows all learning relationships between our players to be interdependent and constantly enriched by feedback. The challenge is to solve this problem by creating a learning organization, not a teaching organization by removing any biases.

Lazy System 2 controllers will immediately be depleted by the math and leave it to System 1 to organize structures patterns based on the past, what is known, but this will lead to repeat errors and sameness. Limitation and separation must be avoided and designed out, not built in.

If this math challenge begins by prioritizing teachers and classes, it sets in motion a linear model around which the school organizes functional subsidiaries such as assessment, evaluation, training, programs, partnerships, management, and even research itself. It perpetuates an industrial mental map and toolbox approach based on the idea that the teacher is all there is (WYSIAT). To solve the puzzle, we need to defy our industrial and delusional mental model.

To begin by dividing the number of same-age (grades and years) students by the number of subject teachers plays immediately into the hands of old biases and assumptions about school management. It creates an operational mindset that is dependent on the myth of the great teacher or the great school leader and denies any accompanying system change.

What allows a teacher to be great cannot be their magical personal qualities alone. All professions have such amazing people able to operate despite the system they are in, but even they cannot counter negative system effects. The stock of such amazing talent is increased when the system in use is designed to trust people and so is better able to release the creativity they have. This begins with key players being able and trusted to absorb and respond to value demand.

It must be the capability of the school as an organization to create the right conditions for learning and for teaching to occur, not just the teacher isolated in the classroom. It starts by ensuring that social and learning relationships begin during minute one of day one. This is not about system compliance and dependence, it is about building a learning consensus in the school based on reciprocity and trust, one that recognizes and cherishes individuals.

Starting school with the single idea of the main service deliverers (teachers) engaging with multiple clients (students and parents) creates a spaghetti of uninformed and malformed learning relationships that can take an age to mature and realize, if indeed they ever do. Schools and learners simply don't have this time. Any such system is forced to manage time, and this means limitation in key areas such as assessment, method, and communication: in effect, limitation and separation of key feedback and support loops. It necessitates an organization high on compliance.

So the question is this: How can a school build learning relationships immediately, strongly, and permanently, and replace wild intuition with genuine support and a more individualized approach? How can schools better identify, absorb, and respond to the value work and maintain all feedback loops among players? The answer is by doing the math differently.

For much of the United Kingdom, Australia, and New Zealand, the start of this answer lies in vertical tutoring and the way the tutor role develops as the critical lynchpin of the school. It is the homeroom tutor role that has to be the learning conduit, the stock that connects all players. For the United States and most other jurisdictions, the key to school improvement has to be the development of the homeroom tutor role and that, as they say, changes everything; at least it does when systems thinking is applied.

# FIVE

# The Real Problem Is the Way We See the Problem

Alice came to a fork in the road. "Which road do I take?" she asked.
"Where do you want to go?" responded the Cheshire Cat.
"I don't know," Alice answered.
"Then," said the Cat, "it doesn't matter."
—Lewis Carroll, *Alice's Adventures in Wonderland*

It's time to take a breather and summarize where we are. If we don't know where we are going, we can be very sure that every road will lead to nowhere.

For example, given well-developed pro-social programs and school polices, we should expect to see a significant decrease in bullying, gun crime, gang membership, dropout rates (staff and students), and even mental health issues. But we don't. What stops us being socially isolated and exposed to such folly has little to do with programs and policies, but instead has to do with the in-group loyalties that shape us.

When a school changes from a same-age means of organization to one based on mixed-age groups, it is able to identify and meet value demand, what people need and are able to draw down from the system to make progress. It does this by building powerful in-group loyalty structures between all key players. These interconnected and interdependent learning relationships are better able to promote aspiration and reflection and absorb complexity. It is a system response to a system problem. There is little wrong with our players and much wrong with how schools are duped into operating.

By getting the school operating in a more connected way and those in and around it talking to each other, then and only then can we begin a discussion on curriculum and standards and anything else. There is an order to systemic improvement and it starts with purpose; this means identifying what we need to measure and what we value as important.

Why? Because purpose determines method. If we only measure passed tests and assume everything else, we shall create a teacher/test-based system, not a system based on intrinsic learning. This may meet the superficial value demand of universities and some employers, but only partially. It may not increase the stock of goodness or make the world a better place. The fact is, we have no idea just how vital schools are to our existence, so we should try and get them right.

Once we understand purpose better, curriculum development will be both more secure and innovative. The intense debates we are having now are entirely based on uncertainty of purpose, which is in turn compromised by command and control thinking. If we throw the dire effects of aggressive capitalism into the mix, we have a perfect storm and a complete mess.

To better develop individual potential (respond to individual value demand) is not just a curriculum matter. It requires the school's learning support structure to be fully functional in terms of building and maintaining the learning relationships and feedback loops needed to maximize support and encourage intrinsic learning.

Poverty, poor access to health care, and ignorance of equity do U.S. children and schools no favors. It also seems that the United States has arrived at a point where there is widespread disagreement on both the purpose of school and how schools should operate as learning systems. The criticisms are legion. While we can do little with regard to the much-lauded version of democracy U.S. style, there is much that schools can do to heal themselves, and at nil cost.

Schools remain stuck in industrial time. They are described as being wasteful of talent, uncreative, and harmful to children, while providing a one-size-fits-all experience that is damaging to life chances. In effect, the current model retains most of its nineteenth-century industrial factory form. While the solutions offered are equally legion, attempts at reform tend only to tinker at the edges and have failed to make the substantive difference needed. While the reasons for this strange state of affairs lie in the past, the solutions do not, despite what lazy System 2 controllers think. But unless the United States can find a way out of this seeming impasse, it will be left with an expensive and ongoing repair process locked in time and with any chance of systemic change becoming ever more remote.

My own intensive work with hundreds of schools worldwide leads me to conclusions and counterintuitive truths that, by definition, are at odds with current change methodologies. For example, there is no shortage of leadership in schools, nor is there any sudden decline in the quality of teachers—quite the opposite. Teachers have access to better books, better technology, and have no shortage of good ideas. Leaders make schools work despite the bigger system.

Otherwise, the curriculum can wait a while—it will always be in essence what politicians decide it to be. Indeed, to concentrate on these factors is delusional insofar as they draw attention away from the real problem, the one we ignore at our peril: how a school works as a learning organization, one that requires people to be effective learners first, and one that is able to build learning communities.

People work and think in ways that are governed by their organizational circumstances, and these combine to create an amalgam of assumptions that determine the broad parameters of how work, our mental models, and our mind maps work. If there is to be any forward momentum regarding school improvement and purpose, it is the school as a complete organization that should command our attention. It is the school that has to change its own operational learning process, and this is a point that can be addressed through systems thinking.

Only when this is done does everything else, including teacher quality, parent partnership, curricula, intrinsic learning, leadership, assessment for learning, and all of the other elements, fall more cogently into place.

## PROBLEMS

*This is a reminder, which is why it is in italicized print!*

*The way schools should change from a horizontal system to a vertical system has already been set out in* The Systems Thinking School, *and is further set out here in the letter, set out in chapter 4. The idea of mixed-age mentoring involving the whole school is so simple that nobody will believe it unless they look at the evidence for themselves and some U.S. bravehearts give it a go!*

*If we know the solution—that the means of transforming schools through a domino effect requires the introduction of mixed-age tutor groups—then the problem has to be the corollary. In other words, the long list of delusions set out earlier is directly attributable to the errant assumption that a school's same-age organizational design can work. The problem is linearity and in particular school organization by grade, peers, or same-age groups alone.*

*The same-age means used to resolve the math conundrum (above) is the problem we have. Math problems are cognitively depleting to System 2 and information light for our intuitive but gullible System 1.*

*Put simply, a school that operates entirely on a same-age basis will always have a factory karma and production methodology with all the problems and practices (limitation and separation) that go with it. Learning relationships between students, school, and parents remain a matter of fortune, not design, and most learning relationships are delayed, limited, and malformed (or not formed at all), and this is hugely damaging to learning and learners.*

*It is not possible to develop a learning organization based on same-age mathematics. We need to look again at the evidence and see why this is a major problem and better understand how it has evaded attention despite the wealth of research evidence that suggests that such dark matter exists. Just because we don't see it doesn't mean it isn't there.*

By the way, after reading italicized, it now looks as though this writing slopes the other way. Kahneman has this illusion covered. It is just our gullible System 1 trying to overcompensate and make sense of things, being a nuisance. The resultant nausea will pass. The print is perfectly normal despite what our System 1 is telling our sleepy System 2.

The task of systems thinking is to secure a better understanding and appreciation of schools as public service organizations and how they go about making work work. It has to explain how a school as an organization operates as a system very precisely. In particular, there has been a limited focus on school management in which far too much remains assumed and taken for granted.

If something is not working as it should in a public service organization like a school, there is almost certainly a fault within the management processes that govern the way organizational relationships work and the way organizational purpose is interpreted and applied. Even the process of learning and teaching is not what it seems. Indeed, the quality of learning relationships between teachers and students is determined almost entirely by the way a school operates, and it is important for this book to set out why this is and to show how it is corrected.

If W. Edwards Deming and Russell Ackoff ever returned to discuss the challenges faced by schools as learning organizations, I like to think they might appreciate my own puny effort with regard to perception, intuition, and assumption, which goes something like this:

> U.S. public schools have a problem. The problem we see, however, is not the problem there is. If we try and solve the problem we see rather than the problem there is but we don't see, we create more problems than there are; this means that the original problem, the one we don't see as a problem, becomes an even bigger problem. If the problems we see were the problems that need to be resolved, we would have resolved them. The fact that we cannot resolve the problems we see means that the real problem, the one we cannot see, is still a problem and remains unresolved. So the real problem is not just the problem we cannot see or even the ones we think we see, but is the way we see the problem. If we can change the way we see the problem, there is a better chance of *dissolving* the problem that causes all of the other problems.

The real problem is linearity and the same-age foundation on which schools have come to depend. We have abandoned or discounted any values-driven purpose and are solely reliant on biases and assumptions. After all, we all understand how a school operates . . . don't we? It's all about good teaching and learning, the bit we see, and that matters most . . . doesn't it? Provide a good teacher and you'll get good learning. Managers manage teachers . . . don't they?

Unfortunately such assumptions turn out to be part paradox, part tautology, part oxymoron, and mostly delusional, while seeming managerially logical and normal. Management biases are hard to unlearn and are ingrained mental models seemingly impossible to challenge.

Systems thinking is very clear on the need for a paradigm shift in education and in its support for learning and teaching. It is overly silent about the operational assumptions deep within the school—it is these that guide the nature of the interdependencies that determine the quality of learning relationships, and it is these that in turn govern the school's performance and the ability to identify and meet customer need.

## THE DANGER OF TOOLBOXES

Toolboxes are used to fix things, make things work better, or to replace old parts. They are peripheral to systemic change. Direct support for teachers and learners, including the application of systems thinking as a "toolbox approach," may well accrue many benefits for schools. It encourages new techniques, new methods of assessment, new confidence, and better learning relationships in the classroom.

However, it is also one that by itself will ultimately delay much-needed systemic change. As a toolbox, systems thinking is single-loop learning and limited. There is no fundamental shift to the underlying structures and the rationale as to how the school operates and why. It doesn't sufficiently challenge the same-age assumption. In part, this is because the common cause of the problem of teacher capability lies elsewhere. Teachers and the classroom are not the problem areas in themselves, and all the time we focus entirely on teachers we remain prisoners of a paradox while the real culprit runs free.

When a lightbulb fails in a classroom, it is regarded as unpredictable and has a *special cause*, one that can be identified and easily fixed. When a light goes out in a child or a teacher, this should have been predictable given the unchanging system in play. This is a *common cause* problem, one that exists deep in the fundamentals of the school's operational methods, and inaccessible to those carrying toolboxes alone.

It is not so much the teacher who needs the time and help to get even better, but more the school managers, leaders, and administrators; in particular the way all of these good people think about schools as learning organizations and as systems. In essence teachers need a system run by managers who are not factory minded, and until they get this, their own performance and the contribution made by parents and students will remain so much less than the potential they have. The fundamental key to improving the poor performance of the U.S. education system is not to focus on teachers alone, but to focus on how the school operates as a service system in its own right.

To emphasize the point: teachers can only be as good as the system in which they operate. It is the school as an organization that is the dominant and final determinant of capability. It can either allow the disciplines of improvement to do their work, or it can't. This means that we must retrace our footsteps and get to know both systems thinking and schools much more intimately than we do. To think otherwise means that we must somehow have a great teacher in every classroom, and that loops us back to a misleading tautology and we've already been there!

# SIX

# Problems, Purpose, Energy, and Complexity

> Of course, we want our children to be well-prepared to attend fine universities and to enter the world of work. But that is not our goal. We see the purpose of schooling as the nurturing of a strong, skeptical mind, a kind heart, and an abiding interest in advancing the greater good.
>
> —Deborah Kenny (2014), New York

The cartoonist Charles M. Schulz once wrote, "In the book of life, the answers aren't in the back." In the book of schools, we seem to have too many multiple-choice answers and none seem to be the right ones for the questions being asked. Every time we think we have an answer, other questions emerge; it is all that systems thinking warns us of. Start fiddling with system elements and other problems arise elsewhere.

In 1999, Kira King and Theodore Frick wrote a paper called "Systems Thinking: The Key to Educational Redesign." The theme is a familiar one and is one I always reference when writing about schools. Their basic thesis is as follows: despite an unprecedented rate of change, schools and schooling have remained largely the same in their fundamental form.

It is a problem that has been expressed repeatedly by pundits, politicians, systems thinkers, and researchers to the point of weary resignation. Fifteen years on, there has been little in the way of substantive change. Their form remains unchanged. Put simply, the dominant model of the universal school remains doggedly in factory mode.

The schools we have today were designed for an industrial society that required students to be sifted, sorted, and batched for delivery, ready for their jobs as factory hands or as managers. In essence, they remain crude production lines, a one-size-fits-all system.

Today, this penchant for sorting, sifting, labeling, and batching remains rife in school management systems. The basic form of U.S. schools has not moved in organizational terms. In fact, reforms have made matters worse, and this ongoing theme of doing the wrong things thinking they are the right things is gathering pace.

Today's technological paradigm goes by several descriptive names, each reflecting a particular bias—the information age, the communications age, the digital age, the knowledge society—and doubtless many others will come along in rapid succession. While the rest of the working world is wrestling with major social and technological shifts, schools remain behind the learning curve, retaining much of their original purpose and form. King and Frick's paper spells out the frustrating parameters of this slow train wreck.

All of this poses questions about the nature of schooling and the capacity of the school to respond to changing conditions. Today, schools seem dangerously disconnected from mainstream culture and any ecological fit—questions about relevance and cost are being asked and the inevitable blame game is gathering momentum. The situation is becoming very messy.

Like so many others, King and Frick rightfully call for schools to be somehow redesigned to be more able to shape the future rather than remain stuck in time; schools, we are reminded, should produce team players, problem solvers, and young people more able to collaborate and synthesize—what Peter Drucker (1959) called *knowledge workers*. Of course, vertical tutoring is based precisely on these ideas and does not require the aid of programs.

The industrial model is stuck in the linearity of time which has to be carefully apportioned. The traditional same-age model has no flexibility—time cannot bend to suit. The school can use only a small part of the information available to it. Unless it limits subjects, assessment, conversations, and partnerships (the learning relationships that make up the school) it breaks down. Bureaucracy increases, time runs out, energy dissipates, and the school overcomplexifies itself.

In effect, the communication loop needed to ensure interconnectivity, renewable energy, and interdependency cannot form in ways sophisticated enough to allow sufficient time for individual reach. What the industrial model ultimately does is create an anxiety about standardized outcomes using restrictive control processes that make real learning difficult and teaching essential. Time doesn't wait if you dare to stop and think, fall behind, or fail to get to the start line in good shape to run. High compliance rules.

An education system is part of a bigger ecological system, but we don't treat it that way, instead paying only cursory attention to values and all that is important for an existence in such a fragile place. It is why more attention should be paid to Steiner, Montessori, and Waldorf schools, in which values and responsible behaviors are practiced rather than assumed. Some refer to this approach as "the slow schools" movement, one that does no harm, cherishes learning, and is ecologically literate.

Having identified and accepted the need for schools to change and be more ecologically connected, King and Frick set out both the challenge and the problem in succinct terms:

> we cannot analyze the existing school model holistically and recreate it from the ground up. Instead, we often remain entrenched in our current notions of education and only tinker at the edges of schools, making minimal changes. With the grandest of ideals, designers often aim towards creating a new school that looks totally different from traditional education, only to find that the resulting system is very similar to a traditional classroom! (p. 3)

It is a quote that haunts systems thinking. Systems thinking is all about holism, seeing the bigger picture, and the school as a system in its own right. An organization like a school, no matter its degree of complexity, should not be able to escape the analytical lens of systems thinking so easily; there has to be far more than what little we see. However, to see more means that the school must be understood at a deep working level, such is its importance, and unless we have that shared systems picture, any hope of redesign is lost. We need to understand how it is that our schools are able to elude, delude, and replicate in the way they do and why they are driven by assumption rather than value.

Note the expression used by King and Frick: *the traditional classroom*. In schools, students end up in classrooms. Part of the delusion is this constant focus on the classroom as the single place where people erroneously think that things go causally wrong and so are most in need of attention. We think the problems and the answers lie here, but to separate the classroom from the school as an organization is an error. To make classrooms better places of learning, the way the school organizes itself must undergo change.

When we do the math, we need classrooms so we shouldn't be too surprised that they still exist. King and Frick know that piecemeal change has failed. Theirs is an appeal to systems thinking to:

> help us determine how our schools will be designed organizationally, how people will interact within the system, and how people and things will move in and out of the system. (p. 3)

King and Frick's assessment and the mission they state is the ironic key to school improvement. The quality of interaction, the learning relationships, and the school's interconnectivity are the keys to better learning in schools, but how to go about such a task? The answer to the challenge of schooling U.S. style is not curriculum reform alone and not teachers alone; both will develop quite naturally by need and through training when the school as an organization is able to redesign itself in a way that is interconnected, interdependent, and more able to understand how energy and information flow in and out of its operational system. It is all about management.

I have already set out the organizational systems answer of mixed-age tutor groups, so we should bear this in mind as we proceed. It certainly meets King and Frick's criteria and explains both the flow of information and the means of building quality learning relationships in a school. VT re-establishes interconnectivity and learning relationships.

Schools have been trampled over by endless observers, inspectors, evaluators, and researchers, and their findings appear to have had little overall effect. The real information needed has to be elsewhere, in those places cloaked with delusion, masked by assumption, and confused by semantic definitions; the dark matter and hidden places where few look and where we need to shine a systems light.

Cady Heron discovered many such places on her first day!

As an aside, when a colleague read the previous paragraph regarding "the dark matter" and "hidden places," he asked whether I meant the school's restrooms, instantly dismantling the flowery metaphors I use to add mystery to the matters in hand. Back to reality . . .

King and Frick then re-examined schools through a systems lens using George Maccia and Elizabeth Maccia's (1966) SIGGs theory in which some of the answers certainly lie. However, this ingenious mathematical analysis, interpreted in part in *The Systems Thinking School*, requires considerable thought and interpretation beyond the scope of my System 2. The basic reason schools are difficult to understand as systems is because we have grown so accustomed to their ways and think we know them well. We are beguiled.

Not only have we become familiar with their ways, most of us quite like schools. Even the wonderful people in them are beguiling. It is almost inevitable that like reformers, school improvers find themselves stuck in the classroom after school where so much (but by no means all) of the important work is done, gazing at the walls and thinking that this, the domain of the teacher and the learner, is surely the place that must change, must "improve."

So it will in time. Meanwhile it remains a dangerous assumption when taken in isolation from the school as a complete organization, and is one that is likely to continue to cause all kinds of repair problems. Barr and Dreeben (1983) use the metaphor of "switching yards" to describe schools as organizations:

> They are structures . . . where children within a given age-range . . . are assigned to teachers who bring them into contact with approved learn-

> ing materials appropriate to age or ability during certain allotted periods of time. (p. 75)

Compare this functional and utilitarian but perfectly valid description with Senge's (2006) description of a learning organization. This will give us an idea of the distance we need to travel, assuming that we can slow down and look before leaving the switching yard and getting stuck on the same universal track.

> organizations where people continually expand their capacity to create the results they truly desire, where new and expansive patterns of thinking are nurtured, where collective aspiration is set free, and where people are continually learning to see the whole together. (p. 3)

If we only see schools as functional units organized to deliver certain narrow outcomes, the key task is to manage any inherent system variation between classes, teachers, students, resources, outcomes, and more besides. The management bias will be toward a closed system, one that limits and narrows, abhors variation, and seeks to eradicate complexity; there is little need for vision in such a teaching-oriented organization.

In a learning organization and in managing cultural change, "sensible vision," to use Kotter's (2012) terminology, is a necessity. It seems that even vision is not what it seems.

The key determinant of learning and organizational performance rests much more with the school itself—its entirety, how it works, thinks, and learns as an organization—and this is an essential part of leadership. The problem is that the linearity of the system necessitates closing down the means of liberating the energy needed for change. The answer is knowing what first needs to change deep in the system, and how to do it.

Otherwise, W. Edwards Deming (1982) was right all along: management has to change. School managers have to learn to see the school in a new way, as a learning organization rather than a teaching system. Only then will a deeply embedded industrial mindset and its accompanying box of inappropriate reform tools be abandoned, as they must be.

Managers must be somehow persuaded to change the way they think about their schools and the way they work, and understand why so much of what passes as normal management thinking restricts and limits. It is this that is holding up the redesign and reculturing processes needed to reconnect schools and their students with more intrinsic learning.

Somewhere in the system, perhaps everywhere, there is delusion at work. I am very aware that psychologists do not like lay people messing around with their words! Delusion, according to *Collins Dictionary*, is "a mistaken idea, belief etc." It enters the psychological domain and becomes delusional when beliefs are maintained despite evidence to the contrary. Teachers are not deluded in themselves, but much of what they are asked to do by the organizations they work for is!

In *The Systems Thinking School,* I sought to explain this, at least in part, as organizational self-deception using Robert Trivers's theories (2011). He regarded self-deception as a means of concealing the truth from the unconscious mind in order to hide it from others. His thesis on self-delusion and its evolutionary benefits (we can all benefit from being natural liars) is very much based on bias. Not only do we possess a remarkable ability to see only our own point of view, but we will argue our case because our deceits blind us to the truth. In this way ignorance is bliss, until we are undone by a perspective we do not share.

Lionel Tiger (1979) in a similar vein, said

> there is a tendency for humans to consciously see what they wish to see. They literally have difficulty seeing things with negative connotations while seeing with increasing ease items that are positive. (p. 146)

People who build systems and maintain them do not wish to know that they might, over time, have it all wrong. For them, something else or somebody else has to be at fault. Changing from a system in which delusion is at work makes letting go difficult if not impossible.

The mixed-age perspective that I claim is the best bet for kick starting such a process has to be convincing beyond being simply a claimed counterintuitive truth. It has to be at least sufficient to make us stop and, in Malcolm Gladwell's (2005) terms, "Blink!" Fortunately, there are now many thousands of schools worldwide who use mixed-age groups as the cultural foundation for building interconnectivity and the learning relationships that support learning and allow for individualization.

As things stand, schools are producing too much waste. The paradox is that in trying to control complexity the school locks itself into a destructive loop and creates more complexity. It fails to deal with what is of value to people, thus creating failure demand (complaints, reworking, bureaucracy, and more besides); this is expensive, exhausts internal energy, assumes purpose, and detrimentally affects outcomes.

Einstein was pretty good at math and physics and figured out that $E = mc^2$. Energy and mass tend to be the same. Trying to control energy can release it elsewhere in an unwanted form that then requires more energy to shift, and it is energy to which I now turn. He also taught us that time needs to be seen differently and that light bends.

## SYSTEM ENERGY

The school's means of dealing with organizational variability and value demand requires a very different, less restrictive, and more open approach to the school's self-organization strategy. Otherwise, math problems accumulate. Frank Betts (1992) wrote an article that still holds particular significance today, and this chapter follows much of what he said over twenty years ago. It is a chapter that provides a conceptual overview, one that underpins much that follows.

For Betts, like King and Frick, understanding a system is our best means of moving forward, which means adopting systems thinking as a guide to organizational improvement. Once a complex organization like a school is understood as a system, it becomes easier to stabilize and thus make it more adaptive to its environment, one that better suits and defines its ecological purpose. Schools should, after all, add to the sum of goodness in the world. Some call it education.

Betts offers us a useful guide that pertains to today. In essence, as schools and society have increased in complexity, we continue to use the same methods and organizational formulae that worked so well in the past.

Any claims to systems approaches have stalled in part because they have reverted to "mechanical models and metaphors" (our industrial and reductionist mindset). Betts states that, "Decision-makers need to fully understand why our current approaches won't work and what is different about the systems approach" (pp. 38–41). Any failure here results in repetition and self-perpetuation, stasis and sub-optimization (behavior resulting from a subsystem's goals dominating at the expense of the bigger system).

Betts sets out five reasons for this failure of transformation taken from Banathy (1991):

- A piecemeal or incremental approach.
- Failure to integrate solutions ideas.
- A discipline-by-discipline study of education.
- A reductionist orientation.
- Staying within the boundaries of the existing system (not thinking out of the box). (pp. 38–41)

The problem, however, is not just an inability to think outside of the box; it is knowing that you're in a box, understanding the nature of the box you are in, and only then trying to figure a way out. Besides, people like boxes. We store our memories in them and they can be a great comfort, but it is never wise to get stuck in one for too long.

For Betts, the reasons for failure in public education can be causally attributed to past success. Schools then had three clear purposes: 1) to transmit core knowledge and values; 2) to provide custodial care; and 3) to prepare students for life beyond school. However, the world has moved on. For Betts, one of the most important aspects of such preparation is "critical and creative thinking for problem solving and decision making" (pp. 38–41).

It is this last challenge, according to Betts, that has proved problematic. While schools have been hugely successful at pattern maintenance, they have found it difficult to respond to changing expectations. Betts calls this "paradigm paralysis," reformers call it "resistance to change," and children probably call it "getting bored." In essence, schools have been unable to adapt to a rapidly changing and more interconnected world. Teachers ironically complain about change, even though there has been none!

There is a further handicap, according to Betts, which is of particular importance. An organization has finite energy to make it work. This means that unless it can import energy from outside or release latent energy from within, it simply loops and repeats in a closed and mechanistic way. It becomes moribund. Innovation and change require energy, but without the capacity to find different permanent sources or utilize available supplies, it requires a transfer of energy from one part of the organization to another, which can have negative implications and high downside risk.

It is important to note that teacher learning and school transformation are inextricably linked, or should be! The way a school moves from one culture (teaching organization) to another culture (learning organization) depends on factors such as innovation, goal clarity, and having the five disciplines in place, understood, and functional. The fact that there has been no school transformation worthy of the name reflects an absence of systems learning and an inability to transfer and mine energy from other sources.

Research into the way teachers learn (Bryk, Camburn, and Louis 1999; Leithwood and Louis 1998; Silins, Mulford, and Zarins 2002) tends to use a theory of change based on cultural and political dimensions of schools and how they operate. Within school cultures, factors such as participative decision making, team approaches, collaboration, openness to learning, a climate of trust, and transformational leadership can, it is claimed, promote professional learning in schools. But without a coherent system that underpins them, they are severely limited.

System change is needed first. We cannot keep working front to back and back to front! We know so much about the "disciplines" and learning criteria, yet not one of these has resulted in any substantive change to the school's fundamental factory form, one that limits the interconnectivity claimed and restricts energy flow and reclamation. More words, more delusion?

These laudable factors in linear schools are not enough and great caution is needed; none excuse the factory nature of school even if these factors appear to lay claim to professional learning. Their development requires time and energy and the linear school system has little left to give. What little it has will almost certainly be robbed from the front-line service. More tinkering.

Like the disciplines, good management ideas require fundamental changes to the school's operational form, otherwise they are merely add-ons, workable until the energy and finance needed to sustain them runs out. To work effectively there has to be a system that allows them to work.

Without a viable supply of renewable energy, a school tends to close as a system, and this causes it to adopt *single-loop learning* as its single means of improvement, trying to do better than what it normally does. Schools merely change existing techniques and amend existing policies, programs, practices, principles, protocols, and procedures. The same energy is constantly recirculated.

Schools tend to shift the deck chairs rather than change the fundamental organizational culture to which they are organizationally blind; their energy supply is simply too depleted to allow them to question accepted underlying assumptions regarding their modus operandi, let alone escape from them. Remember, any failure to absorb value demand requires even more energy and finances to meet resultant failure demand (the complexity paradox).

School management (closed-loop) stays the same as far as the school's underlying operational methodology is concerned. As such it remains dependent on assumption and intuition. Our depleted System 2 shies away from the math problem, allowing the intuitive but gullible System 1 to keep running the show. Eventually, the whole operational load passes to the teacher in the classroom as the last one standing. This is what we see, so that is what we errantly think of as the primary focus of attention.

Otherwise, nothing much changes regarding the fundamentals of the way the school as an organization operates, or for that matter the fundamentals of the wider educational bureaucracy of which it is part. If teachers are doing most of the work, using up most of the energy running out-of-date practices in a place where learning is limited, the chance of reaching escape velocity from such a closed organization is minimal.

## CROSS-BORDER ENERGY

Similarly, if huge amounts of energy are spent dealing with failure demand (mistakes, repeat work, complaints, negative behaviors, etc.), then this too will drive services down as the school enters a cycle of exhaustion and recovery fed by negative feedback loops that attempt to keep the system stable but invariably the same, one of separation and limitation.

A school comprises (or should comprise) a whole complexity of learning relationships and behaviors between key players, particularly parents, teachers, homeroom tutors, support staff, and students. Energy and creativity exist in people and the task of a self-organizing system is to allow people to release as much of their energy as possible in a form that best secures learning. In other words, energy exists in human interaction and in the motivationally intrinsic nature of learning.

Therein is another challenge. To make such a shift requires moving from a high control regime to one far more reliant on trust and a matrix of learning relationships that sustain it.

In schools, the learning relationships between all key players is organizationally restricted (perceived as complexity that needs careful control and limitation). This means that many potential and renewable energy sources are similarly restricted and left to meander around the school in a form likely to result in unpredictable consequences (negative demand and negative behaviors).

Finding a means of maintaining the communication flow between all players and ensuring interconnectivity (building sound learning relationships) will provide the energy so essential to absorbing value demand. When learning relationships are restricted, their latent energy supply cannot be harnessed. We need student energy, parental input, and a school better able to inform itself with regard to assessment for learning. Such interconnectivity also ensures that schools stay in touch with espoused values and value demand.

To tap these sources of energy requires the school to reconsider how all players relate to each other. It is not a matter of speaking about participation, collaboration, and partnership alone; it requires an enabling means.

Restricting interconnectivity (communication between players) does not save energy as schools think. Ultimately it uses it all up and the first to go under are teachers. But to do otherwise requires an open learning culture and a smarter approach to systems renewal and maintenance. Without the operational feedback loops and active informational learning relationships needed to supply energy, the organization cannot innovate, adapt, and revitalize itself and thus stay current.

A same-age school has finite energy and uses more energy than it gets in return; it works near-exhaustion levels. To cope, the linear school simply shuts down its subsystems (information, assessment, partnerships, etc.) or restricts them. We see this in parent partnership, student participation, information quality, and flow. Time cannot flex sufficiently in same-age systems, so it too must be carefully limited and controlled. In other words, same-age organizational protocols not only separate people, but also limit energy supplies to those who need them most. The linear system exhausts itself.

## AN ANSWER

The trick is to find a way in which all learning relationships can be developed to provide a net energy gain to enable learning, customer care, and a better self-organizing capability. This is a system not only able to identify and absorb value demand, but also one that allows for considerable trust and this is far from what we have. Positive feedback loops only require a small amount of energy but can lead to big changes.

Betts tells us that each school has a unique "constellation of relationships" that are in constant flux and seek equilibrium while trying to avoid entropy (disorder and decay). At the risk of repetition, only by creating mixed-age tutor groups can such a constellation of learning relationships be harnessed and achieve steady equilibrium. This means solving the math problem in a different way, one that designs in learning relationships early before the child even gets to the classroom. It is in the homeroom, not the classroom, where the school's learning batteries are charged. This starts on minute one of day one and they remain "on-charge" throughout.

It is the nature of the industrial school as an organization to perceive such seemingly complex communications between so many players as unwanted add-ons that require strict control through minimization, isolation, and limitation. The one-size-fits-all system closes in on itself to cope. Learning relationships like parent partnerships are seen as a cause of energy depletion rather than energy supply. So rather than be seemingly overwhelmed with information and risk instability, the school places strict time limits on the formation of all learning relationships and partnerships, but in so doing it also places individual and organizational learning at risk.

## SELF-ORGANIZATION

Self-organization is a means of creating new and more relevant organizational structures. It is self-organization that enables complexity to be harnessed and embraced as an energy supply powering its own evolution toward the goal of becoming a learning organization. In fact, self-organization should be the normal state of affairs, but it is not, at least not for linear schools.

Self-organization has a very different means of working with the variation people have, one that involves understanding chaos theory, experimentation, innovation, ongoing adaptation, and systemic change. It learns and evolves, tolerates error, incorporates the disciplines with ease, and sees the challenges the school faces differently and holistically, as advantages not handicaps, energy suppliers and creativity releasers.

I have set out very precisely how schools go about this transformation in *The Systems Thinking School* and this is repeated, in part, later in this book. Suffice it to say, teachers are more than capable of thriving in a learning milieu based on a mixed-age dynamic, but managers have to be trained in how to unlearn and readapt their mental models to a very different system and learning culture.

Otherwise, such seeming disorder is not allowed in same-age industrial models. These inflexible institutions are organized and strictly controlled in ways that limit; they are non-adaptive, allowed only so much leeway, and they abhor complexity above all things, not realizing that they are its creator. The consequence is that those who work in them, including students, are restricted by tests, time, and allowances of carefully controlled creativity. The organization becomes dependent on the teacher and high compliance to get by.

A single U.S. school or district willing to learn a new means of self-organization using VT could be a starter domino and change everything. Volunteers, anyone?

In this way, as Betts says, a perceived problem in the classroom may not be due to a teacher's behaviors, but is more likely to be found in a host of other areas such as unrealistic expectations, outmoded support structures, weak parental partnership, target distortion, inadequate assessment for learning, and more, something Kenneth Boulding (1956) suggested over fifty years ago.

How the school manages and maintains all key learning relationships is vital. These should not be assumed or downgraded, and all of these matters are more in the school's control than schools think, but not within the industrial management mindset available to guide them. Too many classroom problems actually have their roots in prevailing school orthodoxies that lie deep within the school's management and organization psyche: the way schools perceive the work they do, their assumptions, and how they attempt to make work work. All of these are deep shapers of attitude, character, motivation, aspiration, and learning.

School managers manage people because they believe that people mess up. They do not realize that the operational system and their own mental models are the real problems. Managers feel obliged to create rule-bound, procedural systems designed to limit what they perceive to be complexity in order to avoid messes. Instead, what they really need to do is manage a system built on greater trust that enables people to work creatively and optimally with others to support the learning of all.

Here is the counterintuitive truth: teachers are not the problem we think they are, and neither are they the direct leverage point for organizational improvement. They will get better when the broken system is recultured to suit today's children, their diverse contexts, and individual learning needs. At least eighty years have been spent trying to fix teachers and train leaders! We have succeeded in changing everything except what needs to be changed: the relationships needed to hold it all together.

That work goes on, but now it is time to start fixing the system.

Schools operate in closed and mechanistic ways (the industrial model) that use up all available energy. What we need are schools interconnected to more of themselves, ones more open as systems and better able to access and release the human energy so readily available. This is not a metaphorical concept but something that is practically achievable with the resources available, but only when schools understand why and how they work in the way they do.

The transformation that schools have to make is from the mechanistic model dependent on single-loop learning to a more organic and open system able to access double-loop thinking and learning. Counterintuitively, far from trying to reduce and control complexity in reductionist ways (which is what schools do and creates more problems), an understanding of how to embrace and engage with complexity is critical to any cultural transformation. This means dealing with basic math.

Betts put it this way:

> organic systems are very complex with many variables, which require a great deal of feedback. The larger and more complex the system, the more energy, in the form of feedback, is required to maintain a dynamic balance among elements.

The more we ask of schools (increase complexity) in their present management form, the more they will limit their operations and appear resistant to change, demanding high investment for little gain.

Their management prerogative is to manage the supply and demand of their internal flow of energy, a kind of life-support system. This invariably results in doing the wrong things, thinking they are the right things. In short, the more schools simplify and limit, the more restricted they become as places of learning.

When this happens, learning relationships fold in on themselves and a negative feedback loop causes reversions to old stable but restrictive patterns. Schools can never emerge from their chrysalis and be the butterflies we need them to be. Even when we reach the point where we are now and realize that things are very wrong, our causal analysis fails; our reductionist ways seek out parts failures (elements such as teachers, programs, policies) and so any attempt at resuscitation tends to meet with a very short shelf life of success and huge (often justified) resistance to change.

Management resuscitation techniques are crude and controlling. We apply the electric shock treatment of increased accountability, financial performance incentives, appraisals, targets, and fear, all the time draining the energy from those we need to be most alive. Turnover increases, students drop out, morale dives. We only have to look back at the road traveled to see the waste and expense of a zillion failed schemes, long-abandoned strategies, and failed reforms; management that fails and keep failing, losses "unknown and unknowable."

As a result, schools are headed in the opposite direction to the one they need to go, that is to say no direction at all. Learning has become a regime of narrow testing. The whole child has been reduced to mechanistic meaning, known only by data sheets of work done rather than by latent human potential. Most pass through schools like shadows, leaving no imprint on their school, invisible, and not known for who they are, let alone who they were meant to be. Nobody knows them well; more loss unknown and unknowable.

As for school "communication" systems, even these are not what they seem. Schools have "information-out" systems and these are an entirely different matter. The last thing a school wants when it sends a letter home is a reply!

Information systems are entirely one-way and limited, traffic out; they are not two-way communications systems at all. In reality they work to seal the school system tight, another feedback energy loop broken, limited, restricted, and assumed. Parents are sold the illusion that they are partners in learning, but these "partnerships" are based on limited information-out. Most are unworkable and unsatisfactory structures and testament to the fact that such an illusion is now a delusion.

As Betts says,

> If the old paradigms won't work, something fundamentally better suited to the task is needed, a paradigm that illuminates the whole, not just the parts; one that is synthetic rather than analytic; one that integrates rather than differentiates.

Of course, when we try to figure out the qualitative features of any new model, it is easy to over-egg what is possible. If we value long-term, supportive learning relationships between our players, then of course we should never ever build more factory schools. There should be a limit of 2,000 students per high school and it should be recognized that the splitting of schools into a three-tier system of lower, middle, and upper makes no sense, and middle schools should be allowed to eventually fade away.

In *Alice in Wonderland* (Carroll 1865), Alice learned much about other schools from the Mock Turtle. She also learned that her own schooling had not prepared her for the world in which she found herself. Alice reflected on the words of the somewhat tearful Mock Turtle and his experience of school. The Mock Turtle spoke of the school he attended at the bottom of the sea and of the school's curriculum. In so doing, he actually describes harm.

> "Reeling and Writhing, of course, to begin with," the Mock Turtle replied; "and then the different branches of arithmetic—Ambition, Distraction, Uglification, and Derision."

We also learn from the Mock Turtle why lessons are called "lessons." It is because they *lessen*.

The Mock Turtle is a sad and confused character, but in his way he speaks a truth about the downside of poor systems and their effect on those who spend 17,000 hours and more traveling through them. He is also a systems thinker and has spotted aspects of the math problem, the blockage of information flow deep within the school's organizational assumptions.

This is where we go next.

# SEVEN

# The Systems Thinking Process to Seeing

People exercise an unconscious selection in being influenced.
—T. S. Eliot

It should be clear by now that while we have been engaging with systems thinking, we have also been gathering information that is less accepting of traditional management practices. In effect, we have been looking at schools from different customer perspectives and we have been checking the system to see what it actually does, as opposed to what those managing it think it does.

So here we are, stuck in the slow Program for International Student Assessment (PISA) lane and feeling left behind. It happened with the car industry, so why not with schools? Management of schools is inherited, static, bureaucratic, ingrained, and going nowhere fast. It adds more unnecessary stuff onto itself as it grows more moribund. Meanwhile there has been no fundamental reappraisal or agreement as to what schools are for, let alone how they might develop as self-organizing entities.

Let's run through systems theory as applied to public services. This tells us what needs to be done and whether the confusion faced is resolvable.

## SYSTEMS BASICS

- Schools comprise teams of people that combine to achieve certain purposes.
- The purpose of a public service like school is defined by customers and what they value (the variety of value demand). There are ethics here.

- The system is there to enable people (teachers, parents, and students) to get from the system what they need in order to make progress (to absorb and meet value demand).
- Any system design must ensure that all players can contribute via an interconnected and interdependent enterprise.
- To ensure such an enterprise, everything that people need is already in the system.
- Any measures in use are derived from purpose. They liberate method.
- This allows the method to be innovative and creative.
- This leads to a better and continually improving service.

So far, it could not be clearer—at least in theory. But in practice, the hapless school finds itself on a continuum of conflicting demand. It is forced to assume values and ignore value demand. Let's continue with systems thinking theory.

The school's purpose is to identify, absorb, and make sense of the variety of customer demand it faces. It must understand the complexity of the value demand being made on it as a system: what customers want. The school's purpose is to enable customers to access and draw down what they need to make progress in the world we have. The challenge is to do this in a way that avoids harm and maximizes good. The sooner that young people read, write, and do sums the better. This flexes time later and reduces failure demand, hence the huge effort needed early on either at home or at school.

Systems thinking too has its own principles and values that cannot be assumed. There are two basic tenets and the first is this: at the very heart of any service sector organization are the people that form it (staff, students, and parents). People are the key. People are innately creative and flexible problem solvers; they are also best placed to determine, understand, and absorb the variety of value demand on the system and are uniquely placed to act.

The second is that everything that is needed by the school as a system is already in the school. If answers are sought by looking outside the system or by copying similar systems, then they are looking in the wrong place. Of course, once the system is functional then you can look. It just doesn't work otherwise.

Let's continue. The key to systems success is to concentrate on *demand* despite the variability of that demand and to ensure *flow*. In essence, *flow* refers to the way communication moves in a system between players. Ideally there should be a smooth and unobstructed passage of information and services around the system that everyone understands and to which everyone contributes. By concentrating solely on these matters (managing the system), systems resources are better used (optimized). It also enables the system to pinpoint *waste* (almost anything that fails to contribute to purposes) and remove it.

Waste occurs when organizational methods and areas of unnecessary bureaucracy are not concerned with meeting demand and enabling flow. Administration of waste is a heavy cost for schools. Waste also occurs in failure demand, the costs in time and labor needed to rectify mistakes and deal with complaints and delays—itself the result of not concentrating on value demand and flow.

## COSTS

This leads us to a neat and misunderstood paradox concerning system costs. It is assumed that the operation of a more individualized system (mixed-age and values-driven) is more complex and requires increased costs. Not so!

If a school focuses on meeting value demand and ensuring flow, costs fall and resources can be better allocated. This is because waste (the really expensive bit) is reduced. If a school focuses on *costs* rather than *value,* costs inevitably increase! So if the school is able to identify the causes of waste and remove them, capacity to improve services increases and resources can be reallocated to continue that improvement. It takes us back to the energy supply discussed previously.

All of this requires a system that believes in and invests in people, one that requires front office systems to ensure flow and not back office (school) systems that block flow and manage waste. Cheap employment, poor training, teaching to the test, rating people by system results, target setting, performance reviews, incentive bonuses, replacing teachers with computers, limiting learning in favor of teaching, all eventually have a negative and long-term systems effect on quality and flow.

They also increase costs, as the United States may have noticed. All cause school managers to manage people because the likelihood of mistakes is greater. When they do this, they are forced to inhibit and limit what people do, an inward and negative spiral of lost energy and creativity. Schools tend to dumb down as they start to build a waste management system rather than a value demand system. Put simply, identifying and switching off the causes of waste is a major cost and energy saver. It increases system capability and capacity.

Here is the point: same-age linear structures are the prime causes of system waste in a school. This industrial structure prevents the information feedback loops on which service systems depend from forming. This separational process not only leads to system limitation and individual underperformance, but kills quality, increases bureaucracy, slows learning, and damages people, forever increasing waste and cost. Trying to repair, motivate, and fix participants only adds to costs with little or no cost benefits.

What is happening globally is not so much a raising of standards but more a dumbing down of the system driven by selective and conflicting interpretations of research. Schools employ cheaply, give subject teachers courses to deliver (scripts), and use inappropriate and limited diagnostics and assessments unhelpful to meeting the value demand needed.

Far from schools thriving on team building, joint decision making, and the like, managers stymy (more restriction and limitation) staff contributions, thereby restricting innovation, creative responses, and interventions. They do this but think that what they are doing is helpful and efficient.

What schools must do is:

- Smarten up on the value side and lower costs by reducing waste.
- Increase salaries over time to maintain stable and better quality levels of learning relationships.
- Identify the variety of value demand and implement the kind of in-service training that enables such demand to be better absorbed and met (a new professionalism).
- Change everything else over time (the subsystems) to better suit the new vertical system (assessment, reporting, meeting patterns, partnership, communications, policies, practices, procedures etc.).
- Remember that purpose determines method. This is why it is important to measure not only cognitive improvement, but also note attitudes and dispositions to learning, that is, take a holistic view of each child. When this happens, method is liberated; the school tends toward learning and higher achievement rather than the paranoia of teaching, testing, and coverage issues.

In other words, managers should manage the system first in order for people to be able to do the value work needed. As mentioned ad infinitum this requires a careful, informed, and collaborative move from a linear to a vertical structure.

## THE CHECK

There are three stages needed to understand an organization as a system and then to change it.

A broad explanation of the systems thinking approach to a complex service sector organization like a school follows a procedure (figure 7.1):

1. **Check:** In many ways, the previous chapters have been part of the check process by highlighting what to look for in understanding the school as a system. Here we have an advantage because we know our destination (the mixed-age school), and the check should

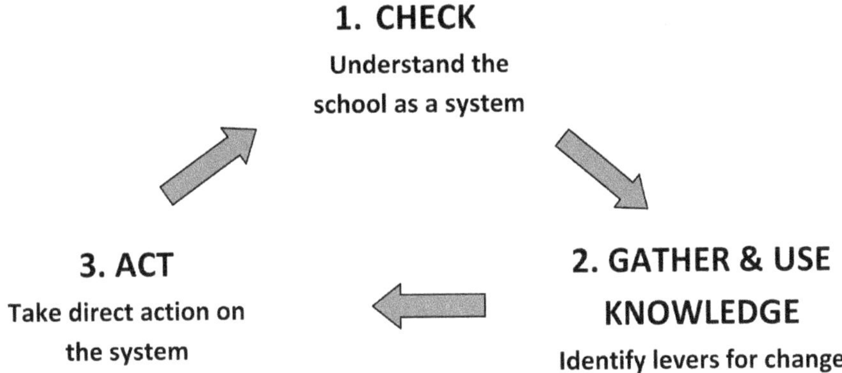


**Figure 7.1.**

show how this conclusion was drawn using systems thinking to seek out incongruities and assumptions.

The check involves an examination of purpose, performance, and management processes needed to identify how and why the school works in the way that it does. In particular the check explores how and where providers and customers interface and the perspectives they have. This process reveals any misplaced assumptions, assumed values, faulty processes, skewed rationales, poor or missing feedback loops, and other inconsistencies. In turn, this generates knowledge about what is actually happening as opposed to what is claimed to be happening.

2. **Get Knowledge:** Gathering systems knowledge has three benefits:
    - It challenges the normal thinking, assumptions, and management practices in use by giving objective and often counterintuitive feedback. This enables managers to take a second and more informed look at the school as a learning operation, given the values and purposes claimed. Remember, questionnaires, surveys, and focus groups are of little use in this process and should be avoided given the bias of interpretation. This is because these self-perpetuate industrial thinking: they are actually *of* the system and are unlikely to effect change. They tend to report on what is received, ad hoc and hand-me-down, rather than on what should be.
    - It enables *unlearning*. When a school is viewed as a system, a host of wrong organizational assumptions, practices, and deeply embedded work patterns are revealed that should no longer make sense to the managers. In this lightbulb moment, much of what passes as normal management thinking

suddenly seems incongruous and no more than hand-me-down assumptions and intuitions. Only by confronting these can they be abandoned and replaced. To change a deeply embedded mental model forged in the furnace of linearity, the culture in use has to be understood for what it is, dissolved, and a new culture created.

- It builds *realistic vision and leadership*. The new way of seeing the school once the veil of illusion is removed reveals a clearer, more achievable, and practical vision and purpose. Values are retrieved from where they were misplaced and these reveal the nature of the key changes that need to be made. The school has to operate holistically, not piecemeal. The joint processes of checking and gathering information counter delusion and promote a more purposeful, integrated, and interconnected organization.

3. **Act:** Now comes the difficult part. Having unlearned the system, we can use the new knowledge to start the transformation process. In this case, the transformation is from a system forged around same-age linearity to one based on mixed-age groups; one better able to jump start all critical learning relationships and employ the key disciplines of the learning organization. One that is better equipped to keep the aspiration gene switched on.

   This means taking direct action on the system to leverage the necessary reculturing process, but even here there is a challenge. It is possible to identify the changes needed (form mixed-age groups), but it is equally possible to leverage change in the wrong way. Schools that attempt this change without some basic systems knowledge, training, and support can very easily find they have reinvented the previous industrial model. Great care needs to be taken at this point and it is important that the school moves as one. The key is to remember that the school is building a set of interconnected relationships involving all key players in the learning process.

Having worked through this systems thinking process with many hundreds of same-age schools, the same organizational failures crop up with alarming regularity during the check phase. The aspirations of the school and the values it claims are always thwarted by same-age approaches to the school's organizational methodology. The school is unable to escape sameness and limitation and abhors anything that might be perceived as complex. In linear factory schools, this means that claimed values and beliefs are invariably assumed and rarely practiced.

To succeed by the measures of the day, the industrial model demands that students arrive aspirational, compliant, or have longstanding and high-ability teachers. However, even these are insufficient for a learning organization to form, creating as they always must a teaching-dependent culture. The ultimate effect is to make a broken system appear to work, and all this does is reinforce the illusion that the industrial model is okay when a good leader takes the helm.

The questions that systems thinking asks are simple but each is loaded with follow-up questions. Remember, questionnaires can never do this, ever! Examples are:

- As a child in your school, what happens to me on the very first day in high school? (We need to be walked through the induction process to test what is happening as opposed to what the school thinks is happening.)
- What is the purpose of the school and what are its written values? What does the school claim to do? What are its purposes? (What does it actually do?)
- How do you assess a student's progress? (What do you mean by progress?)
- What information do school reports home contain? (Is there evidence of limitation against professed values?)
- How and when do parents make contact with the school as a system? (Are these untaken opportunities or are they built into the learning support system?)
- How does parent partnership work? What is its purpose? (Are the learning partnerships real or phony? What data and practice supports them?)
- What is the role of the homeroom tutor? How is this supported? What does the job description say? (We know that this is the key player, the system conduit, for making the vertical system work. It is this player I often find to have been damaged by the existing system.)
- What happens when a child is underperforming or breaking school rules? (Again we are looking at damage to learning relationships so we can test the support system network and how it is supposed to work, as opposed to how it does.)
- How exactly is learning and teaching supported by managers? (We can explore the motivational and support strategies in place, the time and cost involved. Later we may explore why managers see themselves so directly as people managers.)
- What were the last three in-service training sessions the school had?
- How does assessment for learning work? (Here we can explore school outcomes and how these relate to feedback frequency, support, and new learning. It is also a chance to explore target setting, later to be replaced in VT by strategies for improvement.)

- How does the school decide the groups in which a child is based? (Connected to the question above and support strategies.)
- What happens when a child is not achieving all he or she might? (Again the system strategies come under scrutiny. How does learning support work?)
- How is a child listened to and when? (When are there deep reflective conversations about learning, how do these occur, and who is present?)

It is a seemingly endless list to explore and there is no shortage of questions. Most of these questions are not asked directly but tangentially and are explored through the way the system operates. Schools should have a learning culture but too often they tend more toward a factory sifting, batching, and testing system and this means wasted time, effort, and potential. Values, beliefs, purposes, and practices are invariably confused and while none of this is the fault of schools, these are matters all schools can address from within.

Even though the end game for schools is a complete change of culture, managers feel able to give rational and plausible answers to all questions and often feel the need to defend their answers with some vigor until they slowly pick up on how systems thinking works. Managers want change but defend what they have always done to the hilt . . . at least to start with!

Otherwise, as the check proceeds, the answers given start to become increasingly implausible. In an industrial model we can expect to see:

- Separation of the learning process from the school's lauded values.
- An assessment for learning system that relies on testing and the distortions thrown up by targets.
- An absence of individualized strategies for improvement in favor of targets.
- High separation of organizational departments: a silo effect.
- Ineffective parental partnership and student voice or input.
- Students defined and known solely by nefarious grades.
- Students not achieving their potential, let alone having potential recognized and identified.
- An information-out system posing as a two-way communication system.
- Limitation and separation everywhere.

This list too is far longer than set out here. You might think that teachers, like managers, stridently defend what they do; they certainly have that right because it is the linearity of the school as an organization that sets such conflicting behaviors and assumptions in wild motion. In fact, teachers see the systems thinking game immediately. Many are parents (system customers) and they revel in systems thinking. They play out the

Q & A game to the full, adding to the questions they are never allowed to ask and laughing at the many crazy things they are persuaded to do; things they rarely believe, have always known, and which make little sense to them.

The check is not a review process. Reviews, like long-term plans, will achieve little of value and tend toward the superficial. The check is a confrontation between delusion and reality and is a game that must be won and played hard until players see how it works and how it helps mend and heal. It is a board game in which all players start out separately but eventually learn that to win you must help all other players succeed too.

The resultant and recultured model based on mixed-age groups, called vertical tutoring, must replace the horizontality of the universal factory school; one model (the former) is liberating, emergent, and self-organizing, while the other keeps the school as a prisoner of the past.

## THE HUMBLE HOMEROOM TUTOR

No matter how much I examine the factory school, the undoing of it and its subsequent redesign are dependent on management change and the catalyst role of the homeroom tutor. Here is the conduit of the school's communication loops and the enabler of flow, and this is counter to nearly all the usual texts and management theories regarding schools and organizational improvement. The same-age approach is simply wrong, unhelpful, limitational, and broken. It disables learning and the learning relationships our players need to make progress, and no matter how hard a school tries, these can never work well, dependent as they are on high compliance.

Any new school culture has to be completely redesigned and recultured around the homeroom tutor and tutor leadership of mixed-age groups, and this means unlearning long-held management ideas and school structures. It also means doing the math differently. By highlighting the training, trust, and expertise of the tutor, the flow of information around the system improves, energy is released, and learning is better supported and informed.

I have thrown away hundreds of books and papers on school improvement that advise teachers on how they should improve, most written by non-teachers; they contain some well-formulated ideas, but they have no relevant answers for systemic change at the level of the school or the deeper interests of the child and the state. Instead, they all try to make the factory school work better!

While the vertical or mixed-age model described in *The Systems Thinking School* and further underpinned here cannot entirely abolish the universal factory school, it can mitigate most of its harmful effects, revive learning, and start a much better and more reflective conversation about both the urgency and the means of full systemic change.

## STORY

Chef Gordon Ramsay has a certain management style. He is well-known for his TV series in which he turns around restaurants and hotels that are in Russell Ackoff's words, "doing the wrong things wronger." He seems to find very similar management thinking issues wherever he goes, just as I have in every single school of the many hundreds I have worked with.

In a typically failing hotel he discovered high micromanagement and control. The skilled employees comprising the staff team were prevented from making the decisions each needed to make. Any questioning of the owner's command and control management style was not welcomed. Things at the hotel were going downhill fast and customers were walking away and not returning.

In his usual way, Ramsay tested the hotel's performance and its service claims from the customer's point of view (the check). He endured a dreadful meal and found a filthy bed and dead insects in his room. The organizational check process always reveals what appears to be strangely obvious, but which is somehow not seen; so much is assumed to be okay and so goes unseen by those who should see most.

As ever, Ramsay gathered the hotel's management and staff together and arranged a face-to-face meeting with the hotel guests. The guests were adamant that they would not be returning to the hotel and enumerated to the manager the many reasons why they were upset as hotel customers. For Ramsay, there can be no excuses, no intellectual prevarications, and no plausible explanations. The place was a mess and the service culture needed a complete overhaul.

Not surprisingly, the hotel workers, managers, and owner were visibly distressed. The staff always tried to do as they were asked by the boss. Their intention was to do their best and provide a good service; none wanted to be seen as failing and all wanted to do a good job and be part of a great team. Now they had to relearn everything. All knew they could do better. The staff were working hard doing what they were asked, but these were all the wrong things as far as the customers were concerned: the work they were doing did not work!

Ramsay has a wonderful way with the English language and metaphor. He described the hotel as the Titanic and the hotel staff as the orchestra, still playing while the ship is sinking, still doing the "wrong things wronger" in a crisis.

What came next was unexpected and telling despite being typical of the great chef. Ramsay turned to the hotel owner and said, "Don't think you're the (*expletive*) captain of the Titanic, you're not! You're the (*expletive*) iceberg!" It was one of the great management metaphors and it is sad that I cannot repeat it word for word.

What I like about Ramsay is that the process he uses, although perhaps a tad confrontational and a little hostile, is all about changing existing thinking by inviting managers to look again at the performance of their organization as a system, as seen from the customer's point of view. It is a classic approach to service system improvement. It does not need full expertise in systems thinking, but it does need a deep understanding of how people work at their best. Ramsay understands customer value demand, quality customer relationships, flow, and waste removal.

In this case, the hotel manager could see things were wrong but had blocked feedback from staff and customers and so deluded himself that all was okay and customers were happy. He was busy doing all the wrong things like issuing endless instructions and micromanaging people rather than managing the system, building teams, and developing learning relationships with customers. It was an organization that had separated from its customer care values and the hotel owner was unable to figure out that this made him the problem—such is the power of our self-deluding ways. To learn what was needed for success, he had to unlearn all that he had done for years and to stop blaming others and overmanaging them. Training, trust, and leadership were needed.

The confrontational approach used by Ramsay is risky but for grown-ups can be more effective, ensures there is no return to old ways. It is also fast and people generally prefer fast. It is important to see quick improvement.

Ramsay then finds a simple leverage point or two to set in motion a domino effect of cultural change. It could be a new reception area, some basic training, a revised menu, room upgrades—anything that might give customer satisfaction and workers a sense of pride, and a base on which to start the redesign of a better culture. From then on it is a case of building the interconnected teams to deliver the quality service that meets customer needs and expectations.

The great management guru W. Edwards Deming spoke about "joy" in work. It is an odd word for a management guru to use but it best describes the *giving* part of service, and the *receiving* too. As with Ramsay and his hotels and restaurants, a systems thinking practitioner takes a long and broad view of the entire school within its community context as a provider of services designed to meet customer demand.

A hotel has more easily identifiable customers and services. In schools, when you look deeper at the teams at work you see that when schools are at their best, everyone is a customer of everyone else besides being a service provider, and this includes students, parents, and all school staff. All learn so that each can stand on tiptoe.

To spread this management message, I once took an advanced course in school consultancy. We were taught as consultants that we should never offer answers to school leaders but to somehow draw the answers out from the vision of the head teacher by careful and non-threatening questioning. This involved intense listening to school leaders, rather like a psychiatrist, to pick up on clues to help the school leader steer a better course and resolve issues.

I practiced and practiced but learned from the course that I could never be patient enough using such a method and would make a hopeless consultant. Given such a deeply embedded industrial system, it seemed to me impossible to draw out any viable answers to the organizational issues that school leaders face. It is difficult to rescue managers from a mental model and thinking trap whereby schools continually create complexity by trying to control complexity. Their mindset is to control more when the more valid solution is to be less controlling, a near impossible bridge to cross and one whereby vision is rendered impotent.

The fact is that no matter how patient I was, the advanced sophistry, messy justifications, erroneous, assumptions, and appeals to plausibility at which school leaders excel made it impossible to make progress in real terms. Leaders tended to see bits of problems, faulty elements, and would discount whole school issues and even themselves as being at fault.

At that time, I had no systems thinking knowledge, and this meant two people circling each other not getting remotely close to any tangible solutions beyond reconstituting old and failed management ideas. It is what happens today.

Systems thinking provides a more accurate language and this greatly simplifies problem resolution. Today, my preference for tackling wicked school problems and changing the school's culture is very different. It involves the following:

a. Teach some systems thinking basics regarding the link among purpose, value, and method to school leaders so they can look again at the school as a complete system.
b. Walk managers through the school, exploring it from a customer perspective (teacher, student, and parent), especially looking at those places where school and customer make contact.
c. Look at how and what information flows in the system. Seek out barriers and restrictions to flow.
d. Compare what is happening with what schools think and assume is happening.
e. Show schools how the setup of a mixed-age system is different and removes assumption and delusion while absorbing complexity.
f. Show how the transformation process, what schools call change management, works.

By posing simple questions, there is (fortunately) a strong likelihood of getting very different answers from system users and managers. What emerges is usually a healthy and widespread disagreement in the zone where reality and assumption collide. When this happens it is easier for participants to see anew and to question any assumptions. In such reflective moments when assumptions are laid bare, systems thinking comes across not only as an antidote to command and control management, but also a means of climbing out of the aforementioned box. It is common sense.

Unless systems thinking wins the day, school administrators will retain their assumptions and command and control management will rule. This remains the favored method used in the universal factory school. It is a management method born in the United States and returning, it seems, with a vengeance!

# EIGHT

# Background to the Checking Process

> Lying to ourselves is more deeply ingrained than lying to others
> —Fyodor Dostoevsky, *Citizen: Small Pictures* (1873)

A school must be clear on purpose, and this means constantly monitoring the variety and frequency of value demand on its system. As John Seddon pointed out, there is at the heart of any system a defining relationship between purpose (as defined by customers), measures, and methods in use. When this is understood even at a simplistic level, schools discover that the standardized test results, the measures they use to judge performance, are invariable out of sync with value demand. Seddon (2008) puts the case neatly:

> Imposing arbitrary measures creates a *de facto* purpose—meeting the targets—and constrains method, because the work gets designed around the reporting requirements. When measures are derived from purpose (from the customer's point of view), however, and when those measures are employed where the work is done, method is liberated. (p. 82)

In the case of schools, if achieving target scores, the de facto purpose, is all that counts, then these are the measures that will determine the school's method. It is another moribund loop from which escape is difficult without outside help. Value demand, the real purpose, is sacrificed along with real values. The methods used by a school are aligned to achieve test targets, and this encourages a preference for more teaching, more practice tests, more separation by ability, and less intrinsic learning.

There are always unintended consequences when schools treat staff as units of production; these include loss of morale, cheating, antagonism to managers, illness, and frustrations that lead to staff quitting. These same consequences affect students and we can explore these below.

## PARENT CUSTOMERS

Checking a school system constantly reveals incongruities and assumptions that need resolution or designing out. There is a conflict between the espoused values of home and school. The school is desperate to achieve the best test scores it can because these are used to administer punishments or rewards. To comply, the school persuades itself that all other values are being somehow met through the schools operational processes.

The school soon finds, however, that such an approach is not easy without high customer compliance, and all (staff, students, and parents) have to be persuaded accordingly. Buy-in (the so-called leadership bit) has to be achieved. However, this is not easy, and soon the organization becomes dependent upon and defined by seemingly endless policies, procedures, practices, protocols, and principles. This leaves the school with the task of persuading customers, especially parents, that the methods in use are okay (like they have always been) and that the singularity of purpose is what is important.

By following customers through their experience of the system and their contact with the school, it is possible to understand how communication flows between players and, more importantly, what counts as information. Here all is not as claimed.

Parent partnership is a classic example of an assumed information feedback loop. Despite the protests of schools, any valid claim to *partnership* with parents is invariably a delusion, one that increases as the child's school career proceeds. There is almost none worthy of the name, but schools seem obliged to think that there is, oblivious to many parents who can feel overly isolated by the school, struggling to support their child's learning capabilities and disappointments.

A partnership implies a joint purpose and a more equal contribution, but value demand as defined by parents is either assumed or discounted. The numbers don't work: too many parents and too few staff. Schools define virtually all aspects of the relationship between home and school despite research suggesting that the better the partnership, the better a child does in all kinds of ways.

We buy into what passes as partnership as defined by the school rather than any viable definition of a workable learning relationship, one that exhibits outside-in design specifications rather than inside-out. Home–school partnership is what the school *says* it is, not what parents think it should be. Even when the partnership is clearly set out and defined, as many now are, this is rarely sufficient and can actually work to keep the operational system in play the same. It changes nothing substantively.

If such a proposition is right that there is no school–parent partnership worthy of the name from a systems thinking perspective, or even from a less-contorted and more honest definition of the word *partnership*, it must mean that there is limitation and separation at work on an unprecedented scale, and there is. The school sees parent partnership as a complexity that needs to be managed, separated out, and reduced to a need-to-know level. The school defines what minimal information is to be sent home and when, the times of any meetings, the length of meetings, the topic for discussion, the language used, the information to be discussed, and pretty much everything else.

As I have said many times, schools operate information-out systems rather than one based on interdependent communications. In the 450-plus schools I have worked with, every single one claimed parent partnership to be an important value, one that every school held dear. Such beliefs are sincere. All schools are able to recall successful examples of partnership against the odds, but there is collective amnesia on those partnerships that proved more difficult. Whenever value demand fails to be absorbed, it causes failure demand, and the school has to turn expensive somersaults and add another clause to a policy to put matters right.

Every school is able to wax lyrical about their particular version of partnership written large in their school's prospectus. Unfortunately, the written word is one thing, and having such values in your organizational DNA is quite another. The following three statements are among the many touted by schools: parents are free to contact the school at any time; parents are always welcome at our school; we maintain regular communication with home.

In each school I visited, actual practice proved to be a denial of partnership, almost the opposite of claimed intentions, and was more an attempt to manage numbers, that is, to limit, prevent, and control any complexity that might arise should such a partnership actually exist. Parents are offered *opportunities* and this falls far short of any designed-in partnership scheme.

Each school model had far more negative effects than positive, the end result being an undercurrent of failure demand such as follow ups, reworking, uncertain information, more meetings, increased bureaucracy, and delays in intervention. In turn these create confusion, growing dissatisfaction from voices not heard, and complaints. Energy is used up and complexity increases; when partnership breaks down or works ineffectively, the damage caused makes any future resolution difficult, requiring considerable time and effort. Costs rise!

Industrial thinking has not moved one iota. Quite simply, parent partnership can never work effectively in a school that operates a linear, same-age, grade, or year system. The math simply does not allow it to and this is illustrated as we proceed deeper into school assumptions! Everyone is frustrated. In fact the partnership, fed by minimal data sent home, is largely assumed and rarely practiced.

Because industrial thinking is fixed in linear time, all other thinking has to conform to its reductionist and limitational ways. In this way, the semantics of partnership and collaboration are distorted and made to fit existing factory management ethics. This is in part because a viable working partnership with parents was never designed into the original factory school blueprint. This means that parent partnership has to be conceptually added on to the school as another quasi-subsystem, and when this happens, it becomes an additional bureaucracy, one requiring careful management and control, rather than an integral part of the whole.

In systems thinking, this is called *sub-optimization*, a process that perpetuates. Basically, the narrow purposes of the school dominate at the expense of the greater ecological system and society of which it is part. These bigger purposes like increasing goodness, ecological awareness, creating fairer society, and building international understanding are represented in part by the parents and the variety of value demand they make on the school as a system.

At the heart of sub-optimization is a command and control mentality of paranoia, one that depends on a toxic mix of fear, compliance, bias, assumption, and delusion. Some call it *management*. As Deming said, "Our prevailing system of management has destroyed our people." The balance of elements in a system must allow for autonomy and trust in subsystems, sufficient freedom to enable self-organization and information flow more able to contribute to the betterment of the whole. The school needs to look again at partnership, and to do this vertical tutoring and mixed-age groups provide the best way forward.

Otherwise, the partnership process and accompanying procedures too often fail to produce the desired effect (information flow, rapid intervention, joint responsibility for learning, better judgments and decisions, team involvement, mutual support) because they are overly separated from other system elements and overly compromised. The feedback loop is tenuous at best, beset by delays, difficult to manage, misconceived, and prone to breakdown at critical learning times.

## STUDENTS AS CUSTOMERS

If the contentions above are so, there must be evidence that the school's singularity of purpose, the naïve measures that purportedly dominate a school's worthiness and drive methods in use, are far from secure. We need not look far. We can learn much from customers disenfranchised and disengaged from the services that they felt they needed but were unable to draw down from the school system.

The U.S. school dropout survey, *The Silent Epidemic* (Bridgeland et al. 2006) is a testament to the way schools deal with the ambiguity, assumption, and compromise that besets them—the wickedness of the school problem. In Canada, a year earlier, the state of Ontario commissioned a similar report (Ferguson et al. 2005) on early school leavers. Both reports arrived at similar conclusions and both were concerned with capturing the voices of those involved.

These *voices* are important because they are the voices of customers. But among these voices is another even more persuasive voice: the voice of the system. Both reports (above) produced copious advice, but there was not a single recommendation about the Deming question regarding change management: By what method? We all too often end up with a list of what is wrong and what needs to be fixed but little in the way of transformation other than a wish to make the existing system work better.

Any quasi-solutions in schools organized on a basis of same-age groups (especially homeroom groups) can only ever constitute an add-on; this means they can never be elementally connected, designed in, and effectively integrated to form the deeper learning relationships needed in a school. These are likely to increase complexity and costs without decreasing waste and failure demand. Any resulting sub-optimization spreads like a contagion.

Parent partnership policies enacted by schools tend toward the hand-me-down folklore of past practice loosely combined with a cursory and assumed view of what parents are minimally deemed to need to be effective partners in learning. Students are too easily made the victims of a double whammy of limitation and separation.

- The learning relationships they need within school are system limited and defined in part by measures in use (assessments of what is deemed important) that reflect narrow school purposes and an associated need for compliance or buy in.
- The learning relationship between home and school subsequently fails because a) value demand is not being met, b) information home is inadequate (information light), and c) the school strictly controls (perhaps *obstructs* is a better word) flow to reduce what it sees as complexity. The partnership is built on sand.
- Finally, the learning relationship between students and parents is compromised by the same narrowness. The school effectively withdraws from the partnership and this abstinence removes professional guidance, denies personalization, and maroons and confuses the other partners in learning.

While surveys on parent partnership are legion and research is very clear on the value and importance of parent and school partnership in learning, practical application must always fall far short of what is possible in same-age systems. It is rare for any of the hundreds of books, articles, and research papers to point the finger at same structures as a limiter of learning and learning relationships.

Even parental wishes are redefined to side with the system in use. Parents are taught that schools are busy and complicated places, so they learn to ask for so much less than what is needed to maintain a quality learning relationship with the school and with their children. When information is so limited, it makes it appear that flow is okay, but in the background problems accumulate unseen and unknown.

In a mixed-age setting in which the form or homeroom tutors (the people who see the child every day) become the center of a child's learning universe, the organization becomes malleable and learning is relationship dependent; parent partnership is integral, more cogently defined, and parameters flexible and emotional intelligence is practiced and built in. The teacher is part of a team, a partnership, and the person able to make it all work is the homeroom tutor.

Parents are clear on what they want as customers (discussed earlier in chapter 3 and updated below), but need the school to respond in a way that enables those needs (the value demand) to be met. What the demand side requires is a complexity of learning relationships that enable customers to draw down what is needed to ensure support, effective intervention, and progress. Without this the system is compromised.

- They want their child to do well at school and be supported to this end.
- They want their child to be recognized for all they bring to the school as young people.
- They want their child to be known and occasionally listened to.
- They want their child to develop as a good person.
- They want their child's potential to be recognized, noted, and nurtured.
- They want to know that there is a named person at the school (preferably two) who knows their child well and is there throughout their child's time at school.
- They want somebody who not only knows their child well but someone with whom they can talk at critical learning times or when intervention is needed—someone who cares about their child as much as they do.
- They want their child to feel safe and be safe.
- They want to be involved in their child's learning and development.

The challenge for the supply side is to redesign the system in a way that absorbs and responds to the variety of value demand in a quality way. This means an individualized approach whereby there are least two people in the school who know a child well. This means a more sophisticated level of information and a freed-up flow to support its movement round the system. This is the organizational basis for personalized learning and its starting point.

While the school offering is limited and convergent, parents have a much broader and divergent view as to what is best for their child. There is an incompatibility here that is not resolvable in same-age systems. Trace Pickering (2013) believes the answer to this rests within the context of community, the people who live in the area and who want to invest in their school so that the school feels supported, values driven, and able to work effectively. He suggests asking two simple questions of those closest to the school: "How do we want to raise our children?" and "What is the ultimate goal of education?" It is a sublime idea and reflects an understanding of the variety of value demand.

Pickering calls on the three important ideas suggested by Peter Block (2008), ideas actively being put into practice (The Boulder Thesis and the Educational Ecosystem).

- Community: an understanding that within the teams of people and individuals who comprise community is the power to be transformational.
- Abundance: the idea that every community has the capacity and capability to be the change that is needed and to be effective.
- Hospitality: the capacity and willingness to engage with diverse voices in an inclusive way.

But how to get there? Put everyone in a room and they will probably make some improvements, but will never notice what Diana Smith (2011) calls "The Elephant in the Room," the relationships that need to substantively change. Where is the best leverage point to begin such a change? It is to change the way the school organizes itself as a system and it begins with mixed-age groups and the learning relationships these promote.

We should not be surprised if the needs and wants of students mirror those of their parents. Children dislike failure, they need recognition, they like it when someone listens to them; they want to be seen as good, they like to earn respect, they value support, and they need to feel safe and cared for.

The irony is that this is not only what a good school wants, but is something that is eminently achievable rather than aspirational once the barrier of the industrial model is removed. The lists above provide the underpinning means of checking the school's effectiveness. The check asks if such customer needs, what people value, are being met, and how the school provides and ensures such care and support via the learning relationships it has. Unfortunately, linear systems are causal in creating the opposite effect and spend huge effort correcting their own inbuilt system traps.

While it is relatively easy to produce widget children with basic skills, scrubbed down, sifted, sorted, and batched for whatever, it is less easy to individualize such a system into a more customized form and help schools be adaptive, self-organizing, and customer oriented. The oppressive weight of old bureaucracies and management thinking weighs heavy.

## LEARNING FROM THE DISENFRANCHISED

The basic school parameters remain stubbornly in place and the school is faced with trying to resolve the unbending time/math problem. How can a teacher relate to 150-plus students each week and know them and their parents well in the time allocated? It explains in part our bias toward the great teacher in every classroom.

The means by which a school goes about handling this problem goes a long way to defining it as an organization, including its inherent learning and teaching qualities and its outcomes. If the means depends on same-age structures, the school will always return to its default one-size-fits-all industrial process.

The proposal here is that it is well within the remit and capability of schools (and communities) to organize themselves in a new way that can mitigate the harmful effect of the factory school and change from a teaching and testing organization into a higher-performing and values-driven learning organization.

Any first glance at the math problem says it cannot be done. The possibility of treating young people as individuals, parents as partners, teachers as facilitators, and intrinsic learning as needing a three-way dialogue to get it going and support it seems as remote as ever. Surveys of young people who failed to graduate and dropped out of school are testament to the way schools organize learning and manage learning relationships. There have been many such surveys that set out the school's inability to do the math and we need to learn from them.

## WHAT THE SURVEYS SAY

*The Silent Epidemic* by Bridgeland, Dilulio, and Morison (2006) paints a picture of the state of play. The more complex the society, the more that the schools we have are destined to fail young people. We have to come to terms with the value work and personalization. While (for me) the problem is a global one affecting young people everywhere, its most obvious system characteristics are seen in those schools that operate in complex societies, challenging circumstances, and disenfranchised communities. The United States has them all.

Systems analysis says that all factory-style schools have inbuilt restrictions and limitations, practices that are disobedient and assuming of child psychology and what it is to truly care. The reason the factory metaphor has stuck reflects problems with purpose and direction, just as Larry Cuban (2014) suggests. The spiritual tiller is missing; the whole has become separated from values and the bigger purposes that should be driving improvement. Who says so? The young people say so—the customers—and they say it loudest in those places that make the least system sense. It is worth pondering the findings awhile because what we see is never all there is.

Set out below are some of the main research findings from young people who dropped out of school across a number of U.S. towns and cities. The executive summary of *The Silent Epidemic* (2006) states that while some students drop out because of academic challenges, most could and should have graduated. The report further states that,

> circumstances in students' lives and an inadequate response to those circumstances from the schools led to dropping out. (p. iii)

The report tends to ignore structure and has no conception of mixed-age design solutions, so we can expect *people* to figure largely. Because school structure in this report remains substantively assumed, this affects any suggested strategies for improvement. In this respect this *epidemic* is not a teacher fault but a system fault. What we are witness to is a design flaw, not a people flaw. It is a system messing up: blame as scatter gun.

Among the reasons given by young people who dropped out of school are the following:

- 47 percent said classes were not interesting. Of these, 42 percent spent time with peers who felt equally disengaged from school.
- 69 percent said they were not motivated or inspired to work hard.
- 80 percent did one hour or less homework.
- 66 percent said they would have worked harder if more was demanded of them.
- 70 percent said they could have graduated if they had tried.
- 33 percent said they had to get a job and make money.
- 26 percent said that they had become a parent.
- 22 percent said they had to care for another member of their family.
- 35 percent said that failing in school was a major reason for dropping school.
- 43 percent said they missed too many days and could not catch up.
- 45 percent said they started high school poorly prepared by their earlier schooling.

It is a confusion of causes. The report describes the complex reasons for dropping out of school as a process of gradual disengagement, with attendance patterns being an early sign. Young people generally regretted dropping out and 74 percent said that given the chance, they would have stayed in school.

Of particular interest is the report's statement regarding the factors needed to maintain learning in school. These are as follows and what is of interest here is that same-age schools often drive same-age nuanced solutions.

This is what this valuable report recommended, and while the lines are important, reading between them requires systems expertise. Remember, even our dropouts can only describe their experience using mental models forged by a linear, teacher-dependent structure.

- Improve curricula: make school more relevant and connected to work.
- Improve instruction and access to support: 81 percent wanted better teachers and 75 percent wanted smaller classes. Seventy percent believed more tutoring and individualized support was needed.
- Build a better school climate: here the call is for better supervision, safety, and a desire for school to be made more interesting.
- Ensure that students have a strong relationship with at least one adult in the school: 65 percent said there was a staff member who cared about their success. About half felt there was someone to whom they could go to discuss personal issues and 70 percent favored greater parental involvement.
- Improve communications between home and school: 71 percent of young people in the survey felt this was important. Around 50 percent noted its absence, especially when things were starting to go wrong.

Sound familiar? It should. I think I could all but guarantee that students in a mixed-age setting (vertical tutoring) would not be able to make such statements because learning relationships are designed in.

The point is this: when we remove the usual suspects thrown up by distortion and assumption, the respondents in this important survey are describing characteristics and limitations of same-age systems and factory-style schooling. The recommendations resulting from the report, excellent though they are, are made all the more difficult (expensive and bureaucratic) because they are constructed around an accepted school model fixed in the linearity of the existing management psyche. Any suggested solutions tend to be reformulations of old ideas rather than transformational.

When you take a really close look at how schools organize themselves, these tragic disengagements, dropouts, and broken learning relationships are predictable and therefore belong to the domain of *common cause variation* (they are a product of the system's underlying and most fundamental assumptions). They are not *special cause*, unpredictable and fixable by a reform or a new target. They arise from the underpinning assumptions and constructs of a dominant factory approach to a basic math problem.

When we confuse the two, nasty things happen. Deming (1994) put it this way:

> Confusion between common causes and special causes lead to frustration of everyone, and leads to greater variability and higher costs, exactly contrary to what's needed. (p. 315)

Remember that what we see (the superficiality and effects) is not all there is (the underlying assumptions and common cause). The way we intuitively see this problem is the problem! It explains why reformers keep trying to fix the wrong problems again and again when the fault is systemic in origin.

The young people surveyed are describing a system that has no real capacity for listening, no viable means of building in learning partnerships and support, and has a definition of "care" that doesn't live up to its promises. It lacks flexibility for individual adaptation and is slow at intervention when things go awry, a story of broken relationships and partnerships that never formed because they were never designed in. Respondents can only tell how it was for them, how they were taught to see things—WYSIATI.

It is convenient for such reports to try and fix this by highlighting teacher quality rather than the school, and the restricted way it feels obliged to organize and support teaching and learning, as the *special cause* of variation (something apparently fixable using incentives and punishments). Students *see* teachers and blame them; they do this because, like most people, they accept the linear system as somehow benign. What they don't see and thus don't blame is the common cause connection between the two, the system and the way work works, and it this reality that systems thinking points out.

Our view of linear systems always encourages the call for better teachers. But it is a better system that grows better teachers and we need to recognize that the universal one we have is disabling and distrustful of learning. There is no linear model flexible enough to handle complications and variations, let alone understand value demand. Teachers, like students and parents, are all system victims in their own way.

If this large number of young people dropping out of school is a problem, we can all but guarantee that above this water line there is a great deal more disengagement, underperformance, and unnecessary emotional and economic damage. All of this is perpetrated by a system designed for a bygone age and one that specializes in waste management. So we need an alternative.

Set out below are the report's main recommendations with a VT twist. These explain how having a mixed-age basis for school organization meets all of this report's recommendations, at virtually zero cost!

## MIXED-AGE SYSTEMS AND VT (VERTICAL TUTORING)

*1. Improve instruction and access to support for struggling students.*

This section of the report amounts to a plea by students to be in smaller groups and to be recognized as people with individual needs, each with considerable contributions to make. VT is built on this principle and enshrines this opportunity. There has to be at least one short period of time in the day when this is made possible, and tutor time or homeroom time is that time. It does this by building intensely close learning relationships between a) the tutors (there should be two) and tutees, b) all older students and younger ones (not only leadership opportunities and mentoring everywhere, but disruption to negative in-group loyalty by reforming groups), and c) between school and home, and by implication between parent and child. These are the multi-nodal communication loops that drive and support the learning process. VT ensures these learning relationships work and are attended to. They also lead to other system changes such as improved assessment for learning and deep-learning conversations.

*2. Build a climate that fosters academics (learning).*

Here the concerns revolve around safety issues and classroom discipline. The VT answer is to build quality learning relationships between all key players (mixed-grade students and tutors) that grow learners and leaders. This is achieved prior to students even reaching the classroom on entry on day one. When older students start to support younger students, their own learning and attitudes improve (there is at last good research on this); the trick is to transfer this to the classroom by ensuring that all school staff are tutors, including the bosses. This also reduces bullying instantly (good feedback from schools in the United Kingdom) and almost certainly impacts gang affiliation (I have no feedback on this or know of any research on this, but it sounds hypothetically the case) and increases safety. Everyone becomes a learner, a leader, and a teacher. Every human resource is there, on tap and ready. The tutors are the system's information hub, allowing resources to be drawn down as needed.

*3. Ensure strong adult–student relationships within the school.*

The report says that "These young people craved one-to-one attention from their teachers, and when they received it, they remembered it made a difference." The students said that "some of their best days were when their teachers noticed them, got them involved in class, and told them they were doing well." Interestingly, these respondents perceived their teachers to be higher quality when they did this. The report arrives at a counterintuitive truth that quality resides within learning relationships, not test scores (although the two are linked!). VT absolutely enshrines this principle and builds these learning relationships in from the word *go*. VT also guarantees that every child is cherished, known, listened to, appreciated, respected, and cared for in a practical and designed-in sense. They will experience such attention in homeroom time every time, every day. Every child must be a leader and a teacher too, and so must parents. VT enables this. Every child is known.

*4. Improve communication between parents and schools.*

The weight of evidence supporting this theme is vast and comprehensive. Unfortunately and ironically, the means needed to make such a partnership effective is hampered by the education system itself and the linear math problem; the factory system is designed to operate without parents so their influence is diminished. The action taken by schools falls short because of data sheets that have replaced viable and holistic reports, limitations on assessment, absence of viable strategies for improvement, insufficient challenge, a mass failure in recognizing the component needs of emotional intelligence, a misapplication of dispositions for learning, and a mistaken belief that technology can somehow replace human interaction. Once again, VT provides the critical communications hub, and in turn this demands changes to the way we see, listen to, and engage with parents, students, and each other. VT designs it all in, including a comprehensive and in-depth review and reflection of learning, the academic tutorial.

The U.S. three-tier system, like all structures that cause students to move between schools at critical learning times, causes unnecessary disruption to learning relationships. These take considerable time, effort, and information to form in same-age schools, so any further disruption can be highly damaging. Too many critical learning relationships do not form at all, and others malform. It is all a matter of chance, not system design. The former students who comprise this survey tell a story of organizational neglect and of lives wasted, each a tragic tale of waste passed from generation to generation, so much "unknown and unknowable."

It simply does not have to be this way. Learning from failure is essential and these former students describe very precisely what should have made the difference. They are telling us how to design a better school system. Unfortunately the likely response is a request for more money and little substantive change. Jamshid Gharajedaghi (2006) said, "Americans are the greatest problem solvers the world has ever seen. Unfortunately, they solve all the wrong problems."

Any school system should ensure that learning relationships, what students "crave," remain as stable and prolonged as possible, a design for learning requirement.

Education in many districts in the United States is built on a junior high system (sadly exported around the globe) that has no substantive rationale whatsoever in educational, psychological, or human welfare terms. There is no argument remotely strong enough to justify the huge learning disruption, interference, and potential psychological harm caused by the organized mass breakage of learning relationships as young people are parceled off from one school to another every few years.

It seems that too much loose thinking remains configured around an industrial mindset from the 1900s and intuitive assumptions from the 1940s of how education should be enlightened. Now, in the first decades of a new century, the United States is clumsily returning to the structural problems that it created and seems unable or unwilling to undo. I will return later to more of these messy matters that affect schools.

Many education writers include the Hindu fable of the blind men who stumbled on an elephant. Each man offered a different explanation of their experience based on the part they touch. Although often quoted, few read the important lines of John Godfrey Saxe (1872), who ended his famous poem on the subject of the blind men and the elephant with the following two verses:

And so these men of Indostan
Disputed loud and long,
Each in his own opinion
Exceeding stiff and strong,
Though each was partly in the right,
And all were in the wrong!

So, oft in theologic wars
The disputants, I ween,
Rail on in utter ignorance
Of what each other mean,
*And prate about an Elephant*
*Not one of them has seen!*

We don't see the elephant in the room so let us prate.

All of us have experience in schools and most of us attended one, but we don't really see the complete picture. At best we know a little bit about our particular school, our bias. Even with eyes wide open, we only see parts and remember bits like classrooms and perhaps that teacher who was kind or made us laugh. We have an impression. Intuitively, we build a picture from the parts we know. We build a story about teachers and classrooms and how we think schools work and how they might be made to work better. We have opinions. If the teacher is bad, no learning gets done. If students are naughty, the teacher can't teach. Then there is that great teacher able to stride the system like a Colossus. We know that. Ergo we need better teachers. . . . It's all so easy. Except for one thing: it isn't.

# NINE

# Counterintuitive Truths and the Nature of Leverage Points

Travelers, there is no path, paths are made by walking.
—Antonio Machado, "Traveler, there is no path"

Having conducted the systems check and gained a first handle on the difference between the closed factory model based on age and high-stakes testing, an alternative mixed-age system based on values, the decision has to be made regarding the best way to go about changing from one to the other. Every element will be affected, so the question arises as to the leverage point needed to start a domino process of transformation in the school.

While Peter Senge offers useful descriptors and a definition of a learning organization, such organizations have not materialized, certainly not in the universal school system we see. The old system of management still prevails. Schools may occasionally flirt with such ideas. Many lay claim to being learning organizations, but problems of purpose, measures, and method persist and these continue to define and limit learning relationships and determine management thinking.

School managers are locked in this maze and their self-delusional karma is to make it all work somehow; to manage their way through using whatever toolboxes they have. To do this they must a) convince themselves they are right and b) adapt the language of the system to make it cover all eventualities, and c) deter debate. This brings them into conflict with teachers who still cling by a fingertip to the basic ideas of intrinsic learning.

The previous chapter spoke of the variety of value demand that a system like a school has to absorb. For the school this poses a real problem. Young people are complicated and their problems rarely come in ways that are easily fixable. Resolution in a linear organization can require many conversations, decisions on action that cross departments, and require further referral and consultation. The school is divided into subgroups, permission levels, layers, titles, offices, and job descriptions to manage any untoward complexities. The school believes that in order to teach, teachers must be protected from complication.

Unfortunately, dealing with perceived complexity in this way serves only to increase complexity in the form of failure demand. When this occurs, things can go very wrong, with delayed intervention, mistakes, miscommunications, and more besides; ultimately, this makes learning and teaching more difficult. Customers, and this includes teachers, students, and parents, are expected to get in line and use the system in play.

Those on the front line of customer service must use the system procedures, policies, practices, and protocols, while parents access the school through a single back office portal. Above all, people must not use their initiative or suddenly come up with an innovative solution.

Managers invariably subdivide schools into cost centers and task areas to meet all eventualities. Unfortunately, these centers do not allow for the easy flow of information and work; it may take forever for a classroom matter that has suddenly escalated to run its course through the system, with the originator (the teacher or parent) rarely knowing what is happening given the many people involved in the resolution process.

Today, if you want a problem solved, try contacting a call center or customer complaint department. Instead of organizations resolving problems by trusting people, training them to use their initiative against demand and to be innovative, such tasks are contracted out (internally or externally), causing delays, obfuscation, further referral, lost information, and increased costs. Organizations today are slowly learning that this does not work. Whenever organizations fixate on costs at the expense of quality, they drive up costs!

As Forrester (1961) said, managers can usually pinpoint the leverage points most likely to bring about the changes needed, the ones most likely to improve quality and rectify production issues. Unfortunately, having identified where a problem is located, it is often the case that managers leverage the change in the wrong direction. Forrester understood that the policy solutions to urban challenges used in public systems, although full of good intent and seemingly perfectly rational, often had the opposite effect to the one intended.

Forrester showed that that the problems that needed to be addressed were not necessarily the problems being addressed. Problem solving in the public domain tend toward fixing system elements or treating symptoms. It is a theme continued by Dennis and Donella Meadows and others in a stream of work, beginning with *The Limits to Growth* (1973) to an update in 2009.

In the United Kingdom, John Seddon (2008) has mounted blistering criticism on the seemingly endless failure of public sector reform. The solutions used by policy makers to tackle problems not only create more problems, they increase expenditure and too often make the original problem worse and more difficult to resolve.

In a small first school, children often have a single teacher. The teacher uses guile, wisdom, initiative, and emotional intelligence to resolve problems, shares the solution with parents, and to involve necessary others. The teacher is helping the customer pull down what is needed from the system. The home–school partnership is better connected, players trusted, and their roles supported. The teacher too is a customer of the system. She is trusted to do the job, able to use initiative, and is happier and more effective as a result.

As schools get bigger, the way that complication (the variety of value demand on the system) is seen starts to change. Schools are not daft. They can predict the matters likely to go wrong in part through the data they gather, but mostly because of the experience they have. Because small schools do not have much in the way of money, they must design the school in a way that is able to do the value work, a system that Seddon and O'Donovan (2010) call *designing against demand rather than costs*. Customers know not only who will help them but who wants to help them.

As our customers and players travel through the system, things change. We enter the big school, where a child has multiple teachers operating in a world of multiple subsystems. Even so, customer problems remain as predictable as ever, perhaps more so. Unfortunately, the way that problems are dealt with become ever more convoluted, separated, and limited, ever more geared to compliance and keeping things the same.

Senge's three-legged stool is not the metaphor we need and systems thinking is not the fifth discipline at all. If it is a discipline, then it is the only discipline. Systems thinking transcends disciplines. It tells us how to be happy and lead a good life and it is underpinned by values. Systems dynamics is part of systems thinking, not the other way round. Only when we manage the system in a values-led way do the disciplines come into their own.

The four remaining disciplines are all about people, the attributes they need to practice and develop to ward off delusion and enable learning. While I appreciate such an idea, it is not a people problem we face. Most are already trying hard against the odds; most are also reflective, want better, and can develop mastery given the chance. It is not even a leadership problem or a teacher problem. It is foremost a systems management problem and a mindset problem. The real problem is that we don't see the problem and are not as smart at solving problems as we think we are.

## LOOPS

In this way, we enter a closed learning loop or mental model of reform that offers only the illusion of acting on feedback. The four other disciplines (mastery, vision, mental models, and dialogue) are insufficient by themselves. They do not of themselves enable school redesign, and this means they may inadvertently self-perpetuate stale ideas and sameness, adding to delusion rather than removing it. Otherwise, schools become trapped in this whirlpool surrounded by the roaring current of old bureaucracies and the inanity of party politics.

Every school team that I have worked with wanted to improve, regardless of how good they judged themselves to be. Every school realized that same-age tutoring, their espoused theory-in-use, had severe organizational and learning limitations. Every school had examined their same-age system, taken it apart, tried endless fixes, but still could not make their same-age structure work. Frustration and self-doubt had set in and things were getting worse. The schools perceived they had a problem of tutor quality or program appropriateness rather than one of system design and effectiveness. The same old predictable problems from bullying to aspiration issues still raged.

Further, the energy required by same-age schools to make their system work even passably did not match the output achieved. They argued that they had applied their understanding of complexity, they had aspired, and they had participated in endless reflective conversations. Any dialogue was going nowhere other than in circles; they could not leverage the change needed to make their aspirations come to fruition and improve output.

The prevailing system of management thinking from which schools think they are helping their students flee is the same system in which schools find themselves trapped. Who said the United States doesn't get irony? We are all prisoners to some extent of schooling, our formative institutional experiences that not only determine how we think but also why we so often fail. Deming (1994) put it simply:

> I should estimate that in my experience most troubles and most possibilities for improvement add up to proportions something like this: 94% belong to the system (responsibility of management) 6% special. (p. xv)

## THE VERTICAL LEVERAGE POINT (VT MAX)

The introduction of vertical tutoring (VT) is seen by many schools as a transformational means of improving learning relationships, reducing negative demand, and controlling variation (not terms that schools use). Schools initially see VT as a means of creating a better school ethos, ensuring that each and every student takes on responsibility and leadership and is able to develop emotional intelligence. No programs needed! Schools too often see VT at a superficial level, as a means to improve student behavior.

In fact, VT is intended to improve learning and teaching. At a recent training session, a school manager told me that his last school had introduced VT. All they had done was create mixed-age groups. He said that what I was describing was a kind of "VT max." He was right. Schools rarely appreciate that VT is a system in itself that requires a complete cultural and management makeover, and one that is easy to do when understood *as a system*. For me it is the beginning of the route to full systemic change, way beyond the shoreline of this book.

Leverage points are those strange places where a small change like a positive feedback loop can start a significant domino effect throughout an organization. But as King and Frick suggested, it seems to be the case that every part of a school has been examined, tinkered with, and reorganized in some way with no substantive change to any fundamentals.

The school simply replicates itself and all too easily returns to its original linear form as a limiter of expectation, a dampener of aspiration, an acceptor of waste, a creator of bullying, a protector of compliance, an assumer of partnership, and a barrier to innovation—the very opposite of what the good people in schools think they do. Schools try so hard to do the opposite, to escape the chrysalis and fly, but the school's karma is to remain a prisoner of the past. It requires a systemic change for any trust to return as it must.

When PISA points out quality and output problems, the U.S. answer is to first seek out the cause (blame teachers: their training, their pay, their recruitment, their management) and then fix the perceived cause through massive financial incentives that can never work, the kind of evaluative accountability that induces fear and prevents people from attempting the value work.

All are short-term fixes and all cause organizations to freeze and close in on themselves. They exacerbate the real problem of how to enable highly competent, capable, and creative people, our only true altruists, to work better and absorb and meet value demand. They make the problem worse, not better, but think the opposite. The prevailing ideas simply make the industrial mental model even more ingrained as daft and unworkable reforms pile into the mix.

While teachers may seem to be an obvious leverage point for drastic improvement, acting directly on them is not the answer. Acting on the system is! Otherwise teachers will quit, students will continue to drop out, and parents will feel that they too have failed. Our players will suffer in lonely and isolated ways, blaming themselves, not realizing that they have it in their grasp to change what they do by rebuilding the flow and interconnectivity needed, the leadership task of the school.

In *The Systems Thinking School*, I described this situation in the following terms: those who come into schools bent on improvement are likely to walk straight past the fundamental system design issue that causes the problems and make matters worse by using single-loop learning fixes and add-ons. They carry industrial toolboxes. Most schools actually identify the most potent leverage point, the homeroom and tutor time, but weaknesses in organizational mathematics mean they push it in the wrong direction, kill it dead, and then try and apply artificial respiration to the corpse.

Reformers are like aid agencies entering a disaster zone, creating more harm than good by failing to see what is needed, what works, and how the system aligns with its environment and its local context—what people need as opposed to what we insist they have. What surprised Forrester was this self-same oddity. Having done the thinking work and having identified the areas where change might best be initiated, managers leverage change in the wrong direction, making matters worse while believing that they are actually fixing the problem.

In a school, as soon as the leverage point is operated by changing the composition of the homeroom group, all other system elements, such as assessment, reporting, parent partnerships, and re-jigging the academic calendar, have to change to suit. Information must flow.

Any failure to complete the full makeover over time can cause a negative chain reaction, one likely to cause considerable damage throughout the change process, and one that is even more difficult to put right. Systems can unexpectedly go into reverse mode. A school that simply mixes up the students but lacks systems knowledge to complete the redesign in good time can make matters worse. They will discover a world of unintended consequences.

All elements must be realigned and re-engineered to form a new and complete culture, one based on learning relationships, the school as an information exchange lit by a million multi-nodal loops operating with purpose and keeping aspiration alive and switched on.

## INSPECTION

I still work with many schools on systems thinking and vertical tutoring. Six months ago, the headteacher of a school I had trained emailed me. He is the principal of a large, purpose-built secondary school, and following intensive training in systems application and VT (max), the school introduced mixed-age tutor groups for twenty minutes before morning break. In that time, the mixed-age tutees meet with their two tutors, people chosen from all school employees regardless of status.

During that time many productive things happen. Older students support younger ones, discussions take place, there are private conversations between tutors and tutees, work is monitored, there is group activity, and even laughter. Friendships transcend age, responsibility grows, behavior is better, and everyone learns to lead and be a good citizen.

There is no program to follow, but there is an academic calendar that guides the way, and leadership and support are there for all to see. It is an important time in the day. His school is in an area where standards have been in serious decline for decades and this school was built to replace the ones falling apart to exemplify a change to better things. That being the case, the district inspectors adopted a very proactive approach with constant surveillance and ongoing evaluations.

When the district inspection team saw VT in action during March 2014, they were aghast. There was no written program being followed and to them this meant only one thing: no measurable learning. In their mental model etched deep from their own experience of schooling, this meant precious time being wasted. They did not see what they expected to see—program delivery—and this caused their System 1 to go haywire and their System 2 to shut down.

They were unable to see learning relationships building, confidence increasing, leadership developing, aspiration being nurtured, self-esteem rising, mutual respect being shown, improved parent participation, mature learning relationships, and the seeds of better learning and teaching being sown and nourished. They did not see joy and friendship because these were not things they were there to measure.

They did not see that these improved learning relationships extended into the classroom and formed the basis for improved parent partnership and more complete feedback loops. They did not understand flow; it was not in their lexicon of management experience. Neither did they see the variety of value demand being absorbed and students able to draw down the things they most needed to make progress. They saw only what they saw. WYSIATI.

They were clear on what they expected to see—a teacher-led class listening and working—and it was missing. They could not see how there could be a system of learning without a set program. They could see no order, little in the way of preparation, students mixed by age breaking with convention, and to them this meant that nothing was being achieved. It was all too complex for the inspection team, but was completely understood by the staff and the students.

They were hard at work using systems thinking to understand complexity and embrace it. They were engaged in a dialogue of reflective conversations that would spill into the playground, into homes, and later the community beyond. They were sharing vision and each was helping the other develop personal mastery and so maintain aspiration. They were also part of an infinity of positive in-group teams joyous in their well-being and safe in team care. Bullying had nose-dived, intrinsic learning was on the up, and outcomes were improving.

The school principal had changed the system and trusted the staff to do the value work that needed to be done at the customer interface where it matters. It is a system reliant on trust and one that truly invests in people and their need to aspire, to feel pride, to help others, and to master. The payback in leadership, increased self-esteem, and improved learning and teaching is huge, and those who work in the schools have noted the positive change in student attitude, aspiration, and performance. The school understands how feedback loops interconnect and has adopted a system to underpin them and the energy they supply.

The local district inspectors were unable to believe that creative and caring people could work better without programs, targets, evaluation sheets, and the old performance measures. They had noted the long-term underperformance in their area, but their meager bag of tricks contained only the stale reform and management ideas that had failed before. They were factory minded and unable to see systemically what the teachers saw and the students experienced, and wished to see the school return to its old failed ways but done better!

The school principal was disappointed that all his work and practical vision was the target of such mediocre thinking and I supported him as best I could. It is not the students who need to learn, I told him, but those who claim falsely to be their advocates.

## TEACHERS AND SYSTEM CHANGE

Teachers have an advantage: they cherish learning. When invited to look again at a systems problem, they relish the opportunity to both unlearn and relearn, far more so than managers. Young people are naturals and so are teachers. They want to be rid of their delusional mental models.

Their ability to learn is what makes them good teachers, and is why they are so good at what they do. When presented with the counterintuitive and therefore an opposite systems strategy to the one in use, which is what systems thinking allows, teachers will critically listen and evaluate and ask all the right questions. They always reach the end of any systems training sessions long before I do.

Later, they usually say, "It was obvious all along. I knew that was the case. I always thought that." Systems thinking unblocks thinking, avoids the cul-de-sac, barges through paradoxes, and simply finds the right path, the one lit by values and learning relationships. It is a return to common sense.

In other words, organizational mind maps, which we can discuss later, are adjustable and can be reset, but only if everyone understands what the school is trying to achieve and their role in the process. Everyone needs to be part of the redesign needed, the one that is able to return the school to its core values, purposes, and guiding principles.

We are beginning to enter the world of counterintuitive truths. It seems that counterintuition—looking at systems in ways that are completely the opposite of all that passes as normal—actually puts us back in touch with ourselves and our work. It reminds us how we used to think about problems before a hundred years of industrial management grew around us like calcified rock.

It makes the cynic smile! It reveals management truths and returns normal to normal. It is also the quiet language that teachers use when they are not being abused, shouted down to, and asked to do the daft things that prevent young people from learning and from believing in themselves.

Donella Meadows (2009) spoke of the challenge of leveraging change in her book *Thinking in Systems*. She noted the huge difficulty in finding the best leverage points for change in complex systems. Despite the systems thinking application of stocks and flows diagrams, feedback loops, and extensive modeling, it is still difficult to resolve highly complex systemic problems. It is even more difficult in schools in which the perceived feedback and reinforcing loops are malformed, missing, blocked, or constitute examples of erroneous rationalization and reform.

I quoted Jeffrey Conklin (2006) earlier. He placed an interesting observation at the top of his list of defining (school) characteristics regarding wicked problems. It is a statement of wonderful simplicity:

> The problem is not understood until after the formulation of a solution. (p. iv)

This is why this book started with the solution (VT) rather than the analysis of what is wrong. If the solution is built around mixed-age groups or has mixed-aged groups in mind, the critical change to the way the homeroom tutor operates, it is easier to see what is wrong. The math problem can be resolved differently. Because the wicked problem can be seen in the light of the first part of the solution, the school is easier to understand as an organization. It removes illusion and prevents delusion and cynicism from setting in.

Conklin may state the counterintuitive obvious but he is right. It is easy to draw the communications loops and feedback mechanisms of a school after the school's industrial management problem is conceptually resolved.

It was certainly my good fortune as the boss of a large school to work with people cleverer than me. Together we were able to identify the change needed (VT), the precise leverage point (mixed-age tutor groups), and then (the smart bit) to push it all in the right direction (make the tutor the hub of communications and learning support). The teachers liked the idea; it was the administrators beyond the schools who said it was madness and could never work. It was our delight, many decades ago, to prove them wrong.

This was our counterintuitive truth: to reculture our school using mixed-age groups. We then saw bullying decline, learning relationships improve, performance increase, outcomes improve, parent partnerships form and deepen, job satisfaction improve, and so much more fun and energy released. We were also able to do something else. We became our own school inspectors! Because we all understood the system, we all contributed and could easily self-evaluate the work being done and innovate better practice.

We achieved what organizations seek to achieve: to release the inherent creativity of all associated directly with the learning process (students, staff, and parents). We let the dominos of our old thinking fall one by one in rapid succession, policy by policy, until they had all gone, and found ourselves in a very different and far better learning place.

Meadows noted that solutions to complex issues are so surprising that they fly in the face of the rational mind. As one of the great systems thinkers, Meadows knew from bitter experience that when she discovered solutions to complex problems, they were so counterintuitive that hardly anyone would believe her! Of course, readers may choose not to believe that VT is such a powerful leverage point, until, that is, you visit a mature VT school and talk to students who would have their school no other way.

The implementation of mixed-age tutor groups leverages a change that no linear, same-age organization can: the math numbers problem simply doesn't allow it. It is very much like the view of business philosopher Charles Handy. He argued that the best businesses and corporations are like villages in which everyone is an equal citizen and shares information and responsibility. As I have intimated before, we need our schools to be such villages.

There are now businesses and organizations all over the world where work has changed in this way, far from the factory, the time constraints, and the fear. Our schools might have led us to such places long ago had we understood them, supported our teachers, had faith in learning as an intrinsic entity, and seen intelligence as multifaceted, achievable, and malleable.

Our mistake is to overly control learning as a process and to break it down into constituent parts in order to measure progress, something that will always cause problems with method. The management methodologies used to promote such an idea amount to little more than what Alfie Kohn (1999) calls "pop behaviorism." We should do more to show how learning is accessed and made intrinsic. To do this the teacher has to juggle being both the sage on the stage and the guide by the side.

Learning is complex and is why this chapter starts with a poet and a word of advice. "Travelers, there is no path; paths are made by walking." Schools have to create a destiny and a better way. Walking allows time for personal reflection, but as Robert Pirsig (2006) taught us, the journey is what is important given that the destination is never really reached.

I mentioned that one of the foremost systems thinkers and specialists in the field of service sector industries is John Seddon (2008). I repeat his words here for the explosion of counterintuitive ideas that this quote contains.

> If investment has not been matched by improvement, it is because we have invested in the wrong things. We invest in the wrong things believing them to be the right things. We think inspection drives improvement, we believe in economies of scale, we think choice and quasi-markets are levers for improvement, we believe people can be motivated by incentives, we think leaders need visions, managers need targets, and information technology is a driver of change. These are all wrong-headed ideas. But they have been the foundation of public sector "reform."

Whenever I listen at the periphery to systems thinkers and their wisdom, I think of schools and how much we needlessly abuse them, and of the amazing people who walk their corridors. I keep asking: What is it exactly that we are trying to achieve? It is a question nobody should ever have to ask, but one that schools and their communities must.

If Senge's description of a learning organization is right, it is perhaps the best description of what a school should aspire to be. It is a place that builds safe and productive learning relationships, that is interconnected and multi-nodal in feedback, a place that is able to intervene rapidly when problems arise. It is also a place where complexity is not only embraced but is understood as essential to success. If indeed it takes a village to raise a child, then we need our schools to be such villages.

Although this is not what we have, it is precisely what schools aspire to be in the quieter moments between tests, when people are listening to the school orchestra or watching the school play being performed, both of which are mixed-age productions. There are times when a teacher-learner is working with a student-learner, when both experience such fleeting and quality moments. Systems thinking is there to help schools develop learning relationships and to capture more of these quality learning moments than they ever thought possible.

So here we are at a thinking event horizon where one paradigm should be giving way to another and where the way managers think has to change. It is a time for systemic change beautifully set out by Frank Duffy (2007). In that article, he uses a title drawn from Nevis, Lancourt, and Vassallo (1996): "A butterfly is not a caterpillar with wings strapped on its back." Systems thinking is the best means we have of connecting a school to more of itself. We need our schools to be the beautiful butterflies we need them to be—to fly.

By knowing the start of the organizational answer, we can better understand the manager's industrial mindset, its underpinning assumptions, and its outgrown and industrial rationale. Once recognized, we can persuade schools to look again, to unlearn and recreate both what they do and what they have. It is a matter of unlearning and re-learning, moving from delusion to design.

Having named the leverage point—the homeroom tutor and his or her mixed-age charges—schools may choose never to believe it, just as Meadows said.

Having mentioned the phrase "single-loop learning," an explanation is required, and this is where I go to next. The loops provide all we need to understand management.

# TEN

# Learning in Loops

> "When I use a word," Humpty Dumpty said, in rather a scornful tone, "it means just what I choose it to mean—neither more nor less."
> "The question is," said Alice, "whether you can make words mean so many different things."
> "The question is," said Humpty Dumpty, "which is to be master—that's all."
>
> —Lewis Carroll, *Through the Looking Glass*

If we are to rid schools of old industrial ways, it is important to understand how delusion manages to hold schools in such a factory-minded grip. Like any organization, if they become moribund, detached from customers, and unable to learn, they go out of business or become increasingly irrelevant.

The school increasingly limits the way it operates to the extent that the classroom is both isolated and insulated. Communication flow is restricted in and out, values are assumed, and managers and administrators see people, rather than the industrial blueprint that pervades their thinking, as the problem that needs fixing. In other words, we arrive at this section already in poor shape and still searching for a plausible explanation.

Hasenfield (1992) points out an important conflict at the heart of service sector organizations. In the case of schools, staff try to consider the needs of students but must also follow set rules and have an eye on assessment methodology, program coverage, and the measures of evaluation conducted within and by the organization. Unless something is measurable and seen, it is assumed not to be of value. While staff try to be supportive at the point at which they interface with students and parents, the organization is limitational, rule bound, and convergent; it is unable to appropriately support activities and learning relationships that fall outside of functional roles. This dichotomy can take it into a cycle whereby its own clients start criticizing the school.

According to Hasenfield, staff react to contradictions in different ways. Staff may capitulate but still feel good that they are doing the best they can in the circumstances in which they find themselves. They might identify more with the clients (students and parents) than the school, deciding that the school as an organization is a barrier to fulfilling needs. Silos may form whereby staff seek out niches and places that can offer protection from the contradictions that pervade the school.

Teachers may decide to do their work and avoid participation in the wider life of the school, adding to the limitational effect. Others may quit. Some perceive themselves as victims of the way the school operates.

Whatever the case, for schools, these strange divisions persist. In particular, there is a divide between the beliefs the school espouses, the spiritual and moral tiller that should govern direction, and the practices and routines it follows. It is an irony that schools remain very supportive places in all sorts of ways despite their dominant underpinning feature being disconnectedness.

It is Chris Argyris and Donald Schön (1974) who guide us into how organizations think and how managers behave as they struggle to make the work work. They highlighted some strange organizational behaviors and concepts regarding *learning loops, espoused theory, theory-in-use,* and the *mind maps* that connect them. Had educationists picked up on the management implications of these ideas back then, administrators and jurisdictions might have seen schools, their leadership and administration, and the mess all were heading for, differently. Again, we see this business of disconnectedness in organizations and thinking.

It is not unreasonable to inquire what exactly is happening and why. When checked and explored through a systems thinking lens, the strange separations between what schools claim and believe, and what schools actually do, seem to be system endemic. But at the same time, contradictions are all too easily rationalized and explained away by managers and administrators, until revealed through systems thinking to be untenable. Schools can too easily justify what they do, even though what they do when checked as a system may be at considerable variance with what they claim is happening.

These inconsistencies and assumptions, driven as they are by separation from values and uncertainty of purpose, have a delusional edge. It is not simply the case that justifications for improvement and action are rationalized away; indeed, schools try hard to get better and improve. The problem of innovation and transformation to a better culture is prevented by the linear system that ensures that schools stay in a closed loop, one that is unable to learn sufficiently to achieve self-organization.

Teachers, after all, are reasonably well trained (a matter I shall return to), and many are parents themselves. They know much about theories of learning, growth, well-being, and families. They are no fools and comprise some of the most able, creative, and intelligent people we have. However, there is a strange inconsistency between what teachers know and believe and what they actually do or seem compelled to do.

Paradoxes are wonderful things; the way we think creates them, but the way we think is system governed. Even if public school administrators lanced the delusion, forsook values and psychology, and stated categorically that the purpose of our public schools is to sift and batch students using high-stakes testing and a curriculum designed for an enlightenment that no longer holds, they still cannot escape so easily. Values cannot be ignored. They are there to dissolve paradoxes and are the drivers of practical vision and purpose needed for the first draft of any redesign blueprint; they are not an afterthought to be added on, assumed, and redefined to suit.

Besides, if we adjust the examination demands ever upward to maintain standards and prevent too many passing (batching), we persist in creating winners and losers. Such risky cause and effect has consequences for the societies we build. Such a model makes no sense at all and is even more delusional. The paradoxes must be resolved.

John O'Neil (1993) wrote a book called *The Paradox of Success: When Winning at Work Means Losing at Life.* Winners, like leaders, are rarely what they seem. Many have a shadow life deep in their psyche, one of depression, high-risk and deviant behavior, and unhappiness. The paradoxes keep appearing, and what seems to be desirable and a measure of success is not all there is; there is often a big downside when balance to life and relational support is missing, and values go awry. We will come cross this again later when we look at psychology.

Some schools have spotted this. They have noted that high achievers face all kinds of difficulties and stresses and that their happiness can take a hit. The approach of some schools is to believe that happiness can and should be taught. It is the never-ending and wrong answer of an organization stuck in a closed loop: the mistaken belief that deeply emotional and personal matters can be taught, somehow remedied and explained away, using the latest ten-step program.

Citizenship, happiness, and stability should be the natural outcomes of the way a school organizes itself. When this is achieved, then we can look at programs. Relationships come first, before programs, and if they do not, the school has got it wrong.

Among the reasons offered by Argyris and Schön (1974, 1978) for the mismatch between what is *espoused* and what is *practiced* is that behavior in organizations is guided by mental maps, and it is this mental mapping that takes us deep into the psyche of the school as an organization. Mental maps set out the behavioral geography of (in this case) the school as an organization and how people act and respond to given situations.

These mental maps are behavioral guides that undergo constant review and determine actions and responses in any given situation. This means that a split can easily occur between theory, what we know and believe (espouse), and behavioral practices guided by mental maps, what we actually do (theory-in-use).

Our mental maps comprise a whole series of assumptions about ourselves and others in the work environment. The mental map describes the organization in personal terms and offers what seems a plausible explanation for what is happening around us and how we should respond. In other words, it helps us to rationalize and makes sense of our environment and how the organization works. Mental maps govern behaviors (what we do), and in turn these behaviors govern how the organization works, completing the circle. When the loop closes, the system is governed by its own distorted feedback and it simply repeats its behavior and remains static.

This means that inconsistencies will inevitably arise when looking at any complex organization as a system, especially one like a school that is stuck in time. The way people behave in organizations (what they actually do), guided by their mental maps, is often contradictory to what they espouse (say they do).

In this way, the rationalization used to explain organizational behaviors, especially at the delivery or service interface, sounds perfectly plausible. Teachers and school managers can rationalize and explain quite precisely what they are doing and why they are doing it. In effect, factory schooling can be easily justified despite its seeming ecological irrelevance and its waste of human potential.

As Caine and Caine (2014) suggest,

> This results in a tendency to retreat back to the way things once were and to rediscover the certainties of the past.

Beyond these are yet more theories—theories about child care, well-being, child psychology; theories of learning, theories of management, hypotheses about leadership, and more; all of which provide a further overlay for the teacher to recognize and consider. A linear system has to somehow manage within this complexity despite being poorly placed to do so.

The school plays out these conflicts as best it can. Managers and administrators can always provide an explanation to connect theory (espoused) and practice (theory-in-use), but all of this linearity becomes odd when viewed as a holistic system. The actual practice (the theory-in-use) offers only a passing nod to any accepted underlying learning or child development theory. A theory of learning (espoused) can all too easily become a theory of testing (theory-in-use), but retains the same explanation as the espoused theory with a much-stretched linkage, the distance between cause and effect.

When looked at through a systems thinking lens, it is clear that espoused theories of learning, customer relations, and even psychological development are given cursory recognition in industrial models but still serve as the justification that all is okay and functioning normally in the school. Underneath, however, there is more organizational unease and uncertainty than is admitted.

Statistics on well-being, mental health, and happiness are an increasing cause of concern and there must be reasons for why this is. Once again, actual school practice appears to be at odds with what is needed (the value work) and is too often based on assumptions that have limited research validation. The industrial model simply persists in its delusional way.

The school operates on assumptions more so than knowledge: it assumes whatever purposes are suggested it should have; it assumes that learning is underpinned and driven by its values and beliefs; it assumes it is cognizant of research; it assumes it is caring; it assumes it is interconnected as an organization; it assumes well-being; it assumes partnership; it assumes that its means of assessment is useful; and it assumes learning is taking place among groups and individuals. It also assumes it is not doing harm.

In fact, it is assuming pretty much everything through its inaccurate justification that the school's espoused management and learning theories, already contorted to justify a factory ethic, are the same as the theories-in-use they are supposed to inform.

To recap: what people do, their actual organizational behavior, is guided by their mental maps, or as Argyris and Schön (1974) describe it, their theory-in-use—one that is always incomplete, developed over time, and guides action. Players construct an image and rationale of the organization and how it works to inform and justify what actions they might take to make it work. There is no awareness of these maps and different people will experience the same picture but offer a very different interpretation.

There is a split between espoused learning theories, the words used to convey what we do or would like people to think we do, and what we actually do. While what we say (espouse) may appeal to values, research, child development, psychology, and even management theories, what actually happens in classrooms, homerooms, and where customers interact with suppliers is at variance and loaded with assumption. Some describe this as the difference between grammar (the rules) and language (the way we speak), the grey area in which incongruities lurk.

## SINGLE-LOOP LEARNING AND DOUBLE-LOOP LEARNING

All of this means that organizational learning is not what it seems. If there were a true understanding of the variability of value demand and less control of teachers and staff, it would be reasonable to expect high innovation and creativity to manage such complexity. However, it seems that in schools and the wider system of which schools are part there has been little in the way of change. The old industrial model, the factory school based on same-age strategies, persists. The basic organizational patterns and defensive routines are largely the same now as they were when I was a student at school.

Argyris and Schön (1974, 1978) propose that organizational learning is all about the detection and correction of error. In this respect, it is very much linked to special and common cause variation. The first response of an organization to a problem or to something that is going wrong (persistent dropout rates, standards issues, behavior problems, quality issues, etc.) is to seek a solution from within the existing governing variables, the school's working principles, programs, policies, practices, protocols, and procedures, the way the system operates and whatever is at hand, to address the issue.

While it is true that all of what the school needs to improve is already within the school, this is not the same as using repeat variations of existing school practices and policies. If the school attempts *fixes* to system elements using known strategies that have not worked in the past, any success is unlikely.

This toolbox approach from a systems perspective is *single-loop learning*. This approach might mean investing in a new pro-social program, revising a policy, and improving teaching techniques. Such an approach is based on the kind of command management thinking that inadvertently ensures that all of the current and underpinning operational fundamentals in use remain as they are. It assumes all is basically okay, that a few tweaks and greater investment are all that is needed to get past the perceived problem. In this way, the normal routines and assumptions continue without too much disruption and remain largely unquestioned.

Reforms tend toward such an approach, recycling sameness while preaching change; the idea is that variation in performance or output always has a special cause (unpredictable) and a solution can be readily found. In other words, the school keeps trying to fix things using tools from the old industrial toolbox that may have worked in another time. The management system prevails. Single-loop learning seems to assume special cause variation, an unexpected disruption in a process that can be traced back to a particular cause. Find the cause and fix it! This may work well with wonky light bulbs but not so well with people and schools.

Double-loop learning involves a very different approach. The contention of this book is that most of the problems schools face require double-loop learning remedies, the need to question deep-seated assumptions and management practices that have no obvious source. These are unknown until revealed. This involves questioning two fundamental assumptions and operational practices on which the school as an organization has relied for a long time and which surreptitiously govern the strategies in use.

Chief among these culprits is one that no one sees because it seems to be not only benign but unimportant, while the other can provoke tribal warfare, appealing as it does to stretched psychological principles. These are, of course, same-age groupings coupled with the separation that occurs between junior highs (middles) and uppers. These combine to form a perfect storm of damaged learning relationships that prevent the system absorbing the variety of value demand it faces. Both causes have damaging consequences.

While single-loop learning is obvious but organizationally ineffective and follows a normal approach, double-loop learning is far riskier and more challenging. It involves questioning values, notions of the common good, and purpose; it challenges us to look anew at the underpinning system structures and strategies in use. Argyris (1985) described double-loop learning as a process whereby

> The basic assumptions behind ideas or policies are confronted . . . hypotheses are publicly tested . . . processes are disconfirmable not self-seeking. (pp. 103–4)

The reform emphasis, even at its best, focuses on improving management techniques, revitalizing programs, and updating teacher skills without reference to causal learning relationships between key players. It is the domain of the "toolhead" who believes that new equipment, the latest technology, the new reform, the new accountability measures, and the revised targets can make the existing system work better (single-loop learning and thinking). The idea is that these will increase efficiency by improving basic routines, timetables, and practices. None are systemic changes.

In the case of schools, this kind of single-loop approach, if left unattended and unchallenged, leads to an erroneous conclusion: that teachers must be at fault if the school system is breaking down and students not achieving and dropping out. Single-loop learning seeks to improve skills and techniques and, while welcome, such changes are superficial compared to the changes to counter the system's fundamental operational assumptions. Only with system change can learning and teaching skill truly develop in a way that complements intrinsic learning, higher aspiration, and improved outcomes.

Double-loop learning, therefore, is of a different order. Double-loop learning and thinking is less accepting of the status quo and of reform approaches. Double-loop learning questions underlying assumptions and seeks to explore how an organization works at a deep and more fundamental operational level. As such, double-loop learning has very different and very special characteristics. In asking critical questions, it must return to purpose, demand, and identification of the value work, the places where the school is no longer certain.

In the case of schools, double-loop approaches seek out a basic grounding in areas of ethics, values, morals, and spiritual matters. It is almost an insistence that knowledge and research must be applied and the causes of waste eradicated.

## THE LADDER OF INFERENCE

The idea of a Ladder of Inference (figure 10.1) was proposed by Argyris. The ladder is used to describe the way organizations (in this case schools) can move from facts to decisions and hence to actions, often without realization—much is assumed or inferred.

The idea is to show how it is possible for organizations to make progressive errors and wrong judgments. Our starting point on the bottom rung is the safest unsafe point. We experience reality and interpret facts selectively based on experience and beliefs to interpret what they mean (think of intuitive but gullible System 1 and lazy System 2!). If enough people think the same way, this affirms the interpretation. As we proceed upward, we are soon in the realm of assumption from which we draw conclusions. Then we base our beliefs on our assumptions and take further errant action.

When the ladder is used to describe almost any school process, practice, or protocol, it is rarely far before assumptions creep in and judgments become insecure.

Errant mental models of management solidify. As the ladder is climbed, we end up doing *the wrong things wronger,* as Russell Ackoff always said. Judgments are impaired. So the cycle of inference continues. The factory school persists and keeps recreating its own image, accepting the basic organizational and operational premises and purposes to be benign.

The answer of course is counterintuitive: walk under the ladder or avoid it in some way! We have to accept that we all learn from experience and are influenced by the white noise and chatter in the system. Rick Ross, in *The Fifth Discipline Fieldbook* (2000), advises that we can avoid the Ladder of Inference by being more aware of our own thinking (reflection), making sure others understand any reasoning (advocacy), and by asking questions to test any assumptions (inquiry).

In the hubbub of the day, and given the system capability that determines mental models, this is not easy. Neither do I believe it all that helpful against the weight of the system in play in which school vocabu-

**LADDER OF INFERENCE**

| | |
|---|---|
| **6) ACTIONS** | We now start to act on our distorted beliefs and assumptions. For future reference we loop back to rung (2) and reinforce our beliefs, further distorting reality (self-delusion). We are lost but in denial. Unable to innovate a way through problems, and make more insecure judgments. We throw money at problems and regulate more but claim to be expert. In trying to resolve issues, we create more! |
| **6) ADJUST BELIEFS** | On this rung we make adjustments to the way we see things working. We have to create a picture where everything fits in with what we think. The enormous debates around education are evidential of endless adjustments to fit and so persuade others we are right. We join and form like-minded groups. |
| **5) DRAW CONCLUSIONS** | Very strong beliefs now start to emerge regarding the assumptions drawn. Our mental model has formed. The picture of school we create is generated -in part by passion, in part by assumption. |
| **4) MAKE ASSUMPTIONS** | This rung is the most dangerous. From the meanings we have assigned, assumptions are made. We need to justify our view. We start to rationalise based on interpretation rather than fact. Our assumptions are insufficiently challenged and informed. We develop a personalised version of school realities. |
| **3) ASSIGN MEANINGS** | We now attach meanings to what we *see*, the filtered information. We start to interpret selected information regarding school practice and organisation. We haven't noticed we are deviating from values, abstracting, & becoming self-deluding. |
| **2) SELECTED & INTERPRET REALITY** | Here, the raw data of our experience is filtered. We personally interpret what we *see*, the way school is organized and managed and the way relationships work. We show preference for what is important: same-age groups, curriculum, practices, and learning relationships. |
| **1) REALITY & FACTS** | The pool of available information used to explain how schools work. We start by experiencing school & the data available. |

We keep returning to the same model and try to fix it (reform) or make it more complicated by adding more regulation, policy, practices, protocols & procedures. We cement in mistakes and create a learning and teaching problem.

**Figure 10.1.**

laries become distorted to fit. Ask for support in a school and you are likely to be judged inadequate in some way by many.

In the example above, the thinking pattern is difficult to escape. What should have happened is completely hidden from players and is only apparent when the school is designed around mixed-age groups with the multitude of learning benefits that then arise, preventing such problems occurring in the way they do. Trying to fix things in a linear system rarely works. The system has to change first in order for the problem to be understood, and this is the paradox that needs working through.

Just as Kahneman demands objective support to offset errant thinking, so Argyris and Schön show how double-loop learning can lead to better decisions and judgments in organizations. The key, therefore, is to increase the school's capacity for double-loop learning. But to achieve this requires an understanding of how the current structure places strict limitation on learning relationships and flow, cutting off other feedback sources between students, parents, and tutors, and assuming them to be of low importance.

Edmonson and Moingeon (1999) put it this way:

> The underlying theory, supported by years of empirical research, is that the reasoning processes employed by individuals in organizations inhibit the exchange of relevant information in ways that make double-loop learning difficult—and all but impossible in situations in which much is at stake. This creates a dilemma as these are the very organizational situations in which double-loop learning is most needed. (p. 161)

Schools comprise a classic case of organizations made static by a reliance on single-loop learning and assumption. On the very first rung of the ladder are assumptions about people, learning, and age that have gone largely unquestioned and so are accepted as true. From there, every premise and belief becomes exponentially errant and loops back to adapt and redefine further selective facts needed to back up an original falsehood.

Schools cannot be static organizations, but instead must be self-organizing; they should comprise what Argyris and Schön (1978) call "a cognitive enterprise," one in which:

> individual members are continually engaged in attempting to know the organization, and to know themselves in the context of the organization. At the same time, their continuing efforts to know and to test their knowledge represent the object of their inquiry. Organizing is reflexive inquiry. (p. 16–17)

They are, of course, describing a learning organization, and this is not where schools are. Schools can conduct all the action research and participate in deep reflection all they wish, and many do, but if the basic same-age premise is not questioned, they are likely to reach the second rung of the Ladder of Inference compromised, when they should be climbing the ladder of success, innovation, and systemic change.

Those working in schools are operating on very limited and partial information, and thus use theories-in-use largely reliant on intuition, folklore, and assumption. It gets them by. It is the school manager who holds the key to better learning, not the teacher alone. It is the school managers we are reliant on to make the changes needed that enable better learning and teaching.

As Humpty Dumpty so famously said, "The question is, which is to be master—that is all."

Like Robert Trivers, Chris Argyris (1990) showed in his many studies that people consistently make assumptions and inferences about the behavior of others that are often invalid; he also suggested that these behaviors tend to be all about self-protection, and this too makes sense in a school setting in which fear is once again becoming endemic. He explains why focus groups, questionnaires, and surveys are not what they seem and thus have limited use.

Race to the Top guidelines suggest that a more rigorous supervision process will positively influence a teacher's professional development, compensation, promotion, retention, tenure, and certification. Such evaluations, it is suggested, should reward highly effective educators with merit pay and remove those deemed ineffective. It is all single-loop, market force bunkum; ideas born of a Victorian Age and hardly touched since, old bureaucracies cowering behind inadequacies of leadership and a denial of research, and mental maps drawn on the back of an envelope.

Teachers and school managers experience these ravings on a daily basis, placing them in an untenable situation of constantly having to explain and rationalize what they do. To this delusion and schizophrenia we can now add paranoia, the fear of industrial management techniques posing as modern and humane management techniques. An overstatement perhaps, but mental health issues in and around our schools are worrying. The end result is highly defensive behavior, rigid sticking to the knitting, and an inability of the organization to adapt, all made worse by contorting semantics, assumptions, and ideologies to suit.

I end this chapter with the work of John Seddon (2008). His analysis of U.K. housing benefits in the public sector offers a more generalized view of the problems schools face. These are adapted as follows:

1. *Designs for service are based on opinion, not knowledge.* In education reform this has led to a massive increase in specifications that determine what managers do. Unfortunately these specifications are "simply wrong. They do not constitute the best way to design services. Worse, they drive in waste: poor service, high cost and low morale."
2. *Targets do not represent the reality of service from the customer's point of view.* Using specifications, performance targets and standards are dictated. These offer a false reassurance to managers and others that all is well. In fact they drive service down by ignoring the variety of value demand, what customers need to make progress. They also distort the idea of goodness and ecological coherence.
3. *Targets drive people to use their ingenuity to meet the target, not improve performance.* This makes cheating "ubiquitous and systemic." Any such arbitrary measure worsens performance.

4. *Plausible ideas are promulgated without any idea as to their efficacy.* Reform clings to old management ideas that have never worked and can never work effectively in the schools we need. Yet the idea of incentive bonuses, appraisal schemes, back office improvements and more all sound perfectly sensible but have no objective substance to support them.
5. *The regime seeks questionable evidence to support its point of view.* No one wants to admit they were wrong. Proper scrutiny is avoided and there is a bias as to what research is used as a justification and what is ignored. Pilots soon become programs that are later abandoned.
6. *It is the system—the way the work is designed and managed—that governs performance.* This requires a change of thinking. The school as an organization has to be managed as a system to deliver on value demand, with all that this entails.
7. *Taking a systems approach results in performance improvements that would have been considered utterly unachievable if set as a target.* Those schools able to reject orthodoxy and learn about systems thinking and mixed-age structures have discovered improvement in behavior, outcomes, relationships, communications, and so much more. They did not use targets, specifications or extrinsic incentives, and they saved on costs (waste and failure demand) over time.
8. *The reform regime takes a dim view of people.* I cannot better the words of Seddon: "the reform regime is based on negative assumptions about people in general and public servants in particular. Decreeing specifications assumes they don't know what to do, don't want to change and need to be coerced or incentivized to act."

# ELEVEN

# Unlearning and Training a School

> I suppose it is tempting, if the only tool you have is a hammer, to treat everything as if it were a nail.
>
> —Abraham Maslow, *The Psychology of Science* (1966)

Unfortunately, my own training as an educator and school leader (the two are not synonymous) precluded systems thinking. It is a field I discovered after I became a school principal. Had I the books and a management and leadership education based on Deming, Senge, Duffy, Meadows, Ackoff, Wheatley, and so many others, the schools that I ran would have fared better as aspiring learning organizations. As a maverick and risk taker, cynical about the system in play, I unintentionally practiced systems thinking before stumbling on the books describing it.

It was good fortune that my school came up with the idea of forming mixed-age tutor groups as a better means of using data and information to improve student outcomes and parent partnership. I simply felt that with more parental input, students would achieve more, staff pressures would lessen, and I would meet my targets set by appraisal. It was only in the weeks and months following implementation that I began to realize that these changes provided a safer platform to guide our judgments and our practice, and build higher-quality learning relationships better able to absorb and understand demand issues.

It not only provided a neat solution to the challenge of parent partnership, but also seemed to dissolve most of the other problems by reducing bullying dramatically, increasing the quality of learning support, improving learning relationships, and enabling better assessment for learning. Things simply got better; people were happier and student outcomes improved. It also clarified our purpose and beliefs. We were able to walk the talk of our mission statements and values.

It has been my good fortune to have trained hundreds of schools in systems thinking, and early in 2014, I was once again training a full leadership team together with the governors of a large secondary school. It was another school wanting to be better and frustrated that the vast effort they put into their same-age system reaped so little by way of reward. They recognized that theirs was a difficult system to operate and met with repeat failures.

In the United Kingdom there are four basic judgments made by school inspectors: unsatisfactory (in need of urgent attention and possibly school closure or takeover); satisfactory (in need of improvement); good (usually has some outstanding features), and outstanding. School inspectors judged the school I was about to train as *satisfactory,* but the school aspired to be outstanding.

The school leadership team and the principal wanted to know what was missing or wrong that prevented all of their hard work from reaping the rewards they felt their efforts deserved. The crux of the problem, the school had decided, was its same-age tutoring system. They had begun a process that involved visits to schools that had moved to a VT or mixed-age system and liked what they saw and heard.

What the school, which catered to eleven to sixteen year olds, didn't realize was that virtually all of its performance problems, one way or another, related to same-age tutoring and that this defect could be designed out by reorganizing the school and creating a different operational culture. To do this, however, required a school to have a basic understanding of systems thinking that can explain precisely why same-age systems fail.

Without this prior unlearning, it is not possible to successfully implement a mixed-age model, one that improves learning and teaching by rewiring the broken communications linkages and feedback learning loops by changing the back office system to a multi-channeled front office tutor network. Copying other schools is fraught with danger, especially if they have built a system that retains old assumptions (single-loop). Without some basic systems thinking knowledge, this is almost inevitable.

When moving from one system to another, school leadership teams always assume that the management theory that governed one system can be used to implement the other. Schools almost invariably expect me to tell them how to implement vertical tutoring almost as a separate activity, one that occurs in the homeroom situation, not the boardroom. They do not expect a response that bulldozes the existing linear culture and demands a change in the way managers think about work. It is why the Robert Pirsig (2006) quote is so popular with systems thinkers:

> If a factory is torn down but the rationality that created it is left standing, then the rationality will simply produce another factory. (p. 94)

Schools must begin with the check process and with unlearning.

Schools also believe that training involves two linked elements: 1) How to formulate the new mixed-age tutor groups without student rebellion and a parental backlash, and 2) how to ensure that tutors have the skills to manage their new mixed-age groups. Managers are unaware that tutors already have the skills needed; it is the managers' skills that need attention. School managers tend to believe that same-age tutoring fails because the tutors they have are either of insufficient quality or they will not follow instructions.

The fact is that the linearity of schools frustrates school managers, who then blame others for irresolvable problems. They persist in confusing personnel problems (special cause) with system problems (common cause), invariably making situations worse. Both are system victims. There is no fault; it is a simple knowledge issue viewed from the fifth rung of the Ladder of Inference.

As a result, schools being transformed do not expect a systems examination (check) of their modus operandi regarding information, flow, and learning relationships. Neither do they expect an analysis of their linear thinking and their same-age approach to organization, let alone a journey that dismantles the same-age math and leads to cultural redesign. Senge is right. Systems thinking can result in defensive behaviors, but then changing a mental model that has been used for too long is bound to cause some initial unease for managers.

## A TRAINING SESSION

That session in January 2014 began with an explanation of the theoretical background to systems thinking; increasingly I find myself explaining Argyris and Schön and the separation that occurs between the shaky systems *theories* that schools espouse, the mental maps that then form, and how the staff apply *theories-in-use.* I also explain to participants that much of the training they are about to undergo can sometimes feel personally threatening to managers and, though unavoidable, could not be further from any intention.

Unlearning lifetime practices that are de rigueur and considered best practice can be very challenging. Teacher reaction is the complete opposite. They seem to adore systems thinking and seem to get it all first time, every time. They want more not less.

One means of understanding the assumptions that school managers have is to check how the school interacts with parents; another is to roleplay a child's journey through the school in terms of support, feedback, and guidance. Another is to look at the way tutors are managed, supported, and led, given the lofty job profiles they have. It is then possible to compare the theory-in-use with the theory espoused to reveal the ambiguities and the paradoxical assumptions made by the school's leadership team.

Parent partnership is always a case in point and is always a feature of the systems check. Every school that I have worked with around the world has claimed parent partnership to be very important to them and something to be valued. At the same time, I have not found a single school that has even remotely delivered on such a claim, especially when set alongside the kind of criteria and practice set out by the likes of Ross Kanter (1984) and Johnston and Clark (2001).

Neither have I read a single book or seen any research that sets out how such a partnerships works. Espoused theory and theory-in-use are invariably a mile apart and completely out of sync, yet schools continue to laud their practice as being of high quality. A linear system can never be a communications system; the math simply does not work because the school cannot flex sufficiently as a system.

A school faces three basic challenges as an organization:

- Understanding and managing the nature and causes of variation.
- Identifying and securing the value work for customers.
- Ensuring ongoing quality to meet variable value demand.

The means of delivering these is dependent to a large part on having a secure view about what customer care involves (demand) and the organizational arrangements that enable the effective working of such a partnership.

A summary of customer relations from Johnson and Clark (2001) is adapted here for schools. All of the following need to be in place and functional:

- **Communications:** the extent to which there is a two- and three-way (parent/tutor/tutee) dialogue between home and school; the ability to listen, analyze, and agree on strategies for improvement that support learning, sustain aspiration, and maximize outcomes. Partnership is information dependent.
- **Trust:** the degree to which the school and parents depend on the work or recommendations of each other without seeking extra justification or collaboration. In some cases one partner may commit the other to work without prior consultation. It is vital that this relationship is substantive and holds firm.
- **Intimacy:** the process of sharing important information for the benefit of the learner, thus removing barriers to learning through close partnership and agreed support strategies. Student learning is publicly exposed to highly sensitive and personal information. This requires great care and emotional intelligence to manage.
- **Rules:** a mutual acceptance of how this particular relationship operates: what is acceptable and desirable and what is not. This part,

if overplayed, can damage other parts. Customer care is a subsystem.

Because factory-style schools are unable to design in the first three attributes, they "do" rules, provide minimal data, and create an illusion that partnership somehow exists and works. Later we shall see how these four areas link closely with Bronfenbrenner's propositions for successful child development (1977, 1979, and 1980).

As soon as I start to explore with the school's leadership team what passes as parent partnership in the school, it becomes obvious from a systems view that what the school is doing is inadequate. This means there is no viable means of understanding demand. Formal meetings between family and school are short on time, minimalistic, and narrowly defined in terms of information; usually only sketchy data (grades and targets) of dubious use and purpose are shared.

The causal effect is that schools are unable to garner parent input to effect qualitative change and rapid intervention. What should be reflective and quality-sharing moments or deep learning conversations take on all the abstraction of routine. The management system does not enable effective intervention, communication is restricted, trust is not established, and intimacy is unachievable.

When the school is invited during training to confront what it does on the ground (theory-in-use) with what it claims to do (espoused theory), the mismatches, assumptions, and incongruities come to the fore. I tell the school that their implementation of partnership is not only absent, but is damaging to learning and to families. A defensive hand goes up in denial. One school manager objects.

She states categorically that parents can come into the school at any time, that tutors phone home regularly to keep parents informed, and that the data they use for any reports sent home is sufficient and in line with all other schools. Besides, she says, parents can log in any time to see how their child is doing.

Unfortunately, offering *opportunities* that are unlikely to be taken is not even close to partnership, and the claim about regular home contact by tutors was, according to others present, not the case but what was assumed. How could it be, given the built-in blockages to information flow and the perceived poverty of tutor capability?

Besides, if all parents contacted the school, the complexity would quickly overcome the back office system (the math problem) and no teaching work would ever get done. The unspoken aim of the school was to ensure parents did not come into school, and the school's operational setup ensured this was so. In fact the parent partnership system tacked onto the school (every large school) creates the very opposite of a viable partnership and quality learning relationship.

Similarly this school, like all schools, claimed to be great at communicating with parents, keeping parents informed. The school inspectors said as much, after all! Under the scrutiny of the systems check, however, the school was not as excellent at communications as they claimed; far from it. In fact, like all schools, they had no communications system worthy of the name. What they had was a very limited and carefully controlled information-out system. This was managed in a way that ensured that any return information from home did not happen and was not needed.

It was one-way traffic out of hopelessly inadequate data. They had reduced their information home to lists of levels and grades—of minimal use to parents and students. Strategies for improvement were presumed within spurious target grades. After all, the last thing a school wants when it sends information home is to get a reply!

The system that the school said was so good quickly reduced to tatters. It undermined parents, limited learning support, delayed interventions, denied information to teachers, and gave a clear message to students that they held the middle ground—that uneasy wasteland between home and school whereby letters disappear in sports bags and students offer their unique version of what happened in school that day, able to readily explain why there is no homework. Later, those same students will have every excuse for dropping out, claiming that no adult cared or knew them well.

It also turned out that tutors rarely phoned home. The school leader in charge of this area was adamant that regular home contact was being made by all tutors and that the school's open-door policy was effective and used regularly. Slowly, her colleagues began to disagree; the claim was fatuous. So the school began the process of dismantling all that it once held dear, bit by bit. The school's principles and management practices turned out to be little more than wild assumptions, and as each facet of the delusional edifice fell, one after the other, so managers started to unlearn and were able to see their school anew, this time as a learning system.

As we moved on to the critical role of the homeroom tutor or form tutor, I placed the tutor's job profile on the screen. We all agreed that the homeroom tutor's profile provided an accurate description of the vitally important homeroom/tutor role (the key leverage point). I ask what happens in the twenty minutes or so of tutor time that takes place immediately after lunch in this school. Another voice speaks the answer I expect: "The tutor delivers a program on personal and social education."

Delivering anything coherently after lunch is a challenge in itself! Investigations in all other schools I visited showed that the job profile of the tutor represented one of the biggest assumptions of the school; tutors disliked this time and any program delivery ranged from satisfactory to nonexistent.

Tutors were left to make whatever sense they could of the time allowed. I knew that tutor time was more about control and filling time with minimal disruption. The espoused purpose and actual delivery share only the most tenuous link and the chances of consistent quality are so low that an opposite effect is created; the law of unintended consequences hovers permanently over schools like a dark cloud.

So, I ask, if I came to the school I would see sixty classes and sixty tutors all delivering a pro-social program every day for twenty minutes after lunch with reasonable consistency? The reply is a firm, "Yes." I respond: "So you expect me to believe that after taking the roll call, dealing with notices and information, and after lunch, every tutor delivers a program that has been previously downloaded from the internal email system?" The answer is affirmative. As others join in, however, and as we explore the detailed practice, tutor time too begins to fall irrevocably apart as just one more pious management hope, just as it invariably does.

No matter what effort is put into same-age school systems, basic systems crumble, nurtured only by the myth of the great teacher and a heavy reliance on compliance. In fact, this school, like so many of the others, had stifled tutoring. Rather than supporting the tutor's vital role as the hub of home–school communications, the school had damaged it almost beyond repair by the assumptions it held and the specifications it issued.

It was easy to explain precisely how the school had done this, its knock-on effects, and why all of their various efforts at repair had failed. It was also easy to show the negative effect on teaching and learning in general when attempts made to fix one area simply damage others.

It turned out (as it always does) that what happens operationally in a factory-style school system is fraught with management problems, quality issues, and false assumptions. The managers assumed that their organizational strategies were working as planned, just as they had fifty years ago. In fact, teachers often arrived late for their homeroom session and many had not prepared for the lesson to be taught. It was a mess and the school's good fortune that the students and staff were largely compliant and uncomplaining.

Tutor self-esteem was being eroded. Many tutors blamed themselves and felt inadequate for not being able to manage tutor time better. Later these same people would go to the classroom having lost the battle of tutor time. Students in the school regarded tutor time as their "gathering time," which ironically was far closer to what was needed than what was organized.

In fact, the leadership team had not noticed that almost every facet of the school's organization was actively disabling the job description it had set out for the tutors and teachers to follow. Espoused theory and theory-in-use had become dangerously separated.

Critically, the school was unable to see that they had actually identified the key leverage point for their school's improvement (tutor time), but had persisted in pushing it in the wrong direction. They knew what the tutor was supposed to do and be, but had no viable method of ensuring it; and then, as in all same-age systems, they persisted in trying to make it work even though it never really had. It wasn't just that they pushed tutoring in the wrong direction; they tried to push in a direction it simply cannot go.

Incorrect management assumptions meant that not only was learning being undermined, but so were learning relationships between teachers, homeroom tutors, students, and families. In fact, the school was systematically destroying the key to school improvement by damaging teachers and learners through the operational processes in play, processes ironically intended to support learning and teaching.

When I train the whole staff team (everyone employed by the school) on the issue of tutoring and why it should change from a same-age to a mixed-age model, it all becomes abundantly clear. The school's managers are rarely tutors. Not being a homeroom tutor is too often viewed as a badge of honor: a sign that you are now management! The tutor role is rarely valued as much as it should be, and tutoring is rarely effective and often bypassed by a complex referral system and counseling.

There is an interesting cycle. School managers were all once tutors and so were once party to the same-age tutoring system. Had they been effective tutors working in an effective team they should have learned (now that they were school managers) how to lead a successful same-age tutoring scheme. But they did not learn, either as tutors or as the managers they became. They should have learned that same-age tutoring is fraught with challenges that are extremely difficult to overcome, but this never occurred to them. What they believe is that the tutors are not up to scratch, not that the system cannot be made to work.

As we moved inexorably on to assessment for learning, which also failed miserably in the check process (as it always must), it was possible to show how the key information loops between our players had not only become degraded or disconnected, but that most were never there in the first place, at least not in any effective and workable form.

This was nobody's fault. Schools operating same-age systems are unable to dissolve the problems created by the school's linear mathematics. Such wonderful schools are full of passionate people all trying hard and claiming to do the right thing, but too often doing many of the wrong things wronger.

It was also possible to show, just as I had demonstrated to every other school that far from intervening in negative behavior, including bullying and low aspiration, the school was actually creating such behaviors through its errant organizational practices. After creating negative in-group loyalty problems through its same-age structure, schools spend considerable energy, time, and expense trying to repair the mistakes made with copious anti-bullying strategies and programs. They remain blissfully unaware that the school, through its assumed good practice, is one of the root causes of such negative and unwanted behavior.

Schools generally believe that they organize themselves to counter poor attitude and behavior and raise aspiration. Nothing could be further from the truth. This is because the school as an organization does not recognize that much of the causal dynamic of poor learning and its associated problems is to be found within its singular endorsement of powerful same-age groups on which it bases its working and operational assumptions.

This not only undermines teacher capability, but also makes the system appear as though everything is the teacher's fault and that this is fixable by the heavy hand of old management that disabled them in the first place. Such management issues are further compounded through expensive and wasteful delays in interventions, back-up teams, increased backroom activity, inappropriate attempts at repair, and poor home–school partnership, all of which lead to waste, bureaucracy, and failure demand on the system.

At the heart of the school's dilemma is the math problem set out earlier. It is simply not possible to give children individual support and attention and meet their psychological and developmental learning needs in a solely same-age system. There are simply too many children for one teacher to get to know in the time allowed, let alone find quality time to support and liaise with parents. There are too many learning relationships to form, too many back office staff needed.

So the school as a system reduces and limits learning and in such places most students become known through data sheets and grades, not for their contributions as young people.

In training, the industrial model must be exposed as an unworkable and deluding fraud. It must be explained that the reason for the school's apparent brokenness is not the fault of teachers (blaming others is always delusional), but rather a systemic management failure to do the sums using calculus rather than arithmetic alone. As Deming (2004) said, the vast majority of faults in a system are not worker related (4 percent), but are instead faults created by those who purport to manage systems (96 percent).

After three intensive hours, the school leadership team had much to think about. They will spend considerable time reflecting (and recovering). There will be meetings and they will forget much of what we discussed, but they will decide that much has to change and that mixed-age tutoring, done well, has much to commend itself.

I confess that there are certain TV programs that I occasionally catch. As an amateur systems thinker I like the *Sopranos* and am intrigued that

Tony Soprano is expert in waste management and makes a quasi-living from disposal. One of the programs I also quite like is *Undercover Boss*.

When the boss joins the front line teams it is possible to see how the organization operates from a different perspective (theory-in-use). More managers and leaders should try it! Being in the work is essential to understanding what is needed, which is why all staff, including the principal, must become tutors too.

The legendary Tom Peters once opened a seminar to business leaders in this way—and I paraphrase: The people who work for you help out in their children's sports clubs at the weekend, they sing in choirs, play music, do charity work, look after relatives and neighbors, and more besides. They are amazing people; they are creative, caring, energetic, and have great ideas . . . except when they work for you!

It is when the boss crosses the chasm from espoused theory to theory-in-use and between cause and effect that a true picture of the school forms. It becomes possible to see the value work and what is needed, and to understand how people are trying to make the system work optimally. When people are valued, trained against demand, and trusted, they become better and more able people; they also take on a singular individualized form—they matter.

Only when this happens is the manager transformed and able to see the organization differently; one that grows its people as leaders, cherishes them as people, and enables them to learn and innovate on that learning so that the organization learns too.

I have attended many a school administration meeting that resembled a scene from *One Flew Over the Cuckoo's Nest*. This was a run-down institution ruled by the command and control hand of Nurse Mildred Ratched ("Big Nurse") using management techniques of bullying and coercion disguised as therapy. It was the maverick McMurphy who encouraged the patients to think differently about the system and themselves, and to move from the compliance of single-loop acceptance to double-loop questioning.

Too often it is the case that the school improvement process employs increasingly inappropriate management techniques and bad motivational therapy. In any unlikely Race to the Top it will almost certainly be a Nurse Ratched who will get the super's job and a McMurphy who will get the lobotomy.

Nevertheless, it is to psychology that we return in the next chapters.

# TWELVE

# Psychology and Design for Learning

> For a long time, it had seemed to me that life was about to begin—real life. But there was always some obstacle in the way, something to be gotten through first, some unfinished business, time to be served, a debt to be paid. Then life would begin. At last it dawned on me that these obstacles were my life.
>
> —Alfred D. Souza

Research projects occasionally appear that offer a very counterintuitive view of the reality we all too easily accept and then act upon. In the United States there was a minor stir when "Charter, Private, Public Schools and Academic Achievement: New Evidence from NAEP Mathematics Data," made the news.

The research by Christopher and Sarah Lubienski (2006) showed that despite the many obvious advantages enjoyed by the private sector, public schools performed extremely well in mathematics and sometimes better when demographics are added to the mix. The Program for International Student Assessments (PISA 2012) also highlighted that the private sector only marginally outperformed the public sector in the United States in mathematics, a subject likely to be far more dependent on schools than reading.

In 2008, more findings were released by the team that looked at school climate, teacher qualifications, and that incomprehensible word *instruction*. All in all, a whole raft of issues arose from this interesting and valuable report regarding performance outcomes. Some of these concerned difference in teaching and learning styles, teachers' professional development, and school management. These are all areas where the public sector seems to win over the private sector.

This is an opportune time to repeat what has been said previously: public schools perform well in so many ways and the vast majority of teachers who work so hard to make a broken system work are simply amazing. This book never criticizes teachers, but it does criticize the school as an operational system and the effect this has on personnel and performance.

Another interesting report with equally counterintuitive findings, "Differences in Degree Outcomes" (Higher Education Funding Council of England, 2014), appeared in the United Kingdom during March 2014. This one destroyed a myth and a set of learning assumptions about schools and the way politicians and administrators think about them. It has consequently already been forgotten by those who should support change, and immediately downplayed by politicians. But it enjoyed a glorious day in the sun like so many research projects do, and I want to extend its life in this particular chapter. Counterintuitive truths are always to be cherished.

The report analyzed the achievement of 132,000 students over three years. At schools in the United Kingdom (grades 11–12), sixth-form students intent on university follow three or four advanced-level courses (A-levels) in their last two years of school. The grades determine places at universities. Unsurprisingly, students from independent or fee-paying schools tend to perform slightly better at A-levels and proportionally gain more places at "top" universities.

This difference has always been used to highlight how much better the teachers and school managers in fee-paying (private) schools are and how the state (public) schools might learn from their obvious expertise. The many other considerable advantages such as early learning gains, peer support, smaller class sizes, better resources, increased learning opportunities, and parental support are discounted.

The math problem too is easier to deal with! The independent sector (around 8 percent of schools) is able to get proportionally more students through high-stakes tests (A-levels) and with proportionally higher grades. It is a variation to be expected. As in the United States, there is a small difference in outcomes and performance in favor of private schools.

The expectation (assumption) is that these same students (the so-called brightest and the best) will continue that advantage at university and get the best degrees, both first class and higher seconds (2:1s). Surely such an assumption must be true. However, such seeming logic appears to be invalid. The report showed that state school students (public school in the United States) are more likely to gain a first class or a 2:1 degree than their independent private school peers when both have achieved the same A-level grades at school. There is more!

It seems that school performance based on school type is not the best indicator of future performance. The report noted that a male student (for example) from the state sector with BBB grades at A-level was as likely to gain the same higher degree as a private school student with ABB grades at A-level. Even the examinations taken at age sixteen (GCSEs) by all U.K. students provide an inaccurate indicator of future achievement.

Once again, state school students perform better at university than those from the private sector. When students achieving eight A grades at GCSE (students at age sixteen) were compared, 73 percent of state school students went on to gain a higher degree at university compared with 69 percent of independent school students. Similarly, when students from both sectors with eight B grades were compared, 52 percent from the state sector went on to gain a higher degree compared with 43 percent from the independent sector.

In any given year, differences in ethnicity, gender, and disadvantage continued to be significant factors. Thousands of students from the state sector achieved grades that a) prevented them reaching university, b) prevented them following the course of their choice, or c) prevented them from gaining entry to the university of their choice.

It seems that to use high-stakes testing alone and to ignore contextual issues is not a good or cost-effective way of running an education system, and is certainly not the best predictor of future performance. Further, such a system is more likely to confer advantages that later turn out to be unjustified. I highlight these fascinating reports (there really are dozens more) as a lead-in to "intelligence."

## LEARNING INTELLIGENCE

In this respect, psychology offers an opportunity for schools to look again at the various ways and means used to organize learning within a framework that cherishes well-being and supports child growth, especially the more intrinsic traits inspired by curiosity, challenge, and creativity.

In schools, students are often placed in same-age ability groups by subject, usually based on testing. This is perfectly normal and intuitive thinking. It is efficient, it seems to be a sensible use of resources, it is possible to allocate teachers better, it is what parents expect to see, it is based on past learning and tests. (Readers should now be wary of the counterintuitive idea waiting in the wings.) The logic seems impeccable. It is a normal mindset of managers to organize learning and teaching in this way to deal with the math problem that allocates students to classes. What could possibly be wrong? It was always thus.

Many years ago when I was principal of a large high school, an issue arose concerning examination entries for mathematics. At the start of the two-year course leading to the final exam for fifteen- and sixteen-year-old-students (GCSEs), students were placed into ability groups for mathematics. The instructions from the examination board were clear: students were to be placed according to the grades predicted for them two years hence. So there were two classes for students predicted to earn higher grades, two classes for those predicted to earn average grades, and two for those predicted to earn the lowest grades—a process called tiering. This separational process continues today.

Of course, much of this kind of allocation by ability begins much earlier in school careers. The students in each set or group followed a course using texts designed for their ability level. Thus, students in the average groups, no matter how hard they tried, could only achieve an average grade because they sat a different examination paper. Their particular examination paper did not allow for any higher grade to be awarded. This made any movement between ability sets difficult because of the peculiarity of the courses followed. The system places a ceiling on the grade that might be achieved and tends to promote the idea that intelligence is fixed.

While the head of math was perfectly okay with such an arrangement, many parents were upset, and for me too this jarred and seemed somehow wrong—another nonsense among the many I was to discover as the boss of a large school. Things have moved on very little since. Had I been aware of today's research, I might have known better what to do.

Jo Boaler (2005) maintains that 80 percent of children placed in ability groups at a young age (math again) will remain in the same group throughout school. The earlier this practice is introduced, the worse for children and for their learning. Boaler is adamant that the practice of placing students by ability in mathematics results in large numbers of children falling behind.

We need a learning guide to a better-espoused-theory, and on this occasion, the work of Carol Dweck (1998) seems to offer a way forward. According to Ludwig Von Bertalanffy (1968), one of the pioneers of systems thinking, children are "active personality systems," a feature that has passed few teachers by! If the research is right (above), they develop at all sorts of rates for all kinds of reasons.

The way we organize students in schools is based on assumptions that may seem logical and normal, but is one built more on sand and convenience. What is attractive about Dweck's research is its recognition of the relationship between the school as an organization and the effect of its operational assumptions on those who work in them. Her research is both counterintuitive and deeply illuminating, and offers clues about managing learning systems like schools in smarter ways.

Just as systems thinking questions assumptions, so does investigative psychology. Having looked at the delusional and errant motivational theory that dominates school management thinking (appraisal, rewards, accountability, inspection, evaluations, tenures, coercion), could it be that our organization of learning is equally errant? Is there another unexpected and counterintuitive twist that we have missed? Dweck thinks so, and more recent research (below) backs such a view.

Dweck's research indicates that it is possible to develop mastery-oriented qualities regardless of ability and intelligence; she tells us there is no substantive relationship between mastery and ability. In other words, you do not have to have high intelligence and ability to achieve mastery, but you do have to have the right effort mindset, and realizing this is by no means straightforward. (For me this implies the need to change the way we individualize learning and support and this necessitates using mixed-age structures.)

To explain this, Dweck proposes two competing views of intelligence: an "entity" view and an "incremental" view. The entity view regards intelligence as fixed and stable. All the examination systems mentioned above tend toward an entity-type design for schooling. The incremental view suggests that intelligence is more malleable and can change over time. It might be legitimately argued that schools espouse an incremental view of intelligence, while the practice or theory-in-use tends to be entity based.

Problems arise according to how students perceive their intelligence and how they see themselves as learners. Dweck provides a series of fascinating insights into learning mindsets and intelligence. The two underpinning tenants are as follows, and take us into the area of dispositions for learning:

- There appears to be no relationship between a student's ability/intelligence and his or her capacity to master learning.
- It is not how smart a student is that is important; what's important is that the student possesses or develops a mindset that encourages him or her to achieve.

Dweck explains that students who are mastery-oriented try hard. Their learning mindset is such that they pay little attention to how clever they are. They focus on sustained effort and delight in feedback that offers them better strategies for improvement. Such students relish challenge, and worry far less about feeling incompetent or unworthy. It is a clear message for schools that need to think about how they might better support such dispositions and organize learning. I simply do not see how this can be even remotely achieved in schools dependent on same-age structures.

Dweck tells us that many of the students we label bright and able (gifted and talented) often avoid challenge, shy away from putting in effort, and wilt when faced with difficulties. It seems that this kind of labeling can often be inherently damaging. Students regarded as less bright and less able may nevertheless be determined to achieve and may exceed all previous expectations. These students often thrive on challenge, persist against the odds, and accomplish more than predicted. Schools know this, but it is one thing for schools to get these messages and quite another to know how to organizationally respond.

The messages from Dweck and colleagues challenge the way we think about schools as organizations. The clear suggestion is that schools need to know far more about the fundamental bases of learning psychology rather than rely on assumptions from the past that no longer hold true. The focus in schools needs to be far more on creating a mindset of effort and challenge (aspiration in part) than rewarding intelligence alone. To overly dwell on the latter can have dire and unforeseen consequences.

In this respect, Dweck advises great care in the way that students' learning mindsets are nurtured. The key here has much to do with how schools praise and judge students and how students themselves perceive such praise and judgment. The advice and strategies that apply to schools and their students apply equally to parents. Now comes yet more counterintuition.

If a school or the teacher praises smartness, cleverness, and intelligence, students can interpret this praise very differently than that intended by the teacher or even by their parents. According to Dweck, a focus on praise that describes a child as *intelligent*, or any number of similar adjectives, can make students overly concerned with how smart they are and this can make them vulnerable to failure. Such praise can affect their willingness to take risks or to put themselves on the line, which in turn can negatively affect performance.

The child with an entity (fixed) view of his or her intelligence (perhaps one that reflects the school's view) has a mindset that will seek to avoid failure at all costs. This can deter the child from taking on more challenging tasks. This has damaging consequences, resulting in risk avoidance and an underpinning fear of failure. For such children, any hint of not remaining "bright" can have devastating consequences; for them, not being bright means being "dumb" (mindset), which must be avoided at all costs . . . so better not try than risk failure.

Dweck advises that an important requisite for successful learning is the quality of feedback the student receives, and this means being able to offer strategies for improvement and more praise for effort than for intelligence or smartness. Dweck goes further: an important part of the learning process involves challenge. There is little to be gained from making things easy and to do so can remove the joy in work.

If we return to the problem posed at the beginning of this chapter, it is clear that a learning organization would need to approach the way it operates as a learning system with a great deal more care and bespoke sophistication than the factory school can ever allow. For me, Dweck's research has implications both for teaching and the way schools organize themselves.

It confirms VT as the key leverage point, the tutor group, as being central to the design we need in order to develop a school that might be more genuinely called a *learning organization*, one cognizant of every single child as an active personality and learning system. Only VT can ensure every child is known and supported, and information shared throughout learning. Emotional support has to accompany learning support for confidence to grow and for aspiration to be maintained.

Reading this, it is easy to assume (again) that this is all teacher and classroom business, and much is; but it depends entirely on the homeroom tutor or form tutor operating within a house system of mixed-age groups to make it work successfully. Children need to be known and supported as individuals first and foremost, and this in turn enables learning to be better planned and supported within a system that constantly replenishes the organization with information. The teacher, even the great one, is not enough because of necessary delays in forming such learning relationships.

It is within the capacity of a school to escape this bind and become better at self-organizing. If effort, not intelligence, is the better driver of a learning mindset and of mastery, it means that schools need to take great care regarding how they go about organizing learning and the development of assessment and reporting procedures that cultivate a more beneficial and relevant mindset. Effort has to be acknowledged, encouraged, and nurtured.

Such a theory also explains how the excessive use of high-stakes testing can negatively influence self-worth, undermine attainment given its labeling effect, and harm mental well-being.

This aspect of the HEFCE report (above) seems counterintuitive and to defy rational explanation. No one, as far as I could tell, offered a plausible explanation as to why seemingly less advantaged students later outperform more advantaged students at university. The answer may be all too simple. They try harder. They try harder because they have always had to try harder, often against the odds. Their teachers know this and this makes their teachers and schools far better than anyone has given them credit for.

In simple terms, it seems that the grade a school gives a child for effort is far more important and beneficial than the one it gives for intelligence and performance, especially if accompanied by strategies for improvement and the fun of challenge. Given what we know of assessment for learning, this makes sense. If a student's effort report is accompanied by a mutually drafted strategy for further improvement rather than a spurious target, together with a supportive and deep learning discussion (reflection) among homeroom tutor, parent, and student on means, the school starts to promote a mindset oriented toward mastery and improved learning relationships.

It seems that wherever this book takes us, we end up in a similar place. Psychology keeps returning us to learning relationships and the joyous conspiracy of learning that needs to be shared among student, school, and home. It means providing optimal structures that allow staff, students, and parents as much opportunity as possible to support, communicate, and learn from each other. It means managing the school as a learning system and getting it right. Mixing the age groups and understanding systems thinking ensures this can happen through the interconnectivity and substantive learning relationships it builds.

## EFFORT AND INTELLIGENCE

Other research in this area is not only telling, but also supports systems thinking in challenging assumptions and prevailing management behaviors. If schools are organized by graded intelligence levels based on age as part of the sifting, batching, and sorting mechanism, this not only traps students in groups limited by expectation, but can dull potential, limit achievement, and switch off aspiration. A learning organization can never form.

The background research is worthy of note. Claudia Mueller and Carol Dweck (1998) gave high school students three tasks: an easy one, a more challenging one, and then another easy one. Some students were praised for their intelligence and others for the effort that each put into the given task. They found that students praised only for their intelligence:

- Became overly concerned with their intelligence and tended to avoid anything that might damage such a self-view.
- Said they "felt dumb" when faced with a more difficult challenge. The message they were receiving was that success means "smart" and failure means "dumb"—a potentially damaging situation (risk) to be avoided at all costs.
- No longer enjoyed the tasks and were unwilling to self-learn on their own time as they once did.
- Performed significantly worse than expected when they were then given an easy challenge like the first.

Most telling was an additional task. When students praised for their intelligence were invited to write a letter to a friend about their final task, 40 percent lied about their task score, upgrading their results. We flatter to deceive.

Those praised for their effort wanted more challenging tasks, not less. They saw any setbacks as a temporary blip and as a sign that more effort was needed. Not only did they enjoy harder tasks, but they spent more home time working on them. Not only did the "triers" do much better on harder tasks, they were also far more honest about their performance in their letter to a friend.

Recent work by Brummelman and colleagues (2014) also looked at praise, especially that given by parents. In a study of confident and unconfident children, children who had low self-confidence and low self-esteem were given over-the-top and lavish praise (as schools often do with students who lack confidence); the confident children were give more measured feedback on a task. The overuse of praise had a negative effect on the task performance of the children who lacked confidence, the opposite of what is so often assumed. While students with high self-esteem take lavish praise in stride, those who lack such self-esteem seem to take a hit.

How schools handle such research should be important, but this is not how schools tend to operate in the straitjacket that binds them. Theories-in-use are increasingly impervious to new theories about learning and intelligence being espoused.

It seems that while schools subscribe to a view of intelligence based on developing potential, they practice a view of intelligence that appears to be more fixed, despite allowances for limited movement between ability groups. Teachers implement policies rarely of their own making, but act on a mental model based on targets that are externally demanded. The organizational concern is invariably top-end loaded, in which pressures on examination pass rates are greatest and most likely to count as measures of performance.

The measures, not knowledge, will always determine organizational practices and teaching method. What is clear is that the industrial learning design that schools have inherited tends to subsume and assume, and can too often damage teachers as well as children.

There are similar implications with regard to labeling students by intelligence, including the so-called gifted and talented. It is not just the gifted and talented who need and relish challenge, but all students. Dweck also notes that boys often get a harder time at school but get more messages about the need for greater effort, which bodes well for their future, contrary perhaps to that of girls.

Carol Dweck is adamant that schools should be guided by the fundamental concept that everyone can get better, that intelligence and mastery can improve over time, and that effort is the key. Testing should be diagnostic, a means of assessing mastery and finding more challenge, one that allows for better feedback and support regarding strategies for improvement, not a slow learning demise pinned on the sharp barriers of the high-stakes test. The key to such assessment for learning hinges on the tutor as the hub of information and coordinator of support—the chief coach.

All we need do at this point is remember one thing: because the teacher–learner relationship is the only one we see, that does not mean that it is the only one there is. Further, this learning relationship takes considerable time to form, and time in an industrial school is straight-line limited. The industrial linear school with its same-age structures is organizationally anti-learning in terms of this one-dimensional view.

It must sacrifice the many other potential learning relationships available to it (tutor/tutee, all students as mentors and leaders to all other students, parent/child, and tutor/parent) and depend on teachers alone. This makes the industrial model and the factory school a complete paradox of learning operating on 20 percent effectiveness and restricted on creativity, flexibility, and even energy levels. We need to be guided into an organizational matrix in which psychology should inform school design to make all learning relationships fully operative.

Lucas and Claxton (2010) in their book, *New Kinds of Smart*, underline the complexity of intelligence as being not only composite in nature and learnable, but prone to a number of myths (the authors set out eight as a starter). Intelligence is an area where it is wise not to assume too much given the variations within its makeup and the many influences on its development. Lucas and Claxton set out the different facets that make up the complexity of intelligence and how intelligence might be nurtured and developed. Their book is a little treasure chest of research-based ideas.

They reference the research of Duckworth and Seligman (2005) who wondered why children with similar IQ scores produced very different results at school. The all too obvious response is "the teacher" or "the school." Their research explored self-control as a determinant of intelligence. Students with greater self-discipline behaved very differently from those who were more impulsive. This revealed itself in factors such as higher attendance, more time on task, and better application to homework. In fact, self-discipline seemed to be more than twice as reliable as IQ as a predictor of school performance.

If, as it undoubtedly seems, learning dispositions and attitudes are critical factors in shaping and developing the broad nature of what intelligence is turning out to be, then intelligence really is far more malleable in nature than we think, just as Dweck suggests.

All of this has ramifications for how schools set about organizing learning and how they understand what they do, how they do it, and why.

So back to school we go.

# THIRTEEN

# Psychology as the Arbiter of Design

> Education is an admirable thing, but it is well to remember from time to time that nothing that is worth learning can be taught.
>
> —Oscar Wilde

The point being labored is this: if we listen to what psychology tells us about the nature of (learned) intelligence and dispositions to learning, there are critical design implications regarding how schools organize themselves to support the dispositions most needed to enable better learning and keep aspiration alive. We may be in the foothills of new knowledge and exploring new areas, but we need our schools to be ready for the climb and to be good Sherpas.

The current linearity is simply too cumbersome, too slow, and too insecure. The teachers play a leading role, but to meet the complexity they face requires the school to be able to both identify and absorb complexity, gather new information and knowledge, and be able to use it. Everyone, including parents, students, and school staff, have a substantive role to play and these roles need to be both interdependent and interconnected.

Schools need the wherewithal to constantly learn and adapt. We cannot keep saying that teachers should *do this* and *do that* or *be this* and *be that* without first indicating very precisely the fundamental changes needed for the ways schools organize and manage themselves as places of learning. Similarly, the endless toolboxes we offer are welcome but insufficient without (dare I say) training teachers and leaders to think more about how the school as an organization works as an interconnected learning system than the disconnected ones we have.

It is easy to assume, as we do, that all of these implications relate to the classroom and the teacher as the knowledge provider and expert in the psychology of learning. In fact, psychology reminds us that we need to be able to consider even more variation in a system already overstretched. But that is the point. Schools have to understand (customer) demand, while the system (the school) must be flexible enough to absorb and respond to complexity at the level of both individuals and groups. Mixed-age systems are simply far better equipped to do this.

The design of any systems thinking school requires all to be party to the learning cause. Teachers, tutors, parents, and students themselves have to be a team, and this means the homeroom, not teaching in the classroom, must be the catalyst and the first place to change. Once mixed-age tutoring is established, better learning relationships form faster and more securely. These gather the information needed to flex the system and the same learning relationships are transferable to the classroom and the world beyond.

The next stage, once VT is established, is vertical teaching (VTe), a natural extension VT max.

Psychology and research have enormous implications for learning and teaching, but the teacher is only one element, albeit a vital one, in the school's learning system. The teacher depends on the organization being able to learn and be self-organized (the ability of a system to constantly redesign itself, to build new work patterns based on learning and diversification). What psychology teaches us is that there are fundamental counterintuitive truths that should guide all that a school does. Psychology governs design just as Deming said it does.

Daniel Pink's book *Drive* (2009) is concerned with organizational intelligence or the lack of it. He advises us of the many ways in which organizations switch off intrinsic learning through their denial of all that truly motivates us. According to Pink, there is a mismatch between what science *knows* (the research) and what organizations *do,* something that Pink calls "functional fixedness." Ironically, while we are learning that intelligence is malleable, it seems that the schools we have are compelled to remain *functionally fixed* in the form they are.

## THE FUNDAMENTAL DESIGN REQUIREMENTS

Long before we get to teachers and their more cogent dispositions and motivations, the school has to somehow change into a learning organization in a very practical, secure, and doable way. At the immediate point of entry to any school, students must be assured that the school has a working culture that secures:

- A more complete and holistic picture of the whole child beyond grades.
- An immediate means of effective intervention in learning behavior and support.

- Membership of small, nested loyalty groups whereby every child is a leader, mentor, and mentee at all times. (Nearly all of the mentoring and advocacy needed is to be found within the homeroom.)
- Immediate and ongoing support by two adults (tutors) to develop and support positive dispositions to learning and achievement (aspiration).
- Interconnected learning relationships internally and between home and school.
- More coherent assessment for learning; a move from data to knowledge to learning.

A learning organization requires everyone to be a learner and a leader; it cannot be a matter for the teacher alone. The school has to be designed in a way that ensures parents, teachers, and other students are all on *team child* and can operate together to enable learning and maintain aspiration. There can be no separated support systems and no time delays in communications, and all of this requires trust, training against demand, and a less "dim view of people."

These constituent cultural elements are too often absent and assumed in linear schools, modeled as they are on industrial practices based on same-age peer structures. Such system demands are not pious hopes and neither are these matters intangible visions. These descriptors and elements are doable, can be built in by a school, and must be before the child even gets to the classroom. These cultural changes are detailed in *The Systems Thinking School*, further complemented here in completely practical terms, and can be achieved without cost or the need of pro-social programs.

To truly develop as a valid learning organization there has to be a psychological rationale that drives learning, a school philosophy and purpose that is operationally authentic, and constant updating of knowledge, what the research tells us rather than what is assumed. The research (above) tells us we need to get far more from systems than we are. The espoused theory of learning and the operational application, or theory-in-use, must be aligned and designed-in.

For Pink, the key system drivers are the intrinsic and motivational intangibles of *autonomy, mastery,* and *purpose.* For Senge, they are the disciplines of personal mastery, mental modeling, shared vision, team learning, and systems thinking. For Deming, they are appreciation of a system, knowledge of variation, theory of knowledge, and psychology. We have journeyed through most and are approaching the last leg.

Systems thinking is the language of learning and this must replace the language of industrial thinking. The language of systems thinking is the language of learning because of its inherent belief that people are more capable, more intelligent, and smarter than the systems they work in ever allow them to be. Only when this is recognized can an organization truly change. These fundamentals ensure a positive view of people, not a negative one, and include key reasons as to why we should be more positive about people:

- People are capable of ingenuity.
- People want to take the initiative.
- People like cooperating and working in supportive teams.
- People are accepting of achievable vision and a unifying purpose.
- People want to do well and give their best.
- People like to feel part of something greater than themselves.

Most feel better when they do. Haidt's conclusions in *The Happiness Hypothesis* regarding happiness are contained here. But people's behavior is also a function of the working system, so systemic change is a must if people are to be the people we need them to be and they are to be the people they want to be.

However, this can only happen when managers stop trying to manage people and instead learn how to manage the systems that enable people. When this happens, the transformation reduces the distance between cause and effect, complexity can be absorbed, and mental models start to make sense. System redesign is there to make these matters a reality.

This means change, and as Deming always asked, "By what method?" Again we should resist the temptation to ask teachers to simply adapt their approach in ways that embrace all that the research tells us. This is not enough. Teachers will develop more than we ever thought possible when we get the support system right. We cannot depend on teachers alone or on the belief that acting on them is the one option; the school as a system has to change if teachers are to change and learning be allowed to flourish.

If learning dispositions are critical to learning as so much research suggests, the school must respond. This is especially so in those places where dispositions and aspirations have been badly damaged by overly aggressive capitalism and the false mantras of choice and freedom that are so willing to see poverty, health, well-being, and employment issues as collateral damage and as personal inabilities.

There are no "poor" schools. There are some schools that are badly led and there are some schools that serve neighborhoods where the dispositions to learning have been severely damaged by social circumstance and political ignorance. There are schools that need support, having lost their confidence or their way. The real surprise is that so many manage to get by and thrive.

The key here is to seek out the counterintuitive truths and engage with the surprise of the mixed-age management leverage point. Only if the school's full range of learning relationships are designed in (parent-school, parent-child, teacher-parent, teacher-child, student mentor-student, and tutor-mentee) can the design specifications demanded by psychology make the value work work. Learning dispositions are a whole-school matter and any system that relies on teachers as a single element to promote these can only progress so far.

The real learning challenge for schools is a paradox; it is to learn to unlearn and this requires systems thinking. It is to abandon the restrictive practices of same-age structures even if just for a short time each day. While this message must initially seem absurd to schools, it is key to undoing the functional fixedness of management and is the fastest means of unlearning old ways and being able to innovate. Trying to get U.S. schools to engage with this concept on any level will remain a mighty challenge. However, it only takes one state, one district, or even one school to listen and start a conversation about change, people, values, and purpose. Any takers?

## THE VERTICAL TUTOR AS THE INFORMATION HUB

For the school, there has to be a means of organizationally securing optimal learning dispositions for each and every individual learner—one that is fast, effective, and ongoing. Only by securing this essential design foundation will the school be able to improve on all fronts and be more able to construct a strong bridge between players and create a relevant self-organizing mental map between continuously updated and espoused research and theory-in-use.

We should remember that those foolish schools who try and teach happiness, "resilience" (the latest leadership fad), and even "citizenship" will fail. Teaching values and attributes can never be enough in an organization that does not design these in through organizational practice. Schools really must practice what they preach. It is the way that the school operates as a system that is most likely to develop these. Learning relationships in the homeroom between older and younger students are essential to success.

VT ensures that there is an organizational means, a human conduit who acts as the starter domino, the person whose task it is to secure in-school and home–school interconnectivity. Such a task falls to the student's personal tutors in the homeroom who can unpick the industrial model and build a new interconnected and interdependent learning paradigm. The way schools approach this building block and design the learning system around the flow of information is what matters. There must be no separation and limitation.

Where possible there should be two tutors in a homeroom of about eighteen or so students. These people are closest to the child and so are capable of increasing, interpreting, and intercepting the information flow between student, school, and family. This is the basic design principle of the new vertical system. They are the leadership hub, the school's critical leverage point, those best placed to enable such a transformational task.

They intercept work that would normally end up in the school's back office or counselor's (head of year or dean of students) room and this changes the school from being a back office system dealing mainly with failure demand to a front office system dealing mainly with value demand. The co-tutors run one of the school's many front offices, the multi-access link between home and the agencies within the school.

The homeroom is the place where value demand is constantly examined and absorbed through conversation, observation, and information in. It is here that the student and parent customers draw down the initial help, support, and information they need to ensure both progress and ongoing partnership. The student has all the support and mentoring on tap to enable learning and be confident that the tutor and tutor group have their back.

At the same time the same front offices are servicing teachers in the classroom. Vertical tutoring is all about quality learning and teaching. The personal tutors ensure that students are ready to go to class, ready to learn without the teacher having to win the battle of the classroom. Besides, tutors are also teachers. The work done in tutor time transfers directly as dispositions to learning for the work being done during lessons.

The teacher too is dependent on information to make the classroom work. If the students arrive ready to learn, this makes teaching easier and more risks can be taken. If the teacher arrives having just worked with a set of mixed-age students, they are more likely to feel more professional and confident because of the learning relationships that developed in homeroom time.

The homeroom–parent–student trinity also receives information from teachers, and when it does so, a critical feedback loop starts to form. It completes and then constantly informs the critical process called "assessment for learning." Summative assessment is not just about making changes to teaching and learning, it is about developing dispositions and values, but to do this requires reflective conversation between the school (tutors) and home with the student present. This is where summative assessment comes into its own and completes the learning cycle.

It is the unlikely homeroom tutor, the person who takes the roll call and passes on messages, who must step up to the plate. This is the person best able to understand and react quickly to student variation, not as a form of complexity that needs to be limited and controlled, but as potential that needs to be released, nurtured, and grown and so be able to contribute to the school and then to the world beyond. It is this enabling process that undoes and replaces the "prevailing system of management that has destroyed our people."

It is the tutor, like System 1, who is the hero of the piece, the conduit that absorbs and commands information flow and stays alert to changes in pattern and behavior likely to endanger the child. Then the tutor, like System 2, will interpret the information and seek a second opinion and so nurture the sometimes flickering and precious dispositions to learning.

It is the homeroom tutor who is first on the scene, who makes the assessment needed and provides the learning and emotional support by employing the amazing empathetic nature of the tutor group. It is the homeroom tutor who first cherishes all that the child brings to school and keeps the aspiration gene switched on by surrounding the child with all the support needed within the homeroom loyalty group. It is the homeroom tutor without whom all the other learning relationships are so much less.

It would be reasonable to think that during the past 100 years, schools might have discovered much of what there is to know about learning had they been more learning oriented and less deluded by an obsession with tasks, tests, targets, and a dependence on hand-me-down folk management ideas. Unfortunately, the industrial school continues to exert a powerful influence over our teachers, distorting and limiting classroom practice just as it does with politicians, those who should lead change, not perpetuate sameness.

Schools as they are can never get the best out of those who work in them despite the effort put in. This is not to say that our teachers are not highly capable—they are, especially given the circumstances in which they ply their craft. There is simply no telling what they might achieve once the school is reconnected to more of itself and to the families and internal customers it supports and serves.

Systems thinking takes the view that people are capable, energetic, and responsive to a mission, able to use their initiative and more besides, but these qualities can only be made manifest in an organization that understands the variety of value demand on the system and is then able to release such human talent to deal with that demand. This requires management change, training against value demand, what customers need, not the deluded and irrational assumption that this already is the case.

Schools are party to a broken system, but they are not the real problem; they can and do achieve miracles and schools can be dissolved and reconstituted if you know how and are willing to unlearn. It is the way we see the problem that is the problem! Otherwise, the school oscillates unchangingly and becomes increasingly dependent on the maverick leader, a starship superintendent able to somehow engage warp drive and plot a course away from the old bureaucracies of the Borg, and *to boldly go!*

Such a leader is dependent on the crew; another humble homeroom tutor gathering and interpreting information and then engaging others to ensure rapid intervention, good judgment, and the right direction needed to get everyone safely through. In this way all parties can grow their leadership capabilities as they align themselves to the learning cause.

Vertical tutoring connects people. It ensures that all feedback loops work optimally and that everyone knows how the system works with minimal referral and maximum trust. Each player is an essential link, a stock of information in the learning chain. VT secures people loops that allow all parties to use their considerable faculties in the engagement that learning requires. It replaces scripts to be read out and redefines a bewildering jungle of policies, rules, and procedures with all their potential for error and delay. Students need their teachers to be who they were meant to be, not what the horizontal system made them be.

What we have are teaching organizations. Had we developed learning organizations as our teachers constantly advised, schools would have discovered long ago much of what Dweck, Bronfenbrenner, the eminent psychologist Michael Rutter (1979), and so many others advised. But they didn't, and they didn't because the industrial school had other priorities and purposes, many of which haven't changed and most of which are likely to encourage more people management as opposed to system management.

This all cries out for schools able to build and promote learning relationships and improve through sustainable and complex feedback loops—but ones that are easy and fun to manage using mixed-age groups that meet briefly once a day. As Nicole Rivera (2012) says of schooling,

> we are very interested in what does or does not happen during that time. Why? Because today's society is hardwired to label individuals based on their ability to master government-mandated and socially influenced curriculum.

Following in the footsteps of Bruner (1996), who saw schools as places that shape our sense of self with all the consequences this has, Rivera goes on to say:

> What we really need, as a country, is to step back and examine the big picture: how the institution of education demonstrates what we value as a society, and not necessarily the value of children who succeed or fail to meet our expectations.

For me, Rivera is describing problems of value demand. All that can be said is that few, if any, know with any certainty what the purpose of school, U.S.-style, is anymore. The United States demands more of the same and ignores the waste and the damage. It self-perpetuates and has lost touch with its talented citizens, and so many of its judgments have proved wrong; it no longer has any valid claim to lead.

The route to moral purpose only becomes clearer when the fog of the industrial model lifts and a new systems model, counterintuitive in all respects, is enabled to form. The tiny challenge is to use systems thinking to create a school that, because of the way it functions as a complex and interactive human system, has clear intrinsic learning and moral purpose built in, not assumed or added on.

To further underpin the homeroom leverage point needed to change organizational thinking, we need to move briefly from individuals to groups. These too have a huge effect on learning and require smart intervention by schools.

Otherwise we are almost done.

# FOURTEEN

# Drawing Up a Design Spec

> I believe in intuitions and inspirations . . . I sometimes FEEL that I am right. I do not KNOW that I am.
>
> —Albert Einstein

The way the math problem is resolved, how we get past the high numbers and create a system of interconnected learning relationships able to recognize and work with individuals without increasing costs, is the real trick. It is to see the school and the complexity the school faces as a system differently. The aim is to create pattern coherence, and this involves putting together the key learning relationships that need to be permanently in place. The first task, therefore, is to get the size of tutor groups as low as possible, aiming at around eighteen students per group.

1. Divide the school population by the number of spaces/rooms available. This gives a working group size, the tutor group.
2. Repopulate the tutor groups from all age ranges and create balanced groups. This needs care to achieve balance. It is not a group based on friendship.
3. Allocate two tutors per group from all adults employed by the school, regardless of their status and role in the school. This should include the school principal, counselors, the office staff, and teachers. All have a tutoring role to play.
4. Make it a condition of hire that everyone employed by the school will be expected to work as a tutor for twenty minutes per day.

I realize that this may already be too much for school managers, as they quickly invent obstacles and reasons as to why such a simple system is impossible, despite thousands of schools already doing exactly this! The naysayer will immediately come up with a dozen reasons why such a proposal is impossible. Nearly all will appeal to a combination of logistical impossibility and implausibility, anything that avoids values, to prevent any such innovation. Some will invent new dangers while ignoring the ones that already exist.

Those able to move on will discover that the learning benefits massively outweigh the management challenges. To absorb the variety of value demand, the school not only needs all its hands to the learning pump, but managers also need to be practically involved in the work, not separated from it.

In this chapter I want to explain from the point of view of child psychology why the school must redesign itself in this basic way, creating a system able to individualize, increase flow, and be interconnected. Again we return to psychology, and in particular the work of Bronfenbrenner and Rutter, both preeminent in their field.

All we need to know is that the four basic premises above are driven by sound psychological principles that lever a whole series of subsequent system changes set out in the last chapters. Only when this is done and the key learning relationships formed, following the principles and guidelines set out below, is it possible to provide the foundations for the interconnectivity likely to ensure a safe learning passage to better and more intrinsic, independent, and personalized learning.

The school as an organization must have at the very heart of its design a means whereby each and every child is known, and that means each and every *whole child*. The fact is that our children can all too easily pass through schools like shadows, unseen and unknown, perhaps unknowable—students who never had a deep learning conversation with a teacher; students known only by the data garnered from a list of absurdly meaningless tests; students whose parents have been taught by the school that partnership has limitations. Students themselves can all too easily become little more than obscure targets to be somehow statistically achieved.

Not only must the child feel he or she is known and supported in a very deep sense, but there must also be a means of rapid and positive intervention when things go wrong. Similarly, given that sound learning dispositions are vital to the development of a learning mindset, the school needs to ensure that all its human resources support the learner in maintaining effective attitudes and behaviors. It cannot be the teacher alone.

Otherwise, when things do go wrong, the child can enter an endless referral system dependent yet again on good fortune. The school hits the math problem again whereby the grade-level dean, head of year, or the school counselor is charged with the incredible responsibility of somehow knowing and developing a rapport with hundreds of students, each with needs, each wanting to be known, each able to learn given the right support and organizational conditions.

Sir Michael Rutter's seminal work *Fifteen Thousand Hours* (1979) looked at secondary schools and showed that the strange mix of organizational characteristics called *ethos* also greatly influences learning. Rutter identified forty-six process variables (for example, rewards, school uniform, homework) and four dependent variables (attainment, attendance, behavior, and delinquency). His main conclusion is classic systems thinking, but we cannot assume that schools set about this by design:

> Not only were pupils influenced by the way they were dealt with as individuals, but also there was a group influence resulting from the ethos of the school as an institution. . . . Schools can do much to foster good behavior and attainment, and even in a disadvantaged area, schools can be a force for good. (p. 205)

It may seem simple stuff in a way, but its operational implementation, given a rise in mental health issues and fall in well-being, means that change is needed. Schools have to understand how to get the ethos right, and the way in which schools organize themselves to engage individual variation and ensure positive in-group loyalty is critical to learning outcomes and life after school.

A school designed for high-stakes testing as the determinant of method (design) is likely to be one that is not only ignorant of child development but endangering of it. All work and no play not only makes Jack a dull boy but everyone else too.

Rutter's longitudinal studies of the Ceausescu orphans of Romania inform us that despite horrific neglect, children can recover intellectually when exposed to a loving and stimulating environment. The Ceausescu orphans under six months old were largely unaffected by age four when placed with loving foster parents in the United Kingdom. Those over six months old were the ones who faced challenges later on. This study and others have helped us understand an area that needs to be paramount in the minds of teachers: resilience. This is not something to be taught but an attribute that forms when people truly support each other.

Schools can be stressful places, and so can home. Rutter argues that resilience can be built when "risk is reduced through protective mechanisms that change a child's trajectory in life." This can occur, Rutter tells us, when a child (I suspect an adult too) is helped to have a positive view of their *self*. Schools, using tutoring and the in-group loyalty support of older students together with parents, can help young people feel differently about their competencies and abilities.

For Rutter, a child in school (a high-risk environment) can be helped to mitigate risk by accessing a range of support. Such support should be built-in on a daily basis where it matters and not at the end of a referral maze. Schools can reduce risk by establishing vertical tutor groups that ensure attention is paid to individual self-esteem and leadership—support on tap nearby and permanently, designed in every day. Such a system ensures immediate belonging to a loyalty group with a positive view of school and learning.

Bronfenbrenner (1977, 1979) drew up key child development processes that pay regard to the home–school relationship and the vital importance of responsible adults like school staff in the life of a child. His published guidelines, *The Five Critical Processes for Positive Development* (1990), should be written large on school walls as a reminder to schools of what is required and as a means of putting schools back in touch with their values. His processes help establish the basic requirements of the school.

Think parents and tutors and remember that Bronfenbrenner, when asked how long such process should be in play, suggested that pretty much forever would be good!

1. In order to develop intellectually, emotionally, socially, and morally . . . a child requires participation in progressively more complex reciprocal activity, on a regular basis over an extended period in the child's life, with one or more persons with whom the child develops a strong mutual emotional attachment and who is committed to the child's well-being and development, preferably for life.
2. The establishment of patterns of progressive interpersonal interaction under conditions of strong mutual attachment enhances the young child's responsiveness to other features of the immediate physical, social, and in due course, symbolic environment that invites exploration, manipulation, elaboration, and imagination. Such activities in turn also accelerate the child's psychological growth.
3. The establishment and maintenance of patterns of progressively more complex interaction and emotional attachment between caregiver and child depend in substantial degree on the availability of another adult, a third party who assists, encourages, spells off, gives status to, and expresses admiration and affection for the person caring for and engaging in joint activity with the child.
4. The effective functioning of childrearing processes in the family and other child settings requires establishing ongoing patterns of exchange of relationships, two-way communication, mutual accommodation, and mutual trust between the principal settings in which children and their parents live their lives. These settings are the home, child care programs, the school, and the parents' place of work.
5. The effective functioning of childrearing processes in the family and other child settings requires public policies and practices that provide place, time, status, recognition, belief systems, customs,

and actions in childrearing activities not only on the part of parents, caregivers, teachers, and other professional personnel, but also friends, relatives, neighbors, co-workers, communities, and the major economic, social, and political institutions of the entire society.

Together, Rutter and Bronfenbrenner have set out the basic design imperatives of the schools we need, not the ones we have, in which such imperatives are assumptions, despite the miracles performed.

It is the messages from these propositions that the school must ensure are designed in and not assumed. In these five processes there is constant reference to emotional support and learning relationships. They are set out here in full given their importance; think of the homeroom tutor and mixed-age groups and the 20 percent-plus in the United States challenged by poverty and the dearth of affordable health care, and the many above them. The school must design in processes that support all students throughout their time at school. It costs nothing other than a change of mind.

The challenge to schools, given the mathematical conundrum they face, is to recognize the complexity of students' lives and create an organization capable of giving them the individual learning and emotional support they need in order to progress. While schools have already written the means into policies and the tutor's job profile, practical application requires vertical groupings in order for these to work. Bronfenbrenner's critical processes cry out for the homeroom tutor role to be fully developed, and changing the age makeup tutor groups is the best means. It meets the criteria.

Pamela Rutledge (2011) explored how we connect and how the basic drive to be socially connected is woven into our DNA. Like many of us, she returns to the conceptual ideas of Abraham Maslow (1943, 1954) and the motivational *pyramid of needs* he conceived, a concept that has enjoyed endless adaption and play, and one he would no doubt have revisited and revised many times. The emotional stabilizers he promoted remain the foundation for successful child development and personal growth.

Rutledge's concern is not so much the component needs of self-actualization, esteem, belonging, safety, and biology suggested by Maslow, but how these play out in an interconnected way. Life, she says, is "messy," and there is no particular order of events in a world fast changing. For schools, this underpins the idea that what is important is the interconnectivity between the child as an active personality system, the organizational setting of the school, and at least one or two people in the school who know the child well and who remain in the child's corner for the long haul.

It is interconnectivity that enables such needs to be met and this makes Rutledge a good systems thinker, even if such a sensible idea has garnered some unnecessary criticism. Rutledge (2011) refers to this idea as *Maslow Rewired*. According to Rutledge, what we are witnessing today is social networking on a scale that was inconceivable a short time ago with "intricate patterns of interpersonal relationships and collaboration" advancing in sophisticated ways. We are witness to social interconnectivity let loose on a grand scale and driven ever on by new technology.

Rutledge provides a useful guide to school design in her interpretation of how networks and bonds "improve our agency of effectiveness in the environment." While this primitive loyalty driver is not new, it remains important to school design: technology may provide tools, but it is the primitive need for social interconnectivity at a face-to-face level that enables successful growth, one which the school can nurture to drive intrinsic learning. The mixed-age groups are more than capable, when well led, of meeting such needs at school level—one that secures a healthy start and growth.

Once again, such messages help build a picture of how schools can operate and better inform any design rationale regarding the ways schools organize themselves. Not only must the school be deeply interconnected socially as an organization, with all support and feedback loops functioning optimally, but the child has to feel connected to the school and to others at a level far more profound than the universal industrial school model remotely allows.

Technology is not an answer in itself and Bronfenbrenner points out its considerable downside, given it probably does more in the way of harm than good. It is the poorest school means of promoting our primitive desire for connectedness. Neither is it a digital revolution that is needed in schools, helpful though this is in its provision of learning enablement. What is needed to underpin schools is an age of interpersonal and interdependent human engagement or learning relationships, and this is an entirely different matter with entirely different design implications for how schools operate.

Schools that increase parental online access to their child's learning through a digital portal as a substitute for more direct intercommunication are actually practicing separation and limitation, disconnection rather than interconnection. A school full of interconnected technology is a wonderful thing, provided it is not a school full of young people and teachers disconnected from each other. Schools are expert in self-deception and disconnection and it is all too easy to assume that technology can subsume or even replace interpersonal dialogue and emotional intelligence.

## IN-GROUP LOYALTY

The need to belong and feel connected set out in Bronfenbrenner's processes and by Rutter's catalogue of work, and written large here, relates to Maslow's identification of basic human needs. In this respect, belonging-group membership or in-group loyalty plays a major role in any child's development and well-being. Even in positive situations in which a child is a member of a stable, pro-social group, Bronfenbrenner's processes still loom large.

Unless the school establishes in-group loyalty membership early on day one of school, before a child even gets to the classroom, the school will be on the back foot. A child needs the group to maintain pro-school attitudes, a positive outlook on learning, and aspiration. Such a group is better, stronger, and more vibrant if such membership includes children of all ages. This group is not the class (that happens much later) but the tutor group and its derivatives.

Without this, the child is at risk and seek its *self* needs elsewhere. We know what happens when the loyalty group is anti-social, anti-school, and torn between positive and negative behaviors. We know what happens when media influences are stronger than the school in its current form and when gang membership is the provider of solace, self-esteem, and respect. We know what happens when the "hood" provides alternatives to shelter and order, when families become dysfunctional, ineffective, and unsupportive, and when poverty switches off the aspiration gene.

To whom does the child turn to deal with the distress? How should the school cope? The idea of VT is to intervene rapidly on minute one of day one. The school has to be organizationally ready to receive the child, keep him or her safe, and switched on to learning as the way forward.

The systems thinking answer to the school's mathematical and psychological conundrum rests in how the school operates organizationally as an interconnected system. In many ways, the school has to recognize (unlearn) that the pastoral support and counseling strategies put in place for the industrial model are themselves limiting and dysfunctional, not fit for such purposes. They may also undermine the tutor in the initial and important stages of intervention. Of course there should be counselors, but the first line is the tutor.

Maslow has to be *rewired* and so does the school, and this means an alternative and mixed-age approach to the school as an organization.

## DISSOLVING THE WICKED PROBLEM: FIRST PRINCIPLES

The most important thing that can happen to a child on entry to a school and throughout schooling is for the child to be guaranteed membership to pro-social groups more able to protect the child from being overpowered and swept away by the social storms and negative influences that rage not only beyond the school gates, but also in the school itself. This has to be the homeroom or tutor group first. It cannot be the classroom, where learning relationships are many and take much longer to form.

On entry to the school the child meets her two homeroom tutors close up and personal. In customer terms, the student now has direct access to the support needed. The vertical tutors have prepared themselves by garnering available information; they immediately begin the process of dealing with individual value demand and are already starting to save the school time and money in failure demand!

That same child also meets older students from the tutor group. They too will know how to support, lead, and counsel, and they are there every day—leadership everywhere, student voices heard, resilience building and in-group loyalty practiced. The school provides the circumstances that bring out the best in everyone; it not only establishes positive in-group loyalty but weaves the web of learning relationships immediately and sustains them throughout the student's school career.

In effect the school creates numerous front offices. Parents no longer have to access the resources they need through a single school office and the layers of sifting and batching that they have to then battle through to get the advice and support they need. VT allows the organization to achieve a state of flow that improves efficiency. The overall effect of absorbing complexity is to reduce failure demand, improve flow, and remove waste from the system.

Intervention is faster, learning and teaching benefits, and time can be bent to suit. The service level improves when the school reactivates the creative brain power of all staff (remember all staff serve as tutors for twenty minutes each day) and allows decisions to be made at the customer interface. To achieve this the school trains against demand in a school in which everyone understand the system in play and their role in it. All players (students, staff, and parents) can not only draw down what they need from the system, but start to create the system in better ways; they innovate.

Education is a world of unwanted paradoxes that schools are left to resolve. Thus a "great teacher" is actually a great learner and the head teacher is actually the "head learner." The head learner should check classroom practice to ensure that theories espoused are in line with research and in sync with theories-in-use. This means being in the value work, not just directing it from a distant office.

The student is also a teacher and a leader, each a very real test of mastery and of character. It is an imperative that the school is designed in a way that recognizes and supports such counterintuitive roles and the interconnectivity that enables them. It should not assume and presume. Everyone has potential that needs to be realized by the school.

What the teacher is then able to do is to understand and use the rebuilt communications and support network and be party to it. The whole business of vertical tutor groups is to build highly effective learning relationships that move seamlessly from the tutor group throughout the school to the classroom and loop back again, constantly building and renewing with knowledge gained and shared. It is how assessment for learning should work on levels of cognition, character, and emotional intelligence. When put together, spiritual intelligence starts to build.

Vertical tutoring is an interconnected system that needs to be cherished and understood as a system, and is one that requires constant attention and innovation. It is a system that can both create and draw down the energy and information that supports learning and enables teaching. The priority is to get the reculturing and underpinning design principles of the school right so as to create the optimal conditions for learning and teaching given the wicked mess into which schools have been allowed to drift. There is much here to take forward and much to make sense of in terms of school design, school management, and learning.

We now have the underpinning psychology and basic methodology that determines the design principles for our school. This means that we can redefine what it is to truly care and we can understand the conditions required to build strong learning relationships that best support a learning community, one that is able to be adaptive and self-organized. We can also appreciate why this is so important and why the need for rethinking schools is so urgent.

We also know that students spend about 16,000 or so hours in school (K–12). This means that around 15 percent of their time is spent in school and 85 percent out of school. There is overwhelming research that underpins the huge importance of parents in the learning process. At age seven, parental influence is six times greater than the influence of the schools (Desforges and Abouchaar, 2003), and at no time is the school ever the dominant influence with regard to learning.

As parent influence wanes, friends, peers, context, and media start to shape attitudes to learning and aspiration. Poverty adds to the mix in measurable and negative ways. The design implications are obvious to any systems thinker. It is to maintain and enhance the kind of parent partnership and in-school learning support that builds and maintains interconnectivity, not separation. The strength of any school rests in the quality of the learning relationships it builds. School, students, and families must be self-supporting.

It doesn't matter what jurisdiction we are looking at, this basic design capability should be in place. Vertical tutoring is a mixed-age system that ensures this capability and is set out in detail in *The Systems Thinking School* and herewith. Underpinning it are many counterintuitive ideas:

1. Older students do not bully younger students when placed in mixed-age groups. Quite the opposite: they tend to look after them, a new version of "cool."
2. Tutor time should not be taken up with taught programs. Teaching can get in the way of learning. Tutor time is about establishing learning relationships.
3. Everyone who works in the school should be a tutor. In any organization, cultural change is everyone's job.
4. Managers need to manage the system, not the people. They manage the system to ensure people can creatively absorb the value work.
5. Managers need to be close to the customer interface, not sheltered from it. They need to be part of the value work and so they too must be homeroom tutors.
6. Trying to manage costs drives up costs. Costs are reduced when the school is focused on what is of value and provides it. This decreases failure demand, improves flow, and removes the waste caused by poor service.
7. The distance between cause and effect is reduced by VT, enabling better and faster decisions and better judgments regarding actions.
8. Five-year plans are rendered obsolete. The school has to respond to demand and constantly create optimum conditions to meet that demand. Change always has an emergent quality.
9. As an organization, the school can never be managed in a top-down way. Parents and students create an inside-out and outside-in relationship that guides the school's service function and defines value.
10. Concentration on the value work drives up standards, improves outcomes, and has quality and support built in and is less expensive!
11. Decisions take place in the work close to customers and not through remote policies and directives handed down to staff to implement. To do otherwise creates problems of cause and effect, theory and practice, and always results in failure demand. It also stifles innovation by fabricating assumptions and beliefs.
12. When staff are trusted and given this power they are happier and more creative; a learning organization starts to form.
13. When students are trusted, trained, and given responsibility, they respond as learners.

The entire school is redesigned around these basic systems premises.

# FIFTEEN

# Learning from Finland and Other Jurisdictions

Happiness is a place between too much and too little.
—Finnish proverb

The previous chapter ended by setting out some key systems thinking principles that govern school management. Education is complex and culturally defined. Schools adapt to the contexts in which they find themselves. I am saying this because it is easy to confuse culture and education. South Korea, for example, should and will inevitably outperform the United States in PISA measures, not because teaching is necessarily better, but because the culture is entirely different. Theirs, like China's, is a system far more at home with the industrial model. Finland is closer in terms of culture but run entirely on different principles of practice and philosophy.

Without the guidance offered by knowledge of systems thinking, politicians seek out the short cut and the quick fix for the wrong problem. They are guided by bias rather than critical foresight and values. Unfortunately, this leads the United States and many other nations into the minefield and paranoia of comparing jurisdictions when they should be reinventing their own schools and changing direction. Ironically for many jurisdictions, their mistake was to copy the U.S. system, with its built-in flaws of separation and limitation by school and grade.

Senge (2006) got it so right when he said that while benchmarking has a use by opening our eyes to what is possible, it can also lead to "piecemeal copying and playing catch-up." He noted that great organizations have never been built by emulating another, "any more than individual greatness is achieved by copying another 'great' person." An education system should seek answers to the real concerns it has as a society and be ecologically coherent.

While the Finnish system appears to work well as a model, copying what the Finns do requires long-term social change, and any cherry-picking of the "best bits" is unlikely to have much in the way of impact: systems abhor add-ons and fixes and so doing can make matters very messy indeed. Schools that copy each other build in new faults as they strive to eradicate old ones. Not only is such an approach fraught with difficulty and unlikely to work, it reflects an unchanging and moribund mindset that believes delusionally that the basic system in use is okay and can be repaired.

Countries that have worked hard to develop better systems tend to start with purposes and then build the system from the ground up. Arguably, the key to much of Canada's success is not only a redesign process that involved teachers, but its rejection of the United Kingdom's top-down command and control approach epitomized by the then-premier Tony Blair and his government's *delivery unit*. The wonderful thing about "the delivery concept" is its complete failure to systems think, its disbelief in the ability of people, and its subsequent failure to "deliver" anything but mass bureaucracy and higher costs.

That was Canada's smart move, to not copy the United Kingdom and others, but to instead understand how people create organizations that meet individual needs and that work coherently. There was a redesign process, a reculturing that was values led and purposeful, and Michael Fullan was advising. It is the same with Finland, Poland, Estonia, and many other countries that have developed better systems and are now performing well with their better-maintained (but still "factory") systems.

Others like the United States have been less successful. The United States still believes managers can change things when it is management itself that needs to change, as Deming so often said. Throwing money at problems rarely resolves them, and usually makes things worse by entrenching the system precepts even more.

The challenge for this book is to offer systems thinking solutions that cost nothing other than a change of mind. It is to hone in on the school as an organization, a system in its own right, to reveal how it can operate and thrive in order to become more relevant and successful, offsetting many of the harmful factory effects in current play. But to achieve this, the school must aspire to be a learning organization in every sense and know how to make the journey there.

Over time, patterns of behavior develop that we can call a system, the way schools operate to make the work work. Once that system, the way it operates, begins to embed, new challenges arise. It has to learn to be adaptive to the changing conditions of the bigger social system it serves.

Systems must work together and that, in a nutshell, is the problem. It hasn't happened.

## FACTORY MANAGEMENT

When the factory system fails, starts to incur huge costs, and creates significant waste, all that the United States can do is fall back on factory management ethics and techniques intended for another age. Daniel Pink (2009) and Alfie Kohn (1999) produced copious examples of research to show that the management theories of motivation in use not only fail but produce unintended and damaging consequences. In his book *Drive*, Pink says (and I repeat it here) that businesses and organizations "operate on assumptions about human potential that are outdated, unexamined, and rooted more in folklore than in science."

Indeed, the U.S. management industry is driven by the paranoia of fear and failure, an almost religious adherence to inhumane ideas and factory methods that have no substantive research basis. It is this management disease that is spreading (has spread) into schools. There are few that relish the idea of their annual performance appraisal judgment day and more intensive evaluation, and even fewer brave enough to cry foul of such nonsenses.

Marc Tucker, in his book *Surpassing Shanghai* (2013), points out what he sees as the main differences between the U.S. means of school improvement and those jurisdictions that perform better. Ultimately, high-performing jurisdictions have an overarching body in charge that ensures they act in a systems thinking, design way when making key decisions. Once those decisions are made, such bodies generally try and step out of the way. It is a significant point.

Tucker is quick to point out that successfully performing countries (as measured by PISA) have little time for the U.S. management predilection of measuring performance against test scores and almost none for high-stakes testing. It should also be noted that there is a big difference between paying teachers well and performance-related pay as far as motivation is concerned. The former attracts a cohort of highly capable people, which increases competition for positions, while the latter assumes high variation in quality that somehow has to be managed out.

One of the means Tucker advocates for paying teachers more is to have bigger classes, something that other jurisdictions and very different cultures (where high compliance, strong family ties, and intrinsic motivation are more the norm) can get away with. But as I pointed out earlier, money is actually saved by understanding and absorbing value demand. This reduces the cost of management, back office bureaucracy, and failure demand. Despite the research, larger classes are not desirable.

For Tucker, jurisdictions like Shanghai, Canada, Finland, Singapore, and South Korea offer important systems strategies. Thus, raising teacher pay and making access to teacher training more competitive is one strand. Another is to end standardized testing and increase investment. Another is helping schools in challenging circumstances. Others include a more challenging curriculum better able to produce the creative problem solvers it is perceived the United States will need. These are important matters and all need to be considered as elements. The last on this list, "developing problem solvers," remains an irony!

The so-called characteristics of higher-performing jurisdictions are regularly reflected in PISA reports, and the latest report (PISA 2012) is no exception. There is no evidence, for example, that the application of market forces to schools and to the art of teaching has any positive effect—quite the contrary. In high-performing jurisdictions, high-stakes testing is delayed in favor of diagnostic testing used to inform a more individualized learning and teaching process. Routes into teaching are controlled by standards, aptitude, and high-quality training, consistent across the board. So the list goes on.

Deep in the Finnish system, Finland recognizes the importance of customer care and inclusion (demand). Instead of providing limited, universal services dressed up as entitlement, it has built an education system that is able to provide more tailored services. It is able to actively practice what other jurisdictions preach. Slogans such as "No Child Left Behind" remain vacuous and forlorn aspirations in the United States, another example of a worthy vision without a system able to deliver on such rhetoric. The U.S. reaction is to relaunch the idea and throw even more money at the problem. Finland has little need of such slogans: values are built in, not assumed and added on. In Finland it is anathema to leave a child behind.

The predilection in Finland is to trust schools and to use a light touch. This develops professionalism and reciprocity in teachers and hence to students. This is possible because Finland has a coherent system that works for them. Unashamedly, Finnish schools have a deep purpose: to do the right thing, to intervene as much as possible in the transmission of unequal life chances from one generation to the next (Sabel et al. 2011).

They approach words like "freedom," "care," and "choice" from a completely different standpoint to that of the contortions used to justify overly aggressive capitalism in the United States. Finland knows it has to maintain the economic drivers that such a small country requires. They need all of their people to be productive and successful; they cannot afford luxuries like waste and staff and students dropping out. They know that investing in the value work drives costs down. The United States invests in making a broken system work better and drives costs up.

Neither can the Finns afford the limitations of single-loop learning with its emphasis on technique, reform, and ever-new programs. To create a school that reduces the waste of children left behind and who don't really matter requires a wider social culture that must be individually enabling and learning supportive. The school is part of an integrated whole. Finnish teachers are no better than other teachers; the difference is their system.

The United States has an industrial mindset locked in the past that believes people require firm and coercive management through targets and incentives: it is the Trivers syndrome whereby managers transfer their own lack of capability on to others. The underlying reason that teachers are likely to mess up is not one of competence but because the organizational system in which they work doesn't work. It is no longer fit for purpose. The United States doesn't have a social support network that works, which for some is "anti-American."

Finland's mindset is that it pays to manage the system so that people are able to work better and be trusted. This method is also far cheaper and more effective when this is thought through. The received analysis of how Finland achieves so much more than other western jurisdictions rests with factors that are almost entirely external to its schools, including the early acquisition of language and reading skills, high-quality teacher training and recruitment, and comprehensive child welfare policies. This makes copying Finnish schools very easy in some ways; copying the rest of the support system that makes it all work is not so easy.

In Finland, there is wide cultural agreement regarding action to offset any detrimental effects of social and economic disadvantage. We might note:

- Well-trained teachers, competitively selected, who enjoy high prestige and professional autonomy, perhaps in exchange for less pay than in other jurisdictions.
- A simplified national curriculum that provides guidelines rather than endless programs of study. This allows teachers to decide what is best and offers time to do it.
- No high-stakes testing, no published school comparisons, and little in the way of inspection (replaced by sampling).
- Exceptionally high literacy rates that start early on in family life and that are seen as a family responsibility. This includes high library use.
- A highly effective and accessible welfare system and family-friendly policies that combine to better support childrearing and schooling (double-loop learning and systems thinking in part).

This list goes on and on! Finland invests in what is of value because it is cheaper. It is a system that seeks to challenge industrial thinking but has yet to entirely escape it. When it does eventually decide to explore mixed-age approaches, as it no doubt will, it will achieve even more.

So which, if any, of these factors should the United States copy, and which one is the silver bullet, the magical key, the leverage point needed to unlock the door to a better system? The answer is not easy and most of these desirables remain unavailable to the United States in its current form, which is why schools should examine an alternative way.

The point about systems thinking is that each element must work coherently with every other element, and it is this that is the strength of Finland. One element without the others simply does not do it, and this makes copying and cherry-picking very risky as a means of managing change. Yet this is the favored method of schools and of jurisdictions driven on by an unhealthy and irrational competitiveness.

It is no surprise that so many systems thinkers demand full systemic change to access a better learning paradigm. Tucker suggests that equitable and targeted school funding would be a start, followed by standardized teacher training and time for in-house professional development and collaboration—paid for by the government. All are not only desirable but necessary elements.

The comparative headlines that Finnish young people start school later, are better cared for, have less homework, and do no standardized tests until they are sixteen years old seem to defy all that passes for normal U.S. management thinking. They are counterintuitive. Finnish schools also have more breaks during the day in early years. They insist that teachers also take breaks.

We can imagine the lazy System 2s of bureaucrats and administrators considering such matters: "Now which things from that scary list can be cherry-picked to fix our system?" To sufferers of repetitive stress disorder, this must all seem like madness. To the thinking that pervades U.S. school administration, such elements seem counterintuitive, so best ignore them and concentrate on teachers as the non-system problem that needs fixing. Even then, all is not what it seems to U.S. prisoners of the past. The confusion doesn't end there.

Many claim that Finnish schools don't test young people. Not so! They do, and at a very early age and extensively so, but in ways that are interconnected, diagnostic, communicated, and informative to learning and to purpose! They are not high-stakes tests. Finnish teachers do not rely solely on their own evaluations; instead, they work in strong, highly professional teams geared toward intervention, support, and developing learning strategies that counter disengagement. It is a values-driven system based on equity. Little is assumed.

The diagnostic process is also continuously evaluated and is one that involves teachers in the refining process, providing a stakeholder reference point for intervention, planning, and monitoring. This approach makes the operational system process more coherent, planned, and holistic, rather than being broken into stages and levels. In the end, it remains the case that what happens operationally inside the school is extremely important, but it is the external social scaffolding that is so vital. The system promotes and enables organizational effectiveness, which in turn ensures teacher effectiveness. For U.S. public schools, it has to be the opposite way around.

The fact is that the differences between jurisdictions have far less to do with teacher capability and far more to do with culture and social systems. U.S. teachers would thrive in Finnish schools (some do) should they ever recover from the damage of previous management thinking. In the end, it is the fundamental end-to-end learning and teaching process that children experience that matters: how the school operates culturally, organizationally, and managerially to enable learning.

What Finland has been able to do is avoid rebuilding the massive, ineffective, and broken command and control bureaucracies inherent to the United States that create waste, consume resources, prevent flow, repeat errors, and stifle leadership and innovation. It is the same bureaucracies that believe their system to be fixable by having "a great teacher in every classroom," by measurements of performance and target setting. Finland opts for an effective teacher in every classroom.

Finland has been able to move from a system of command and control to one that believes in people—it devolves trust. It has also managed to escape the preoccupation with mass education by paying attention to the individualized tailoring needed to support learning. It has changed the learning culture and reduced regulation, doing the right things, what needs to be done, given the clear purposes and values it has that drive it on. It is far from perfect, but at least it is coherent as a semi-linear system.

Finland is only partway there. What Finland seems to have in part discovered are values, clarity of purpose, a more ecological fit, and a way of making education work optimally. It has rediscovered and developed the interconnectivity and interdependency needed to create effective learning relationships in school.

So what messages can we take that are most likely to help us identify false assumptions and help with any unlearning and redesign? There are many, but here are some starters:

1. Intervention and support early on to support family life is cost effective. Welfare is important for well-being, which in turn is important for learning, which in turn is . . .
2. Diagnostic testing early on to inform professional practice and process is sensible. A system should enable people to identify and draw down the resources they need as easily as possible to achieve the purposes it has. This makes learning stable and systems secure.
3. Professional organizations like schools must have a genuine working partnership with parents and among all key players (almost nonexistent and all wrongly defined in most non-Nordic countries, despite claims otherwise).

4. The idea of "no child is left behind" and "every child matters" should never be slogans but system implicit. These are not aspirations or targets but system design factors.

It should be noted that PISA ranks *equity* very high as an improvement criterion, and Tucker reflects this, but there is a problem. The cultural point is hammered home by Pasi Sahlberg (2013), director general of Finland's Centre for International Mobility and Cooperation, who points out some of the wrong-headed misconceptions but normal thinking promulgated in the United States. These include the following:

- *Attracting more high-level (whatever that means) teachers is a silver bullet for improving U.S. schools.* False. It is commonly thought that teachers and the classroom account for 20 percent of variance and the school climate, facilities, and leadership account for another 20 percent. The rest, including family background and motivation to learn, is beyond the control of the school.
- *Effective teachers develop once they are in the system, not beforehand.* False. In Finland there is an emphasis on quality selection and rigorous teacher education prior to system entry.
- *Effective teachers can overcome all barriers of poverty and background faced daily by 23 percent of U.S. children.* False. The solution is to elevate children out of poverty using systems external to the school, not to hope that great teachers can fix an errant system that denies equity.
- *School culture and leadership matter little compared to teachers.* False. Maintaining focus on learning, producing a positive school climate, setting high expectations for all, developing staff skills, and involving parents—in other words, school leadership—matters as much as teacher quality.

I believe that VT can help in each of the above.

Sahlberg doesn't stop there regarding his challenge of the "prevailing system" of U.S. management ideas. He points out that the United States has 1,500 different teacher training programs, creating huge variance; that high-performing countries have no fast-track teacher entry system; that the United States is in the bottom four in a recent United Nations review on child well-being; that among twenty-nine wealthy countries, the United States is second to last regarding child poverty measures.

Sahlberg is also adamant that the "toxic" use of teacher and school accountability should be abandoned; teachers place great value on professional autonomy and better working conditions higher than their pay. A survey in Finland showed that 50 percent of teachers would leave teaching if performance were related to standardized test results. The United States should note this.

For me, Finland will get even better when it realizes that there is still more energy it can tap into through mixed-age student mentoring. The point being labored here is that it is quite right to seek best practice, but such practice must be part of a complete system. It is precisely the point endlessly promoted by Frank Duffy (2014) in his many reports on systemic change.

In her book *Reign of Error,* Diane Ravitch (2013) echoes similar sentiments, starting with recommendations for good prenatal care and high-quality access to early education. These are followed by smaller class sizes, proper medical and social services for the poor, and the elimination of high-stakes testing. So, once more, the list of absent or broken system elements grows.

## MORE DESIGN IMPLICATIONS

Politicians are invariably the first to espouse values but the last and least able to implement them.

What is of interest is the diversity of opinion used to describe how the universal industrial model (the factory school) works best. In the west, it clearly works best as a system only when the factors external to it are family friendly and more equitable, or (in the east) when the culture is unquestioning, compliant, hypercompetitive, and accepting of it, and that is the bottom line.

Besides, why should the United States bother, given that it does so well? It has an aggressive record of securing more patents than the rest of the world combined; it also manages to produce more Nobel Prize winners than any other country. Presumably, all of these people were taught in U.S. schools. It can also tolerate waste and inequity more than all other western countries, preferring the delusion of the American dream to the responsibilities of equity.

Few talk about changes that schools can make or alterations to the U.S. three-tier school system both wrongly assumed to be benign. Schools, however, cannot wait, nor must they. They need to know now what they can do to make their school better despite the managerially moribund context in which they operate. So what really needs to be done is what can be done by schools themselves: it is to show how a school can change the way it thinks about itself in very practical management terms. This means doing the right things *righter* rather than the wrong things *wronger*.

Otherwise, we need to take great care. The point of the past is to understand it and learn from it; it is not to repeat it. The debate we are having needs great caution because it seems we are having the wrong conversation about direction, one guided by our deep, deluded, and inbuilt assumptions perpetrated by an industrial model that no longer pertains, a system that prevents us from seeing and thinking clearly. Such instinctive biases must be challenged and better informed to realize better system judgments.

If we are to learn one thing from systems thinking, it is that the alternative counterintuitive view, the one that few recognize and the one most dismiss, just as Meadows said, is likely to be far more potent than what passes for conventional wisdom. It is this world of counterintuitive truths, the chaotic world of the neutrino, the charm, the quark, and the dark matter we don't see, that offers the best means of escape. The same-age structures have to be undone first, and when this happens, the way we think about schools will also undo.

We need to see the school from the user point of view and revisit the space-time-numbers problem. I like to think that even Victorians and Prussians who invented the factory school using their state of the art knowledge and enlightened view of their time would be aghast that the managerial thinking blueprint they created is still in universal use.

# SIXTEEN

# Learning about Customers

Your most unhappy customers are your greatest source of learning.
—Bill Gates

Herein is the ultimate delusion of management in my view. Students are peer grouped—they are all in the same grade or year pretty much all of the time. To continue with this as the basis for school organization is simply an absurdity, delusional thinking based on a whole gambit of false assumptions and beliefs.

## THE GOOD NEWS AND THE BAD NEWS

Schools operating same-age groups, especially in tutor or homeroom time, eventually reach a hiatus. Having tried numerous ways to make the espoused tutor support model work, school managers eventually see, just as Forrester predicted, that all is not as it should be. What was it Peter Drucker said? "There is nothing so useless as doing something efficiently, like that which should not be done at all." It seems that the old adage is right. School managers and administrators know everything about their school except how to improve them.

While few notice that the hoped-for information pathways are blocked, placing limitations on the knowledge needed, almost none have worked out the same-age mathematical cause of the blockage. It is not made clear to schools that what is claimed as a strength (control of complexity using information limitation and separation) is actually a system weakness. At the same time, innovating a design solution is not easy for schools, given the nature of the organizational thinking that dominates.

Having discovered this leverage point, it is possible to completely redesign the learning culture of the school from the inside out—something set out previously in *The Systems Thinking School*. This means changing the school from a one-way information-out system to one that has an active two-way communications system.

## DOING THE MATH

Once the counterintuitive leverage point is decided, it is important to push the leverage point in the right direction. Once understood, the schools will say, as they always do, that they knew the answer all along and couldn't believe they were doing the wrong things thinking they were the right things. Only then is the unlearning complete and the management delusions of a century left behind.

Problems of mathematics require mathematical solutions with a twist. This is how I suggest schools should resolve the industrial equation:

1. Divide the number of students in the school by the number of spaces. This should (hopefully) give you a number around eighteen to twenty or less. This is the size of the school's new homeroom/tutor group.
2. Now carefully create new tutor groups based on students from across all age groups to achieve a balance of gender, ethnicity, ability, and behavior.
3. Next, add up all the staff in the school, including administrative staff, managers, counselors, librarians, support staff, and anyone employed in a professional capacity. Train them to be tutors and explain the system.
4. Carefully allocate two members of staff to each tutor group, according to the school's judgment on leadership, need, and team capability. Status is not a consideration, nor are logistical concerns.

Of course there is considerable expertise and further guidance needed, but what such a school has done is create new pro-social in-group loyalty and a mentoring and leadership system more able to generate self-organization. It is the counterintuitive mixing of students that will undo the linear, industrial school and start an inside-out reculturing and redesign process of ongoing improvement.

Counterintuitively, bullying (all vertically tutored schools tell me) will decline immediately when such a system is understood and implemented with care and an understanding of how the system operates and is built. Everything should get better.

Surely separation by age enables the school to control unwanted behavior? No, the counterintuitive opposite is true. What about gang membership? Surely older ones will encourage younger ones to join gangs and schools should not facilitate this? My personal experience and the counterintuitive argument is this: tutor time is supervised time. When all older students are trained (against value demand) to mentor and lead. Instead of recruiting youngsters they tend to care for them, give them sage advice, and be protective toward them. They are put back in touch with deeper instincts that they sometimes lose somewhere en route.

Only when this is done will the school's full potential start to be released. Such a school will:

- Have purpose and aspire to be a learning organization.
- Know how to allow energy to cross boundaries.
- Have an underpinning of positive psychology.
- Build powerful pro-social in-group loyalty that will reduce bullying and gang membership.
- Build on-tap support and leadership everywhere that will ensure every child is known.
- Enhance parent partnership and support to families.
- Offer every child in the school leadership and mentoring opportunities.
- Transfer better learning relationships and raised self-esteem to the classroom.
- Be confident, innovative, and self-organizing.
- Complete the assessment for learning loop (formative and summative).
- Ensure that every child matters and is known and that none are knowingly left behind.

. . . and so the list goes on and on as the school begins to adjust, the dominos of the old industrial model start to fall, and a better culture builds.

The school now needs a guide to show precisely how learning relationships develop and are steered by the revised academic calendar and learning need. Once the interdependent learning relationships are interconnected, complexity and the energy and information that come with it is no longer limited. It is absorbed within the system design. In other words, the new learning culture enables information to flow and be used to support learning and teaching.

In this way, each and every student is surrounded by a strong support network including every other student in the group. All that remains is a series of tasks:

- For the tutor to build the learning relationships needed without the need of programs.
- For the school to construct the new information highways and multi-nodal communications hubs around each student and tutor.
- For students to understand their new leadership and mentoring role.

- For managers to manage the system and allow the domino effect to change all other constituent elements such as assessment, reports, and partnerships.
- For parents to understand how the new partnership with the school works and their role in it.
- For teachers to take advantage of the new learning culture and take more risks in developing challenging and innovative learning.

School managers can now set about their task of managing the system. The list provided below offers initial guidance and the opportunity for innovation and creativity. The tasks and the matters that managers should consider ensure that the value work is prioritized and that managers remain *in* the work, not just directing it.

Managers should now manage the domino effect to change all other constituent elements, ensuring that:

- Data sheets and reports are enhanced by clear written strategies for improvement and better information that enable tutor, student, and parents to support learning, reflect, and strategize.
- New methods of reporting including face-to-face, deep learning conversations involving school, parents, and student (around forty-five minutes minimum) are designed in. These meetings take place at identified critical learning and reporting times, requiring a redrafted academic calendar.
- All learning relationships are identified, in place, functional, and system supported.
- All policies, practices, protocols, principles, and procedures (cultural dissolution and redesign) are realigned to the new system.
- Leadership and training are developed to suit and outcomes monitored.

The list is as long and innovative as the school's ability to be imaginative allows. All that is required now is an idea of what else the gradual transition from a teaching culture to a learning culture entails.

# SEVENTEEN

# Managing the Change Process

## *The Implementation of Vertical Tutoring*

> Culture does not change because we desire to change it. Culture changes when the organization is transformed; the culture reflects the realities of people working together every day.
>
> —Frances Hesselbein, *The Key to Cultural Transformation* (1999)

This is the penultimate chapter. If you have made it this far, you will appreciate the letter in the fourth chapter and understand the solution to the math conundrum set out in the previous section.

There is a concern that I need to share. Having spent many years working in and with schools, it is easy to predict the errant practice inherent to linear, same-age systems; it is also possible to identify places where schools are likely to go wrong as they move from one system to another. Managing such a change is fraught with challenge. While it is possible to work out the fundamental process for internal redesign of the school to enable better self-organization, it is not always possible to eradicate old management thinking.

I train schools as best I can; it is a hobby, not my living, something I do because I am a teacher and a learner. I teach because it makes a difference to many lives that otherwise may have been wasted or gone unrecognized. I learn from schools more than I teach them. Robert Greenleaf (1970) set out a counterintuitive idea about leadership in an essay, "The Servant as Leader." The idea is this: the leader of a school has to be a servant first, driven by the desire for the well-being of others. It is a noble philosophy and ensures that leadership stays in the value work and minimizes distance between cause and effect. It is a systems thinking philosophy that values people and ultimately creates better organizations. It does no harm.

But I cannot stop leadership teams deciding to make exceptions and adaptions that diminish purpose, undermine people, and disregard values. They may feel they can follow their System 1 whims because the few hours of systems thinking training I offer cannot always overcome a lifetime of single-loop learning. It is all so much unnecessary ignorance and arrogance, and something that teacher training institutions should tackle.

Many leaders prefer to be isolated in ivory towers by the distance between cause (their decisions) and effect (long-term negative consequences). Such managers and administrators create more work because they themselves are not part of the value work needed. They too easily forget the servant that once helped them through.

Unlearning is difficult, and denial born of self-delusion has a habit of clinging on regardless. Most schools and teachers take to systems thinking easily because ultimately it is about care, spiritual intelligence, and personal growth. They are more able, in Deming's terms, "to adopt the new philosophy." Most are grateful to be back on track and in touch with their values, who they are, and their higher purpose to make a difference and increase goodness. Managers and administrators feel far more challenged than teachers by cultural change. Teachers just get it every time because they are doing the value work at the customer interface at which learning relationships form; they are in the work where it matters and not isolated from it.

Set out below is the general framework that in my experience best lights the path to successful change, remembering there will be as many pathways as there are schools. Dangerously absent is the training that gives teachers the chance to have their questions answered and to be inquisitive and learn more. Teachers also need the reassurance garnered from the many successful schools that have made the switch to vertical tutoring and the stories of their journey. Just as a sage on the stage can never truly replace a guide by the side, so a book is a poor substitute for a learning conversation with those still able to listen.

While each school likes to think that vertical tutoring can be adapted and implemented to their particular school, such a notion requires caution. Those principals who, through arrogance and/or ignorance, mess with organizational change without a clear understanding of their current industrial system will never unlearn sufficiently to make any new system good. They will be left exposed to the failure of management and organizational reform as an antidote to the wrong illness. In turn, this will result in almost irresolvable problems and expensive errors that will prove difficult to undo. The irony is that schools that ignore systems thinking principles and human values will leap into the negative areas of denial and eventually return to their deluded industrial preferences.

The sequence of the school's management change process set out below guides the transformation of a school as it moves from a closed, linear, and same-age model (horizontal system) to one dependent on leadership, communication, and mentoring (vertical). It is at best an *idiot's guide* and should be used with care, though enthusiasm may take schools far. All I can urge is that schools learn as much about systems thinking as possible and that teacher training and leadership institutions ensure this topic is high on any teacher training agenda. Leadership is not the problem we think it is—leadership without systems thinking is.

In the United Kingdom, where most of my work is done, there are about 800 secondary schools that now claim to be vertically tutored schools, a number that increases annually. I suspect I have trained half of them. Those that have not been trained are unlikely to have ever heard of systems thinking as a concept and a principled study. This means that they have come up with models that are almost certainly disobedient of systems thinking management principles, and consequently are much less effective than they should be.

A few are poorer for the rudderless changes made and a few have even reverted to their former linearity, having made a leadership mess of the change process (usually by not bothering with training and information, copying other schools and assuming they had the management understanding and capabilities needed).

Many untrained schools have made life for learners worse, not better, by introducing unnecessary paperwork, not changing practices, and remaining ignorant of key elements of the changes needed. The few that have abandoned vertical tutoring claim that it "didn't work for us." I hear from the teachers of such schools that "VT didn't work" or that "it created more work," only to discover that no one at their school had been properly trained, no one had heard of systems thinking, and that their schools were simply copying other schools, building faults in rather than designing them out. Managers hadn't changed, so the system couldn't change.

Even some of the schools that I trained can be affected by their old industrial ideas and thus reintroduce unneeded elements they should have abandoned. They try and push the tutorial leverage point in two directions at the same time. They tinker. Most of those schools whose leadership teams underwent systems training (the process of unlearning, gaining knowledge, and applying new learning) have thrived beyond recognition and even the inspectorate has commented positively on the benefits VT brings. Some of these schools are even creating a new future by exploring mixed-age teaching and with great success. Once innovation starts, there is no knowing where it might lead.

I simply don't know whether the U.S. system, with its unhelpful changes of school and rigid grade system through elementary, junior, and high school, can embrace VT. Most may see it as an interesting oddity of schools in the United Kingdom, Australia, and New Zealand rather than a learning system for themselves. Having liaised with a few educationists in the United States, I like to think it is worthy of a try and some mavericks and visionaries doubtless will give it some thought. I have seen that some U.S. high schools and junior highs already have mixed-age homerooms, and this is a start.

## CONSIDERATIONS

A knowledge of systems thinking applied to schools as organizations is more than useful. Set out below are the main areas of professional development set over a three-month timeline.

*1. Take advantage of leadership and governor training.*

The process begins with understanding the basics of systems thinking and the challenging process of unlearning. Only then is it possible to reexamine the school's organizational purposes and values as the stable platform on which to build. From there a check can be made against these values and purposes, and this means examining the school from a customer perspective (really understanding the value demand on the system), preferably with the help of a systems thinking facilitator.

Look at the school from a user (staff, student, parent) point of view set alongside research, best systems practice, and what works. Note all the places where parents and schools interact. It is a first attempt at showing the informed reality of what is happening in the school and identifying as much as possible any assumptions and biases. By following customer experiences, especially at points of interface, judgments can be made about the learning process in play, measures, and method. These will reveal all kinds of restrictive practices on which linear or horizontally organized schools depend.

By critically dissecting the linear model, it is possible to see how a vertical system deals with issues such as parent partnership, interventions, reports, and assessment, and how these can be managed more effectively. Only then is it possible to introduce mixed-age groupings (vertical tutoring) as a systems thinking solution capable of ticking all the right cultural and learning boxes. It should be noted that the vast amount of management information offered at this stage is intense and requires more work later.

*2. Provide full staff training.*

All staff require similar training, and this means everyone who works in the school regardless of their role or status. A school can only work effectively if everyone understands how the system works and how each contributes.

Remember that everyone (staff, students, and parents) is a service provider and a customer of everyone else. Remember, too, that everyone employed in a professional capacity by the school is expected to be a tutor (involved in the value work). Once a day for a short time, all silos will be abandoned for the joint enterprise of tutoring, the school's expression of what it is to care and to focus on its primary investment in learning. It is the place where IQ (learning intelligence), EQ (emotional intelligence), and SQ (spiritual intelligence) start to coalesce.

The training provides the before and after window. School workers, parents, students, and the community at large have to be stakeholders, and this means understanding systems thinking and owning the changes. Once they know and can appreciate why the existing industrial system is so difficult and so limiting, it is easier to understand the need for change.

Knowing precisely how a mixed-age system works is vital for the other dominos to fall and a new culture based on learning to emerge. For the school's management or leadership team to do this alone requires considerable certainty as to why the old management ways should be abandoned and how the new system will work. Remember that the staff really need to know how the system works more than they need training in how to mentor.

*3. Train all students for their leadership/mentoring role.*

Before any changes to tutor groups, existing students need to understand the new system and what's in it for them. Many students may not be convinced that moving from the comfort of their grade or year-based peer group, even for such a short time, is in their interests, so achieving student buy-in is essential. Bringing older students to the point at which they understand their new leadership and mentoring role and the payback they get (the leadership, team, and problem-solving skills needed beyond school) needs thought. Some are likely to have one single thought: resentment at the loss of friendship (albeit for twenty minutes a day). My own research from school feedback says that no friendships are lost and a whole lot more are gained!

A preparatory training session for students in leadership and mentoring will help. Developing these transferable workplace skills and being encouraged and enabled to practice them in tutor time builds trust, self-esteem, and better learning dispositions; it also develops emotional intelligence, including empathy and aspiration through the support given to others in their new group. They learn that the more you put in, the more you get back.

As schools develop vertical models, students become the best ambassadors and advocates of change. I have seen young people deliver inspirational talks on VT to teachers and other students. I remember being told by many employers and colleges why they hired so many students from my school, and these reasons related to traits like confidence, problem solving, resilience, balance, character, and personality. All are products of vertical tutoring relationships. They were better prepared for their next move and all without a requirement for pro-social programs.

*4. Visit schools that use vertical tutoring.*

There will be such schools. Take students and staff to see schools using vertically tutored groups (after training) or arrange a teleconference. This is to reassure students and ensure that schools do not copy potentially bad practice. Sadly, the United States needs to start virtually from scratch, though that is not a bad thing. The benefits to students, parents, and learning are high when counterintuition and innovation are embraced and self-determined. There are U.S. schools that have mixed-age tutor groups, but most have yet to go further and fully develop the rest of the system (VT max) and build a complete and interconnected learning culture.

*5. Conduct a parent consultation evening.*

Parent consultation is a vital part of the change process—hence the draft letter set out earlier in this book. Parents do not like unexplained change and will want to know what they and their children get out of vertical tutoring, so the school must be confident about how VT works as a system. The parents actually get a redefined partnership with the school, a shared learning relationship that for the first time is built genuinely on two-way communication.

Parents and caregivers also have the assurance that their child's vertical tutors (homeroom tutors) will know their child well as a complete person. This is because the tutor is the key information hub in the revised system and is able to intervene rapidly to support and guide progress. Of course this can only work with other changes, especially the reporting and assessment information used to underpin deep learning conversations or academic tutorials (see number six).

*6. Define critical reporting and meeting times when academic tutorials are needed.*

In the lives of parents, students, and teachers, there are critically important occasions when school, student, and parents need to reflect, talk, and agree on strategies for improvement. These occasions are not at times convenient for school logistics but at critical times for learning. Such annual or bi-annual occasions should be identified with parents to ensure students get the best support at the most important times.

These may be (for example) the two or three months before an important test or six weeks after starting school. The school will need to review its academic calendar and ensure that these occasions are identified and are the first to be plotted in, especially as these will be important signposts directing tutor action. One of the advantages of VT is that critical times are spaced throughout the year according to the age of the student, and this is advantageous in spreading workload.

*7. Understand the academic tutorial (deep learning conversation).*

By making the vertical tutors the conduits of an enhanced information and communication system, the school is changing from a back office bureaucracy to a more accessible and high-quality front office system. It is the vertical tutor who becomes the primary link between home, school, and student. It should be noted that that there are two key occasions (formal) when progress is discussed between home and school. The evenings when subject teachers and parents meet are still necessary.

However, these are complemented with a much longer session, the academic tutorial, involving the student, the student's personal tutor(s), and parents. This enables four critical sources of information and viewpoints to be communicated, recognized, and acted on—the school's assessments, the parent's observations, the student's voice, and the tutors' summative view. The quality of this session depends entirely on the information supplied by the school (beyond grades), parents, and the student concerned. Identifying and agreeing strategies for improvement and support is the name of the game.

Working with students and parents and having better assessment information available enables a much more sophisticated process of learning support. The results, agreed-on strategies for improvement, are fed back into the summative assessment process. Deep learning conversations or academic tutorials, lasting about forty-five minutes or so, are stress free and enable more general strategies for achievement to be mutually agreed and supported. Academic tutorials also inform the tutor and help define the tutor role in terms of the nature of the support needed in tutor time and elsewhere.

In turn, this spreads the assessment load and ensures necessary complexity is integral to the learning system, not limited by it. It also fulfills much of the definition required of a learning organization.

Remember that high among parents' wishes are four important customer concerns. Every parent wants their child to do well at school. Every parent wants to be part of the learning process. Every parent wants the school to know what their child is good at and capable of. Every parent wants someone in the school they can talk with, someone who cares as much as they do, someone who knows their child well, and someone who values their contribution to the life of the school.

*8. Revise assessments and reports to ensure inclusion of written strategies for improvement and dispositions to learning. Increase the information in the system and from the system.*

Assessments need to be diagnostic and individualized as well as standardized and must always be complemented by written comments and especially (again) strategies for improvement. Targets alone can cause all kinds of unwanted and misleading distortions. Parents, students, and tutors can only be as good as the information they receive, so the dominant grade assessment methodology of U.S. schools needs qualification to enable learning and not limit it. Always beware of targets, praise, and punishments, and their tendency to distort learning behaviors!

At the same time, this process must enrich the learning relationships that students, teachers, and parents need. Without vertical tutoring and improved parental and student input, summative assessment and assessment for learning as a concept remains so much less than what they should be.

*9. Restructure the school to enable the previous points to become organizationally active.*

VT is a nested system comprising schools within schools within schools. Thus, each older student leads a small group of younger students, the tutor leads the VT group, the head of house leads their house, and the principal leads the school. The school is subdivided into houses or colleges and each head of house acts like a school principal in their own right. Theirs is a leadership role that embraces classroom quality. Heads of house should work from the same base to share ideas, manage the system, and make any system changes needed. They drive innovation.

It is critical that heads of house ensure tutors are the first port of call regarding tutees, especially when intervention (managing variation in part) is needed. This process is not easy. It means changing the way the school is managed and organized. The school will also need to address its own senior management or leadership team accordingly. It is an area requiring considerable skill and judgment and one that many schools shy away from.

*10. Dismantle all horizontal same-age groups and create new mixed-age groups.*

The mixed-age or vertical groups are the key to resolving the numbers, space, and time issues (the math problem) of the industrial model. They are based on an equitable distribution of gender, ability, and behavior so that all new tutor groups are reasonably similar. It is advisable to keep numbers as low as possible, with eighteen being close to an ideal base size for a tutor group. Consult with staff on the final group makeup to determine changes before any final decision. Ensure that students who are a bad influence on each other are separated. Do not ever base these groups on friendship! How tutors meet their tutees for the first time should be given considerable thought and needs to be personalized (see number fourteen).

*11. Mandate that all adult staff are expected to be tutors regardless of role and status.*

From this point, no one should join the school in any professional capacity (this includes principals and administrators) without realizing that they will be trained and expected to be vertical tutors. Tutors do not teach programs, though there may be rare occasions that sometimes warrant such an approach; otherwise, their role is too important. They are there to advise, lead, mentor, support, check progress, form learning relationships, and communicate in their role as information conduits and as advocates.

Once the system is understood, the culture of tutor time builds. The mystery of what happens in tutor time is not included here simply because prescription needs to be avoided and schools need to find their own path. However, I have seen many fun activities, many great assemblies, great discussions, quizzes, students supporting the learning of other students, students leading and teaching, and even a session based on speed dating! This is probably the most joyous but challenging area of the whole process when done well.

Every person employed in the school should be involved in tutoring and mentoring, and so should all students over time. This includes senior staff, librarians, counselors, and support staff. Tutors are selected on their ability to be a tutor, not on their status or their other roles. The main qualification is to be vaguely "human." As a school principal, I was also a tutor and the head of house was my boss for that time. The process of forming the balanced teams of tutors needs the same care as forming the tutor groups. Once done, decisions need to be made on allocation to tutor groups, and again staff consultation is recommended to avoid mistakes.

*12. Ensure that all weak readers and special needs students who need support are identified and tutors are made aware.*

One of the key roles of the tutor and the VT group is to support children designated with special educational needs (SEN). Part of the preparation for leadership of older students is to teach them how to support and mentor those with learning challenges. Training older students to deliver individual support in (say) phonetic reading is very effective. It should be normal practice to see this happening in tutor time.

This ensures that younger students have ready access to the expertise of older students each day. This dynamic and interactive process is the key to success and personal growth. The vertical tutors become key players in all learning support.

*13. Allocate time for lead and co-tutors to meet to review tutee data and files and special educational needs issues.*

Prior to meeting tutees for the first time, the new VT team of lead tutor and co-tutor must be given time to meet each other and jointly review the progress and nature of their individual tutees by garnering information and studying any student files available. They should check on special issues regarding learning, but also get the bigger perspective, such as participation in sports or the arts, behavior, and social background. Tutees need to feel that their new vertical tutors know them as young people, while tutors themselves need information necessary to fulfill their professional role.

*14. Arrange the very first meetings between tutors and tutees as advised.*

These meetings are of critical importance. One of the most important intentions of vertical tutors is to quickly establish new and positive pro-social in-group loyalty and to be able to intervene immediately should anti-school and anti-learning attitudes arise. Indeed the whole VT process is very much concerned with the creation of positive attitudes that maintain aspiration by creating the positive pro-social groups that best support individuals.

The very first meetings between tutors and tutees should not be vertical, but instead be in same-age peer groups where the students feel most comfortable. It is a very simple meeting, short and to the point, but again, there is much more to this brief but vital session than is set out here.

The tutor should warmly greet these students (preferably there should be no more than four). The tutor introduces herself and her co-tutor. The tutors explain their role, what happens in tutor time, what is expected, how it all (the system) works, and how the tutees can and should contribute. Students should leave that brief meeting knowing that their tutors are sincere, supportive, empathetic, and will be a permanent fixture in their learning lives while at school. The tutor should leave this first meeting having achieved honorary membership of a student in-group (team child).

What is also happening is something I learned from Kahneman. The meeting ensures that interference and unwanted speculation from System 1 is minimized and System 2 more engaged. This ensures more accurate judgments, greater trust, honesty, and mutual respect. Later, these traits will transfer to the classroom

So the vertical system starts to take shape. From there on, it is a question of managing the system, lest it revert and start to manage you! Why does VT win every time? The short answer is that it cherishes people, builds and develops their expertise, and values their contribution. It defines the value work. It ensures each of our players is listened to. It makes each person, each parent, child, teacher, and tutor, part of something bigger than themselves, part of Jonathan Haidt's definition of happiness. It is also innately spiritual at its finest and entirely values driven. At the same time, it enables better judgments and decisions based on more pertinent and informed information. It is a system that removes assumptions and biases and allows System 1 and System 2 to work harmoniously. It secures trust.

# EIGHTEEN

# From Delusion to Design

> It's frightening to think that you might not know something, but more frightening to think that, by and large, the world is run by people who have faith that they know exactly what is going on.
>
> —Amos Tversky

It is time to ramble to some sort of close. The math puzzle that started this book was the same I was faced with too many years ago when I was appointed principal of a large secondary high school. The letter was long ago sent (misplaced participial phrases are so much better!) and was much shorter.

I knew the conundrum's parameters. It was to organize learning for 1,200 students ages eleven to sixteen (five grades) with sixty-plus teachers, a dozen support staff, office staff, a librarian, and a dozen or so subjects. The parameters included 2,000 parents, all of whom wanted their child to be successful, and the knowledge that at least half the students in the school shared a certain ambivalence to all the fuss. Our resources were limited and we had the typical horizontal, age-based factory system indelibly written on every practice, one we all knew from experience didn't quite work as written on the tin.

As a visually based learner, I knew I had to draw on paper a viable model of how the school might work as a learning system, not just a teaching system, one that even I might understand and one that I could easily explain to everyone else. Without that, I knew life in our school would be difficult.

As a school, we became one of the first to assiduously gather and use performance data. A local software company helped us and we were soon able to track and crudely predict the performance of every child. This was a useful tool in the 1980s given the organizational purposes we had. The problem was using the data and turning it into useful information that could better enable learning. Parents had to play a role and so did students. The challenge was how to do it.

In those first days and weeks as a new school principal, you are granted a brief respite of time, or what psychologists term a "halo effect." People are yet to judge you. Kahneman (2011) describes the halo effect as "exaggerated emotional coherence." The school's System 1 intuition doesn't have all the information on the new school principal and thus offers a best early picture based on the limited information gleaned (looks smart, wears a suit, seems interesting, might be intelligent, smiles, talks to students).

System 1 follows the principle of WYSIATI (what you see is all there is) and therefore has a view that automatically fills in any gaps with all kinds of biases from which all kinds of further assumptions can be made that may or may not prove valid. The occasionally alert but generally lazy System 2 puts these biases on hold and will delay any judgments until more is known.

The fact is, I struggled to make sense of it all as newly appointed school principals inevitably do. I asked for a flip chart to be placed in my room and started to draw systems models. Back then, systems thinking was an unknown concept to me and I couldn't conceive a model that worked. I must further confess that I got the principal's job under false pretenses. The appointments panel believed that *appraisal*, the annual performance review and the "hot" new management tool of the time, was the key to making any school work better. I did not, and I disliked the idea. Now that I have grown older and wiser, I dislike it even more!

Under the pressure of interview, it is extremely hard work for (lazy) System 2 to hold and access the information needed to answer so many loaded (and biased) questions. When the question on appraisal was asked at my job interview, the one I was dreading, I hesitated. In that moment's hesitation, I suddenly found that my dark passenger, my intuitive and eager-to-please System 1, had taken over the interview. It seems that my System 1 detected that I (System 2) was depleted, about to lose control, and about to get argumentative and be rejected for the job.

Instantly (I prefer to think) System 1 was reading my vital signs and simply took over. I sat there while my System 1 waxed lyrical about the "obvious benefits" of annual appraisals and the annual performance review, reading the panel and giving them the answers they wanted. It was a brilliant, if (for my System 2) completely wrong and delusional account of motivational management. I seemed to let System 1 take over my System 2 and eloquently fabricate on my behalf.

I later justified my fabrication on the lines of the greater good. I continue to dislike the whole idea of appraisal but *chose* to feed the delusions of others that it was all a marvelous idea and a teacher's *right* to be so assessed and given performance targets to improve.

In those early days as the new boss, I couldn't dissolve the factory model and redesign how the school should work, but I knew the elements, the teacher, the tutor, the student, the parents, and the information each needed but systemically kept secure from the others. The simple linear factory school is what it is because of the lack of knowledge it has. It is like System 1. It operates within the limitations and biases of the information it has (WYSIWTI). This feeds partial information to managers and the view that variation is a special cause problem in the form it is seen.

Over thirty years ago, as a rookie principal, I was awoken early in the morning by System 1, who had clearly been messing around with the parameters that had been on my mind. It seemed that I was suddenly handed the completed model and its simple instruction sheet on how to make it work.

In the time between sleep and wakefulness, when there is less environmental interference, it seems that Systems 1 and 2 work optimally and spark fresh ideas. Haidt seems to be right; the emotional tail really can wag the rational dog! All I had to do as I lay there was to check it, remember it all, and share the simple eureka moment with colleagues, students, and parents regarding how it all worked. The important thing about problems is not to overthink them, but to be patient and trust that the solution will emerge in quiet and unsuspecting moments from the library of memes we all have. It is a question of being still and quiet. Systems 1 and 2 can be a great team but should be careful to behave properly at interview.

To work, the model required two completely counterintuitive ideas. First, it required tutor groups to be mixed by age and all communications to be redesigned around this principle. The second was to improve learning and teaching, but not through appraisal and heavy duty evaluation, but by improving learning relationships and by allowing them to form outside of the classroom first.

The new vertical model is simple beyond words and rewires the system. When it does so, it redefines what it is to care, to assess, to communicate, to value, to create, and to build the better learning dispositions more likely to keep the aspiration gene switched on and to improve outcomes. Every child, teacher, and parent would be known and valued for their contribution. VT is the practical application of this model that makes it work optimally (VT max).

Bullying declined, behavior improved, results went up, and the system started to both heal and redesign itself. School became a much more joyous and interconnected enterprise. The tutor room, not the classroom, became the first key information hub around which the system pivoted, with everything else redesigned to suit. The tutor room provided the key that enabled learning in the classroom.

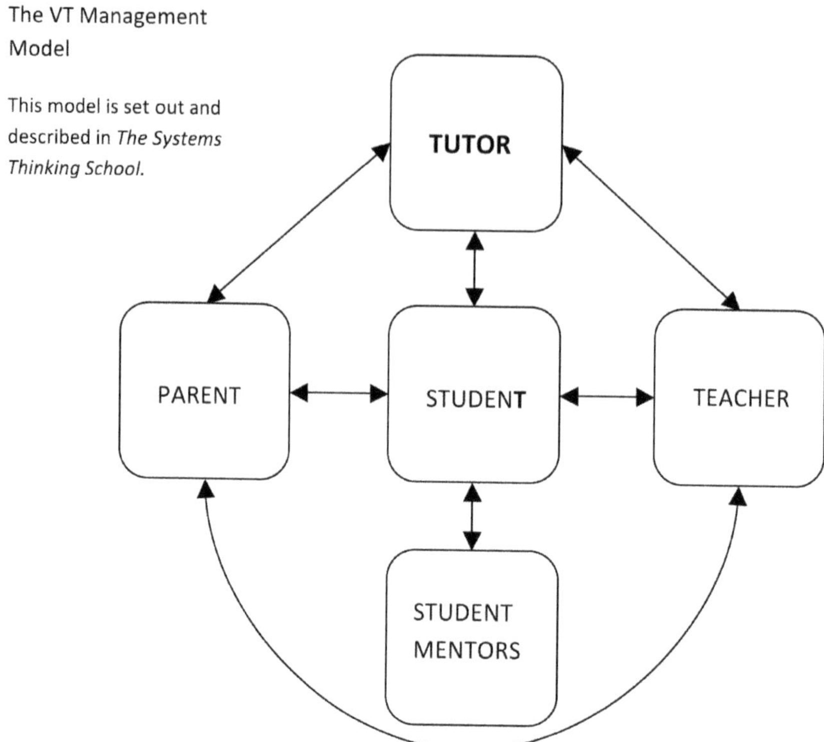


**Figure 18.1.**

Teachers felt less pressurized and able to take more risks. The school was more fun. The real formula for success was not great teaching but great tutoring first; this led to better teaching by implication. The latter enabled the former. By creating a system able to give back to teachers, students, and parents—the leadership, respect, responsibility, and trust that the factory school degrades—customer care also began to redesign itself. We understood and redefined value demand.

To the students we were able to give something else that they desired to complement their growing self-esteem. It was possible to give them trust, respect, and an opportunity to lead and to practice emotional as well as cognitive intelligence. It was also possible to give students a deep sense of what it is to be more genuinely "cool" in front of others. We put the "cool" back into school, where it mostly belongs.

The school became a giant information warehouse dependent on feedback loops, which of course enable feed-forward to better decisions, better strategies for improvement, more focused effort, and more informed judgments. It became a school that recognized individuality and one able to engage complexity.

Kahneman would doubtless correct my theory. He would explain that life is more complicated than we think and it is Kahneman who will enable me to conclude this book.

## FACTORIES AND SCHOOLS

I have tried to point out the organizational delusions thrown up by our acceptance of so many deep-seated assumptions and the common cause of variation schools face. There is so much more to a school than what we see; any view that keeps returning to the teacher in the classroom as the problem is a bias, a misperception, and a delusion perpetrated by a broken, same-age system.

I have been critical of factory methodology, and especially of its industrial nature, and yet this model is universal. It seems that schools are run on a System 1 basis of WYSIATI, which means information is limited and decisions are always biased and gullible. We see the school wrongly and need to see it more clearly for what it is and what it is more genuinely for.

VT takes us part of the way. It creates a system that is more able to access information, appreciate complexity, and understand variation. This enables it to be more purposeful, responsive, and bespoke to individual learning, development, and support. The hope is that this first phase (VT) creates an adaptive, self-organizing school, an information-sharing system able to promote better decisions and better judgment regarding direction and purpose.

I have no doubt that the second phase involves massive innovation and even mixed-age teaching and learning. But to do this, the school as an organization will need to make better judgments as to its purpose and be able to decide what is of real value. Method depends on getting purpose spiritually right.

This means the school must orchestrate a move from unreliable and heuristic beliefs based on guesswork and assumption to ones that are more certain. It is a move along a continuum to which there is probably no end, but the direction is important and is the learning journey we share. Schools will always be factories of sorts and even in the industrial and inappropriate ones we have the human spirit shines through; a surprising number of young people seem to just about survive, at least that is what we think we see.

Organizations like schools are essential. Humans need guidance when deciding matters; we are just not that clever and the delusions herein pay testimony to that. Kahneman (2011) ended his book not by describing people but systems. I shall set out in bullet points what he said and my (biased) interpretation, because they help us see our schools, leadership, and how work works not only better, but differently:

- *Organizations are important because they are better than individuals when it comes to avoiding errors. They think slowly and impose more orderly procedures.* The better and more reliable the information, the better the decisions on learning. Learning involves decisions: students need help as much as teachers do to get the decisions right. Better therefore to be slow, to involve students and parents in guiding judgments and supporting learning long, rather than short.
- *Organizations can have useful checklists, engage in forecasting, and have pre-mortems as well as post-mortems.* They can think before they act, in part, but need a distinctive vocabulary that everyone understands. The one we have is loaded with assumptions, biases, and distortions. It is all so much *Alice in Wonderland*. As Caine and Caine said, we talk past each other.
- *Organizations create a distinctive culture wherein everyone looks out for one another,* especially when approaching minefields, let alone walking through them. Families need schools as much as schools need families. Children need both to be in their corner and on the sidelines shouting encouragement rather than derision.
- *Organizations may well be basically factories, but whatever else they are, they are places that must manufacture judgments and decisions.* Schools will make much better decisions when they are adaptive, self-organizing, and reconnected to more of themselves.
- *Organizations must have ways to ensure the quality of their products in the initial design, fabrication, and final inspection.* Schools must be accountable, but first should be able to give a rational account of their purpose and their value work and how it delivers in a quality way. Quality lies in relationships, while outcomes reflect the quality that went before. Schools must become their own inspectors.
- *Organizations must be able to reframe the problems they face to make the right decisions needed.* Ackoff's wisdom on the dissolution of wicked problems is accurate. When problems become wicked and irresolvable they must be dissolved and a new culture built. During this process they need our support, not more crazy reforms or more of the same.

We keep reinventing the same schools in part because we prefer our lazy ways and our deluded intuitive guides. In every book I have read on school improvement, it seems I am reading another instruction manual for exhausted teachers rather than any redesign blueprint for managers of our broken systems. We keep projecting our own fallibility onto those that do the real work rather than ourselves.

We judge on what we see rather than what there is, and thus rarely make progress. We fail to make the right decisions and exercise the hard work, risk, and sheer effort needed for redesign. Our vocabulary has become blurred, research ignored or hijacked to suit. Even so, many schools are already incorporating this list (above) by thinking things through, looking anew, and realizing that counterintuitive truths work. Deep down, most already know this.

So one final quote from the master: it is the one with which Kahneman (2011) ends his book. It makes me think not of lofty places but of humble schools and management and leadership teams who face such mighty challenges each and every day. But then in my sort of school, everyone is a teacher, a leader, and a mentor, and so all contribute to the stock of sophistication and to better learning decisions.

> There is a direct link from more precise gossip at the water-cooler to better decisions. Decision-makers are sometimes better able to imagine the voices of present gossipers and future critics than to hear the hesitant voice of their own doubts. They will make better choices when they trust their critics to be sophisticated and fair, and when they expect their decision to be judged by how it was made, not only how it turned out. (p. 418)

In January 2014, Patricia and I were in Las Vegas for two days—just two more tourists about to drive to the Grand Canyon and then back to Phoenix. We were to take the Old Mother Road, the mythical Route 66, from Kingman, a journey that will stay with us forever. In Vegas, the two faces of the United States were there for all to see: the famous "strip" with its extravagant hotels, astonishing shopping malls, the Bellagio Fountains, and the endless opportunity to decide whether or not to throw money away.

We both love the United States, the kindness of its people, the vast landscapes, the optimism, and so much more. But wherever we go there are the many destitute people holding their cardboard signs asking for money. One sign read, "I admit it, I need a beer!" The guy should have been snapped up by a marketing agency for his creativity, honesty, and ability to make us laugh—and part with our money. I'd rather invest in this down-and-out than any machine with bells.

Just off the strip and parallel to it are shanty areas and tent communities worthy of any third-world country. The fact is, some of us go to bed with superficial matters on our mind, others with problems about how to get food, kick habits, get a gun, take revenge, afford health care, pay back loans, get a job, get out of the gutter, and get back into some kind of shape. They too will wake with ideas, some high-risk and dangerous, because any alternatives have been reduced and limited; others might be more fortunate and wake with an idea they might be able to one day sell on, or simply get them through another day on the strip. Seventy percent will not make it out.

In Nevada, I understand that taxes are low to encourage gambling. Unfortunately, they are too low to help the destitute. Too many young people enter this game of economic Monopoly to find all the houses sold, the hotels already built, the community chest raided, and that all that is left to them is the "Go to Jail" card or "Take a Chance." It is a system that doesn't work, but one that is justified on warped and delusional views of freedom, choice, and the American dream. I prefer systems that work and ones based on equity—ones that enable me to look others in the eye rather than pass them by.

This brings us back to school systems. We might postulate a number of theories. Intuition is great when it is right, but when it is wrong and our thinking is impaired by delusions thrown up by system assumptions, it is counterintuition that holds the better truth. Counterintuitive ideas work because they snap us out of our malaise and free us from the weight of illusion, our intuitive assumptions and the fast System 1 thinking that can lead to repeat mistakes when System 2 gets lazy.

If an education system such as Finland's is performing well, those running the system will be quite sanguine. They will like the feedback from PISA and they will not be prone to take risks, preferring small incremental gains of ongoing system improvement. They will use slow, rational decisions based on research and the judgment of professional teams so that what they are already doing continues its steady progress.

They understand that beyond the school, health access, poverty reduction, early learning, and parental support, all have to be part of the same learning relationship system. They understand that it is much cheaper to get it right and that most of the important factors that drive school improvement happen outside of the school. At no time is the school the dominant player, despite the miracles they perform daily.

It seems that when a system like the multifaceted U.S. education system performs so badly for so long when judged by many performance measures there is anxiety and an overreaction caused by loss bias and one or two other biases besides (there are at least nineteen others!). Considerable money is put in, more than any other country, for lower output. The investment is lost and the instinctive and biased reaction is to get it back as soon as possible by gambling again: the Mickey Rooney syndrome, and this means bad decisions.

This loss leads to risk-taking behavior and unedited System 1 thinking. To get the investment back, limited System 1 intuition suggests two things: the first is to pour even more money into the system to make it work better; the second is to return to the industrial management styles of the past, ones that are more coercive, target oriented, and the only one it knows. Both will ensure sameness, the opposite of what is needed. Both are judgments more at home in Las Vegas than in educational administration.

The slow thinking that looks at research and suggests systemic change is perceived as the risk rather than the solution, and so the system self-perpetuates and deludes.

For those old bureaucracies that command the U.S. system, feedback from PISA confirms underperformance. The intuitive reaction is that there is a teacher quality problem and this poor judgment call leads to bad decisions. The lazy and self-delusional bias of systems administrators is that they are right—after all, how could they be wrong—while those operating the system, the school workers and teachers trying to make it all work, are blamed for doing things badly.

The universal, industrial school is part of a giant sorting mechanism with a purpose that is at best dubious and at worst dangerous and wasteful, one linked to an abstract hierarchy of subjects and of mind. Students enter school and are prepared for a world that no longer holds and a future that none can predict, but one that looks bleaker by the day.

Chazal once said, "The ring always believes that the finger lives for it." A system like a school and schooling per se must have a higher purpose that not only increases the common good and the development of human potential, but one that is connected ecologically to other systems. To do this it must first reconnect to more of itself and to its intrinsic learning values. The best way to begin such a process is to understand the delusional nature of the current system and the intuitive weaknesses of reform strategies.

A jurisdiction has to get to grips with value demand. Only then can a school reconnect to more of itself, to those who work in our schools, and the families they support. In the end, the ring must fit the child.

In *The Myth of Sisyphus* by the French writer and philosopher Albert Camus (1942), the King of Ephyra was forever condemned to roll a large boulder to the top of a hill as a punishment, only to see it roll down again. For Camus, this pointless repetition illustrated his philosophy of the absurd. He once famously said, "Nobody realizes that some people expend tremendous amounts of energy merely to be *normal*." Schools will understand this, given the delusion that surrounds them, and many must wonder if there is any point. They too must search for meaning in circumstances that can seem futile, unintelligible, and sometimes absurd.

But that's the thing about schools and those who walk their corridors: they don't give up. They will roll that boulder every day until someone tells them to stop, that they have been punished enough for situations not of their making. What vertical tutoring (mixed-age tutoring) contributes to design and systemic change is the capacity to create a virtuous circle of reinforcing feedback and balancing learning loops that should, when understood and managed as a system, change every policy and practice in a school—a shift from delusion to design and to a better learning culture.

It is the smallest protection for schools and our teachers from the nonsenses of absurd management ideas and a life in which the teachers' real purpose, to make a difference, has been stolen from them. In turn, this creates humane learning relationships, a learning organization that is better able to nurture aspiration, embrace difference, and cultivate more intrinsic learning. It not only achieves quality in learning relationships, but may yet be the best way of allowing an informed conversation on the full systemic change that is needed.

So what advice to offer my colleagues in U.S. schools? I was born with a maverick disposition and held dear to one idea: observe the direction of travel taken by the many who, as Amos Tversky said, claim to be right. Then go in the opposite counterintuitive way with your school; it will always be the fastest way to the future.

We don't need a great teacher in every classroom. They are already there. But then, you knew this all along . . .

# Glossary

## *A Systems Interpretation for Schools*

**Balancing feedback loop (sometimes called a negative feedback loop):** All loops are causal. If the school as a system restricts information in and out (fails to absorb the variety of value demand on the system) this can lead to failure demand—complaints, more work, and increased costs. The school might respond by hiring more back office staff to handle complaints, thus increasing costs and failing to resolve the problem that caused the failure demand. Instead of removing waste, it shifted it elsewhere. It is often the case that linear schools respond in this way. The answer is nearly always more money! While the balancing loop seeks to stabilize things, a reverse or negative effect is created. Ultimately things stay largely the same. People are managed instead of the system.

**Common and special cause variation:** Special causes are associated with unexpected events external to the process the school is operating. The lights fail, we find the cause, and fix the problem. A flu bug hits the school, disrupting examinations, so we reschedule. These events were not predicted. Our penchant is to allocate a special cause when things go wrong and fix things so they work better. Common causes arise from within the system itself and relate to the way it operates: it produces expected variation within tolerance levels such as assignments lacking in challenge or poor sequencing. Over time things tend to balance out. The contention of this book is that we confuse the two. When things go dramatically wrong (students fail to graduate, teachers leave, results decline, well-being falls) in a public service system, we allocate blame (special cause) to teachers, programs, curricula, or whatever. In fact, we should have predicted these problems. Common cause is illusive. The contention here is that the root of all school variation is a system that separates and limits because it uses an industrial structure based on same-age groups. This requires redesign and the removal of delusion to release flow.

**Complexity:** We often hear talk about taming, reducing, and controlling complexity. In school, we can define most of the complexity as the variety of value demand that so many individuals (teachers, students especially, and parents) make on the system. The school has to somehow respond to the divergent needs of customers, but its inherent linearity disables any ability to flex and innovate. The capability of the school to respond is further influenced by conflicting demands from government, employers, and universities. The school's party trick is to delude all parties into believing it can perform such a task and organize itself as a system able to absorb value demand (what customers need to draw down from the school to make progress). It is forced to do this by a process of separation and limitation. While this appears to exert organizational, control complexity increases to eventually run rampant either in school or out (well-being, psychological harm, bullying, lost aspiration, wasted lives).

**Double and single loop learning:** These seem to me to be akin to common and special cause variation. Argyris and Schön (1974) put it this way: when matters go awry, we try and put things right or improve things (schools for example) by working *within the governing variables* of the system. We seek another technique, a program change, or a new strategy; reforms tend to take this single-loop learning approach. We seek out things (like teachers) we think we can fix when reforms inevitably fail. The system's (the school's) fundamental assumptions and organizational methods remain largely unchallenged, unquestioned, or rationalized away. They are assumed to be benign and so remain fundamentally the same. **Double-loop learning** challenges the status quo. It questions "the role of the framing and learning systems which underlie actual goals and strategies." Importantly, the latter involves consideration of goodness. In this book, double-loop learning challenges the same-age structure as the source of the learning problem. The school must increase its capability for double-loop learning.

**Feedback loops:** Schools are like an information warehouse in which information needs to flow around the system among players to enable learning and teaching. Teachers, students, and parents depend on feedback to support progress. Systems thinking can explore these causal loops by examining the places where the main players (staff, students, and families) interact and exposing what is actually happening, as opposed to what is assumed to be happening.

**Flow:** If a loop is missing or damaged, or obstructed information doesn't flow, there is a cause and an effect. This can result in delays, wrong decisions, and system damage. Parent partnership is a case in which limited information home obstructs learning support needed to make progress. Flow is also a psychological state. The enemy of school is boredom. The assumption of schools when students (say) are watching a video or listening to a lecture is that they are paying attention and on-task and thus are engaged in learning. Work by Csikszentmihalyi (1990) sees flow as a *state of being* when a student is truly absorbed in learning unfettered by time restraints and too much direction. This optimal learning state (the point at which challenge and individual capability to meet challenge collide) is difficult to achieve in a highly regimented, separated, and limited system like a busy school. Teachers can help by using systems thinking to promote engagement, but so can the organization by ensuring that the child is part of an interconnected and personalized system using VT. We need a system that can learn more about the child (absorb value demand) to enable the value work.

**Linearity:** Schools operate using design assumptions based on the industrial past. The model is the factory and teaching follows the conveyor belt in a completely arbitrary way. Cause is assumed to equal effect. The paradox is that this approach can switch off intrinsic learning and aspiration (it controls flow and the nature of engagement, robbing the child of time to stare and to explore), that is, such an approach to teaching can get in the way of learning. It is a product of industrialization whereby learning is ever more equated with memorizing facts to pass tests. The pass grade is seen as the dangerous and dark measure of intelligence. Vertical tutoring intervenes by creating a means of absorbing the variety of value demand and personalizing learning (support) by rebuilding interconnectivity between players. It mitigates linearity and begins to return the school to the 99.8 percent of engaged human learning pre-industrialization. VT is non-linear and should eventually lead to vertical teaching and on to systemic change and the learning organization. It creates and flexes time.

**Open system:** This is one that is not only able to absorb value demand and rebuild interconnected learning relationships, but one able to connect with the environment and be ecologically coherent. This allows energy to cross borders and recharge the system, enabling self-organization. Schools claim openness but practice closedness and sub-optimization. An open system, in effect, is open to learning. **A closed system** remains insular, unable to access external energy (say, from parents and research), and dependent only on the balancing but negative feedback loops described earlier.

**Quality:** For our purposes, I have used the David Langford and Barbara Cleary definition (1995). First they warn us about imitating and trying to copy other schools. Quality resides in the learning relationships among players that support and enable learning. This means looking anew at the structures able to optimally promote such quality. Vertical tutoring achieves and ensures quality by creating a multi-nodal and interconnected structure based on the counterintuitive idea of mixed-age groups—the platform for the school as an organization. These quality relationships transfer to the classroom and eventually to society, increasing learning capabilities and the stock of goodness. However, they demand changes to what Deming called the prevailing system of management.

**Reinforcing feedback loop:** Vertical tutoring creates these loops. These are ones that can accelerate change and create a virtuous circle by reigniting innovation and re-establishing learning relationships among players to promote intrinsic learning. These cannot form or be managed using prevailing management methods that attempt to directly change people rather than the system. Managers have to completely change their behavior when these loops are formed. They cannot exist in command and control structures (industrial). The loops can also run uncontrollably if left unattended!

**Resilience:** This is the ability to bounce back from adverse effects. Some believe resilience, like happiness, should be taught! Systems thinkers believe that system structure is the root of system behaviors. Get the system right, and resilience and happiness enabled, and de rigueur.

**Self-organization:** The capacity or capability of a school to be able to redesign itself, innovate, and learn. This enables it to personalize learning and cope with value demand.

**Sub-optimization:** This occurs when one part of a system acts in a way that dominates at the expense of the bigger system of which it is part. Schools themselves (arguably) operate practices that are out of sync with their claimed values, practices that are not coherent with ecology. They do not contribute to the stock of goodness, but self-perpetuate a pervading but perverse kind of management. If we treat schools as low-cost, standardized, profit production centers designed to sort out winners and losers, costs go up, waste increases, people drop out, and society suffers. Waste is not removed, failure demand increases, costs rise, and the stock of goodness declines. Instead of fixing teachers, we need to fix the system and manage it to prevent sub-optimization.

**System:** A system is characterized by an interconnection of parts (elements) designed to achieve a purpose. You cannot have a system without a purpose. In schools, many purposes (like values) are assumed. The measures we use to judge schools (test results) define the de facto purpose. The measures tend to define the methods used by schools. This is a balancing but negative feedback loop that keeps things the same (stable), but also prevents change.

**Tutor group or homeroom group:** Schools tend to organize themselves by separating students into grades or year groups and then allocating students to tutor groups. The tutor may not teach the group but is there to follow progress and support students. The tutor follows students through their school career. However, such a system is high-risk, poor flow, and anti-learning, besides being inadvertently pro-bullying. Schools rarely see this until they change the structure to a mixed-age economy. Vertical tutoring (below) changes this structure with surprising results.

**Vertical tutoring:** A means of organizing a school as a learning system based on establishing mixed-age tutor groups. It is a system driven by the demand of those using the system and relies on being values driven. Managers manage the system to optimize flow. The management principles are described herein and detailed in *The Systems Thinking School*. VT enables *flow* and *quality*, two critical drivers of intrinsic learning (above)

# Bibliography


Ackoff, R. L. 1974. *Redesigning the future: A systems approach to societal problems*. New York: John Wiley and Sons.

Ackoff, R. L. 1979, February. The future of operational research is past. *Journal of Operational Research Society*, 30(2).

Ackoff, R. L. 2004, May. Transforming the systems movement. Speech at the Third National Congress on Systems Thinking, Philadelphia, Pennsylvania.

Ackoff, R. L., and D. Greenburg. 2008. *Turning learning right side up: Putting education back on track*. Upper Saddle River, N.J.: Pearson Education.

Argyris, C. 1982. *Reasoning, learning, and action: Individual and organizational*. San Francisco, Calif.: Jossey-Bass.

Argyris, C. 1985. *Strategy, change and defensive routines*. Boston: Pitman.

Argyris, C. 1990. *Overcoming organizational defences: Facilitating organizational learning*. Boston: Allyn and Bacon.

Argyris, C., and D. Schön. 1974. *Theory in practice: Increasing professional effectiveness*. San Francisco, Calif.: Jossey-Bass.

Argyris, C., and D. Schön. 1978. *Organizational learning: A theory of action perspective*. Reading, Mass.: Addison-Wesley.

Alpaslan, Can M., and I. I. Mitroff. 2011. *Swans, swine, and swindlers: Coping with the growing threat of mega-crises and mega-messes (high reliability and crisis management)*. Stanford: Stanford University Press.

Banathy, B. H. 1991. *Systems design of education: A journey to create the future*. Englewood Cliffs, N.J.: Educational Technology Publications.

Barnard, P. A. 2013. *The systems thinking school: Redesigning schools from the inside-out*. Lanham, Md.: Rowman & Littlefield Education.

Barnard, P. A. 2010. *Vertical tutoring: Notes on school management, learning relationships and school improvement*. Guildford: Grosvenor House Publishing.

Barr, R., and R. Dreeben. 1983. *How schools work*. Chicago: University of Chicago Press.

Belbin, R. M. 1996. *The coming shape of organisation*. Oxford: Butterworth Heinemann.

Bertalanffy, L. Von. 1968. *General systems theory: Foundations, development, applications*. New York: George Braziller.

Betts, F. 1992. How systems thinking applies to education. *Educational Leadership*, 50(3): 38–41.

Block, P. 2008. *Community: The structure of belonging*. San Francisco, Calif.: Berrett-Koehler Publishers.

Boaler, J. 2005. The "psychological prison" from which they never escaped: The role of ability grouping in reproducing social class inequalities. *Forum*, 47(2&3): 135–44.

Bock, M. 2009. What quality guru W. Edwards Deming had to say about public education. Retrieved from www.daytonas.com.

Boulding, K. E. 1956. *The image*. Ann Arbor, Mich.: University of Michigan Press.

Bridgeland, J. M., J. J. Dilulio Jr., and K. B. Morison. 2006. *The silent epidemic: Perspectives of high school dropouts*. Seattle: Bill and Melinda Gates Foundation.

Bronfenbrenner, U. 1977. Toward an experimental ecology of human development. *American Psychologist*, 32(7): 513–31.

Bronfenbrenner, U. 1979. *The ecology of human development*. Cambridge, Mass.: Harvard University Press.

Bronfenbrenner, U. 1980. *The ecology of human development: Experiments by nature and design*. Cambridge, Mass.: Harvard University Press.

Bronfenbrenner, U. 1990. Discovering what families do. In D. Blankenhorne, S. Bayme, and J. B. Elshtain (eds.), *Rebuilding the nest: a new commitment to the American family*, pp. 27–38. Milwaukee, Wisc.: Family Service America.

Brummelman, E., S. Thomaes, B. Orobio de Castro, G. Overbeek, and B. J. Bushman. 2014, March. "That's not just beautiful—That's incredibly beautiful!" The adverse impact of inflated praise on children with low self-esteem. *Psychological Science*, 25(3): 728–35.

Bruner, J. 1996. *The culture of education*. Cambridge, Mass.: Harvard University Press.

Bryk, A., E. Camburn, and K. S. Louis. 1999. *Professional community in Chicago elementary schools: Facilitating factors and organizational consequences*. Washington, D.C.: Office of Educational Research and Improvement.

Caine, G., and R. N. Caine. 2014. Education cannot get where it wants to go because it cannot see where it needs to go. *F. M. Duffy Reports*, 19(1).

Camus, A. 1942. *The myth of Sisyphus*. New York: Penguin Books.

Carroll, L. 1865. *Alice's adventures in wonderland*. New York: D. Appleton & Co.

Csikszentmihalyi, M. 1990. *Flow: Psychology of optimal experience*. New York: Harper and Row.

Coffield, F. 2012. Why the Mckinsey Reports will not improve school systems. *Journal of Education Policy*, 27(1): 131–42.

Conklin, J. 2006. *Dialogue mapping: Creating shared understanding of wicked problems*. Chichester, U.K.: John Wiley and Sons.

Covey, S. R. 1989. *The 7 habits of highly effective people: Powerful lessons in personal change*. London: Simon & Schuster.

Cuban, L. 2014. Schools as factories: Metaphors that stick. Retrieved from larrycuban.wordpress.com.

Deming, W. E. 1982. *Out of the crisis*. Cambridge, Mass.: MIT Press.

Deming, W. E. 1994. *The new economics for industry, government, and education* (2nd ed.). Cambridge, Mass.: MIT Press.

Desforges, C., and A. Abouchaar. 2003. The impact of parental involvement, parental support, and family education on pupil achievement and adjustment: A literature review. *U.K. Research Report RR433*. Department for Education and Skills.

Drucker, P. 1959. *Landmarks of tomorrow*. New York: Harper and Brothers.

Drucker, P. 2010. *The five most important questions you will ever ask about your organization*. San Francisco, Calif.: Jossey-Bass.

Duckworth, A., and M. Seligman. 2005. Self-discipline outdoes IQ in predicting academic performance of adolescents. *Psychological Science*, 16(2): 939–44.

Duffy, F. M. 2007. Strapping wings on a caterpillar and calling it a butterfly: When systemic change is not systemic. *The F. M. Duffy Reports*, 12(2).

Duffy, F. M. 2010. *Dream! Create! Sustain! Mastering the art and science of transforming school systems*. Lanham, Md.: Rowman & Littlefield Education.

Duffy, F. M. 2014. *The F. M. Duffy Reports*. Retrieved from www.theduffygroup.com/publications/reports.html.

Dweck, C. S. 1998. *Mindset: The new psychology of success: How we can learn to fulfil our potential*. New York: Ballantine Books.

Edmonson, A., and Moingeon, B. 1999. Learning trust and organizational change. In M. Easterby-Smith, J. Burgoyne, and L. Araujo (eds.), *Organizational Learning and the Learning Organization*. London: Sage Publishers.

Ferguson, B., K. Tilleczek, K. Boydell, and J. Anneke Rummens. 2005. *Early school leavers: Understanding the lived reality of student disengagement from secondary school*. Final Report. Ontario Ministry of Education and Training.

Forrester, J. W. 1961. *Industrial dynamics*. Cambridge, Mass.: MIT Press.

Galagan, P. 1991, October. The learning organisation made plain: An interview with Peter Senge. *Training and Development*, 37–43.

Gharajedaghi, J. 2006, April. Systems thinking in education workshop. Interview with Trace Pickering. *The F. M. Duffy Reports*, 18(2).

Gladwell, M. 2005. *Blink: The power of thinking without thinking*. New York: Penguin Books.

Graziano, C. 2014. Public education faces a crisis in teacher retention. *Edutopia*. What works in education. The George Lucas Educational Foundation.

Greenleaf, R. K. 1970. The servant as leader. Westfield, Ind.: Greenleaf Center for Servant Leadership.

Haidt, J. 2001. The emotional dog and its rational tail: A social intuitionist approach to moral judgment. *Psychological Review*, 108: 814–34.

Haidt, J. 2006. The happiness hypothesis. New York: Basic Books.

Handy, C. 1989. *The age of unreason*. London: Business Books.

Handy, C. 1998. *The hungry spirit*. London: Hutchinson.

Hasenfield, Y. (Ed.). 1992. *Human services as complex organizations*. Thousand Oaks, Calif.: Sage Publications.

Hattie, J. 2012. *Visible learning for teachers: Maximising impact on learning*. London: Routledge.

Higher Education Funding Council. 2014. Differences in degree outcomes: key findings. Ref. 2014/03 Issues Paper. Published by HEFC UK.

Hogarth, R. M. 2001. Educating intuition. The University of Chicago Press, Chicago.

Johnston, R., and G. Clark. 2001. *Service operations management*. New York: Pearson Education.

Kahneman, D. 2011. *Thinking, fast and slow*. London: Penguin Books.

Kanter, R. M. 1984. *The change masters: Innovation and entrepreneurship in the American corporation*. New York: Simon & Schuster.

Kanter, R. M. 1998. *When giants learn to dance*. London: International Thompson Business Press.

King, K. S., and T. W. Frick. 1999. Transforming education: Case studies in systems thinking. *Systems Thinking: The key to educational redesign*. Paper presented at the annual meeting of the American Educational Research Association. April 19, Montreal, Canada.

Kohn, A. 1999. *Punished by rewards: The trouble with gold stars, incentive plans, As, praise, and other bribes*. Boston: Houghton Mifflin.

Kotter, J. P. 2012. *Leading change*. Boston: Harvard Business Review Press.

Langford, D. P., and B. A. Cleary. 1995. *Orchestrating learning with quality*. Milwaukee, Wisc.: ASQC Quality Press.

Leithwood, K., and Louis, K. S. 1998. *Learning from leadership: Investigating the links to improved student learning*. Minneapolis: University of Minnesota Press.

Lubienski, S. T., and C. Lubienski. 2006. A new look at public and private schools: Student background and mathematics achievement. *Phi Delta Kappan*, 86(9): 696–99.

Lubienski, S. T., C. Lubienski, and C. C. Crane. 2008, November. Achievement differences and school type: The role of school climate, teacher certification, and instruction. *American Journal of Education*, 115.

Lucas, B., and G. Claxton. 2010. *New kinds of smart: How the science of learnable intelligence is changing education*. New York: McGraw-Hill Education.

Maccia, E., and G. Maccia. 1966. *Development of educational theory derived from three models*. Project No. 5-0368. Washington, D.C.: U.S. Office of Education.

Maslow, A. H. 1943. A theory of human motivation. *Psychological Review*, 50: 370–96.

Maslow, A. H. 1954. *Motivation and personality*. New York: Harper.

Maslow, A. H. 1966. *The psychology of science: A reconnaissance*. New York: Harper & Row.

Meadows, D. H. 2009. *Thinking in systems: A primer*. London: Taylor & Francis.

Meadows, D. H., D. L. Meadows, J. Randers, and W. W. Behrens III. 1973. *The limits to growth: A report for The Club of Rome's project on the predicament of mankind*. Washington, D.C.: Potomac Associates.

Mueller, C. M., and C. S. Dweck. 1998. Praise for intelligence can undermine children's motivation and performance. *Journal of Personality and Social Psychology*, 75(1): 33–52.

Nevis, E. C., J. Lancourt, and H. G. Vassallo. 1996. *Intentional revolutions: A seven point strategy for transforming organizations.* San Francisco, Calif.: Jossey-Bass.

O'Neil, J. R. 1993. *The paradox of success: When winning at work means losing at life.* New York: Penguin Group.

Orbach, S. 2012, spring. The sad truth. *Royal Society of Arts Journal.*

Peters, J. T. 2014. *Pivot points: Five decisions every successful leader must make.* Hoboken, N.J.: John Wiley and Sons.

Pickering, Trace. 2013. Educational ecosystems & community building: Conversations and practices for the transformation of learning. *The F. M. Duffy Reports,* 18(2).

Piketty, T. 2014. *Capital in the twenty-first century.* Cambridge, Mass.: Harvard University Press.

Pink, D. H. 2009. *Drive: The surprising truth about what motivates us.* New York: Riverhead Books.

Pirsig, R. M. 2006. *Zen and the art of motorcycle maintenance: An inquiry into values.* New York: HarperCollins.

Program for International Student Assessments (PISA). 2012. Organisation for Economic Co-operation and Development. Paris: OECD. PISA 2012.

Ravitch, D. 2013. *Reign of error: The hoax of the privatization movement and the danger to America's public schools.* New York: Alfred A. Knopf.

Reigeluth, C. M. 2006. A leveraged emergent approach to systemic transformation. *Tech Trends,* 50(2): 46–47.

Rittel, H, and Webber, M. 1973. Dilemmas in a general theory of planning. *Policy Sciences,* Vol. 4, pp. 155-164. Elsevier Scientific Publishing Company, Inc., Amsterdam. Reprinted in N. Cross (ed.), 1984. *Developments in Design Methodology,* J. Wiley & Sons, Chichester; pp. 135–144.

Rivera, N. 2012, April 5. Opportunity and education: The culture of education. *PsychEd.*

Ross, R. B. 2000. In P. M. Senge et al., *The fifth discipline fieldbook: Strategies and tools for building a learning organization.* New York: Doubleday.

Rutledge, P. 2011. Positively media: How we connect and thrive through emerging technologies. *Psychology Today.* Published by Pamela Rutledge November 8, 2014, https://www.psychologytoday.com/blog/positively-media.

Rutter, M., B. Maughan, P. Mortimore, J. Ouston, and A. Smith. 1979. *Fifteen thousand hours: Secondary schools and their effects on children.* Cambridge, Mass.: Harvard University Press.

Sabel, C., A. L. Saxenian, R. Miettinen, P. H. Kristenson, and J. Hautamäki. 2011. Individualised service provision in the new welfare state: Lessons from special education in Finland. *Sitra Studies: 62.* Report prepared SITRA and Ministry of Employment.

Sahlberg, P. 2012. Pasi Salhberg Blog: Finnish education reform. Retrieved from www.PasiSahlberg.com.

Sahlberg, P. 2013. *Finnish lessons: What can the world can learn from educational change in Finland?* Columbia University: Teachers College Press.

Sax, J. G. 1872. Six blind men and an elephant: A Hindu parable.

Saxe, J. G. 1873. The poems of John Godfrey Saxe; complete edition. Published by James R. Osgood and Company, pp. 77–78, Boston.

Seddon, J. 2008. *Systems thinking in the public sector: The failure of the reform regime and a manifesto for a better way.* Devon, U.K.: Triarchy Press.

Seddon, J., and B. O'Donovan. 2010, May. Why aren't we all working for learning organizations? *e-Organisations and People,* 17(2). Retrieved from www.amed.org.uk.

Senge, P. M. 2006. *The fifth discipline: The art and practice of the learning organization.* Revised edition. New York: Random House.

Senge, P. M., et al. 1994. *The fifth discipline fieldbook: Strategies and tools for building a learning organization.* New York: Doubleday.

Shukla, M. 1994. Why corporations fail. *Productivity,* 34(4): 269–639.

Silins, H., W. Mulford, and S. Zarins. 2002. What characteristics and processes define a school as a learning organization? Is this a useful concept to apply to schools? *International Education Journal,* 3(1): 425–46.

Smith, D. M. 2011. *The elephant in the room: How relationships make or break the success of leaders and organizations*. San Francisco, Calif.: Jossey-Bass.

Strauss, V. 2013. What if Finland's great teachers taught in U.S. schools? *The Washington Post,* May 15.

Sweeney, L. B. 2014. Learning about systems. Courtesy of Linda Booth Sweeney, www.lindaboothsweeney.net/learning

Taleb, N. N. 2011. *The Black Swan: The impact of the highly improbable*. New York: Penguin Books.

Tiger, L. 1979. *Optimism: The biology of hope.* New York: Simon & Schuster.

Trivers, R. 2011. *The folly of fools—The logic of deceit and self-deception in human life.* London: Basic Books.

Tucker, M. S. 2013. *Surpassing Shanghai: An agenda for American education built on the world's leading systems.* Cambridge, Mass.: Harvard Education Press.

Wheatley, M. J. 1999. Bringing schools back to life: Schools as living systems. In *Creating successful schools: Voices from University, Field, and the Community.* Christopher Gordon Publishers. Available at http://www.margaretwheatley.com/articles.

Wheatley, M. J. 2004, March. Is the pace of life hindering our ability to manage? *Management Today*.

Zohars, D., and I. Marsahall. 2001. *Spiritual intelligence: The ultimate intelligence*. New York: Bloomsbury.

Lightning Source UK Ltd.
Milton Keynes UK
UKHW030752280820
368652UK00018B/410